"In today's volatile world, business leaders are well advised to analyze globalization carefully and pursue a fact-based strategy that strikes the right balance between global scale and local adaptation. This book is a helpful companion on that journey."

—**FRANK APPEL**, CEO, Deutsche Post DHL

"Pankaj is unique in his ability to connect theoretical rigor to practical decision making on the ground. I highly recommend this book—and Pankaj's sensible approach more generally—as a crucial voice to counter the oftentimes bombastic nature of our current dialogue on the future of globalization."

—from the foreword by **N. CHANDRASEKARAN**, Chairman, Tata Sons

"The new book by Professor Pankaj Ghemawat could not be more timely. As a brilliant and sensible voice in the field of business strategy, his insightful analysis has long provided useful elements for companies focused on growth—not for growth's sake but to create lasting value for customers, stakeholders, and communities worldwide. Now Professor Ghemawat connects new dots to show that the challenge is not to opt between local retrenchment or pursuing a mindless globalization but to find the right balance in leveraging the competitive advantages that allow any company or organization to create sustainable value while also contributing to the achievement of inclusive development for all—and in the process to help build a better world."

—**FERNANDO A. GONZÁLEZ**, CEO, CEMEX

"With the speed and extent of change in many industries adding new levels of complexity to business models and decisions, Ghemawat provides an excellent and updated framework for discussing the present and future of globalization in our business."

—**ENRIQUE OSTALÉ**, EVP and President, Walmart Latam, UK, and Africa

"Pankaj Ghemawat's book highlights important perennial truths about globalization that are frequently overlooked because of wild swings on sentiment around the topic. *The New Global Road Map* provides a useful framework to strike the right balance between where and how to compete, as well as help tackle the increasing anger towards global actors."

—**CARLOS TORRES**, CEO, BBVA

"Pankaj delivers his views on globalization based on a wealth of facts and data. He pivots globalization on the strength of each local market, an approach that keeps at bay emotional perceptions. In this more complex world, Pankaj proposes avenues for business leaders to strategize and execute on their internationalization programs. His work helps balance better the global-local spectrums. An important read for all companies who move in the larger world!"

—**JEAN-PASCAL TRICOIRE**, Chairman and CEO, Schneider Electric

THE NEW
GLOBAL ROAD MAP

THE NEW
GLOBAL ROAD MAP
Enduring Strategies for Turbulent Times

BY PANKAJ GHEMAWAT

HARVARD BUSINESS REVIEW PRESS
Boston, Massachusetts

10 9 8 7 6 5 4 3 2 1

Library of Congress Cataloging-in-Publication Data

Names: Ghemawat, Pankaj, author.
Title: The new global road map : enduring strategies for turbulent times / by Pankaj Ghemawat.
Description: Boston, Masachusetts : Harvard Business Review Press, [2018]
Identifiers: LCCN 2017044296 | ISBN 9781633694040 (hardcover : alk. paper)
Subjects: LCSH: Globalization. | Business and politics. | International business enterprises.
Classification: LCC HF1365.G524 2018 | DDC 658.4/012—dc23 LC record available at https://lccn.loc.gov/2017044296

ISBN: 9781633694040
eISBN: 9781633694057

अनन्या के लिए अन्य किताब

CONTENTS

FOREWORD

Pankaj Ghemawat has been a pathbreaking thinker and strategist throughout his career, and it is my privilege to have been a friend for many of those years. I first met Pankaj in 2001, when he shared his expertise on globalization and its context for strategy development at Tata Consultancy Services (TCS). Founded in 1968 as India's first software company, TCS is a member of the Tata group of companies and has over 371,000 employees operating across forty-five countries across the globe.

Pankaj became an anchor of TCS's core strategy group, and his ability to dispassionately analyze issues and to read the tea leaves on the trajectory of the global markets—often contrary to the prevalent rhetoric—has been extremely helpful to the organization's overall growth and success. Back in early 2001, when the Asian financial crisis and its aftermath were keeping us awake at night, Pankaj maintained a steady view that the gloom and doom was overdone. Before the global financial crisis, when the world was supposedly becoming flat, Pankaj persuaded us that it was not a foregone conclusion—not even for Indian software companies. His counsel was so valuable that we soon referred to the core strategy meetings as the "Pankaj Ghemawat sessions" and, later, the "PG sessions."

In *The New Global Road Map*, Pankaj continues to insightfully question betting on globalization extremes. He examines a topic that has come under scrutiny again after Brexit and the election of President Trump, interweaving his experiences as an academic and a strategy consultant to portray a more pragmatic and balanced view. As always, Pankaj sets himself apart by using robust data to bring his story to life. His work on the DHL Global Connectedness Index (he tells me, an accumulation of almost two million data points) supports his view that globalization will neither disappear nor expand at warp speed.

As a business leader, the yo-yo of localization versus globalization he speaks of has strong implications for our companies. In the first part of this book, he guides managers to take a measured view, cautioning against both a leadership cadre's becoming too enthralled by the extent and impact of globalization and its succumbing to excessive pessimism about globalism's prospects. Amid the overheated rhetoric and violent market swings, Pankaj manages to find stable patterns that can help business leaders steady themselves and their organizations. These are the patterns he calls the *laws of globalization*.

The second part of his book addresses many of the practical issues that concern even the most seasoned manager. Should firms scale globally or strengthen locally? Should organizations decentralize power to regional management, and if so, how? Pankaj outlines various ways that firms can improve organizational readiness in the face of globalization through levers such as culture, innovation, and his novel take on public affairs engagement.

Pankaj is unique in his ability to connect theoretical rigor to practical decision making on the ground. I highly recommend this book—and Pankaj's sensible approach more generally—as a crucial voice to counter the oftentimes bombastic nature of our current dialogue on the future of globalization.

—N. CHANDRASEKARAN

Introduction

When I wrote my first book on globalization, *Redefining Global Strategy*, in 2007, the prevailing sense among executives was that companies could safely bet on globalization continuing to increase. As I finish this book a decade later, some business leaders, such as Alibaba founder Jack Ma, still believe that more globalization is inevitable.[1] But most of the talk about globalization has turned pessimistic.

Some of the negativity reflects, of course, recent shocks, most notably Brexit, as in the United Kingdom's vote to exit the European Union, and the election of Donald Trump as US president. (I refer to these two events jointly as *Brump*.) But the mood had already soured before then. In May 2016, a month before the Brexit vote, Jeffrey Immelt, then chairman and CEO of General Electric, told the graduating New York University MBA class that it was time for a "bold pivot" toward localization in response to rising protectionism.[2] Brump continued this shift: having a global strategy seemed to swing from an absolute necessity to an outright risk. Only a week after Trump's inauguration in January 2017, the *Economist*'s cover announced "The Retreat of the Global Company."[3]

In figuring out what to make of such opinions and, more generally, the state of globalization, we need to remember that the present turbulence is not entirely new. While the process we now refer to as globalization has been going on for hundreds or perhaps even thousands of years, people's hopes for it have tended to overshoot reality and then come crashing back down for centuries as well—what I call the *globalization yo-yo effect*.[4]

While yo-yos are fun to play with, the globalization yo-yo effect is dangerous for firms and economies—making it more like yo-yo dieting than harmless childhood play. As venture capitalist Peter Thiel put it back in 2008, "for the past three centuries, the great rises and falls of the West track the high and low points of the hope for globalization . . . [as have] the peaks and valleys of the stock market. Almost every financial bubble has involved nothing more nor less than a serious miscalculation about the true probability of successful globalization."[5] Postscript: Thiel, a major donor to Trump's 2016 campaign, agrees that with Trump's election, the globalization yo-yo is on a downswing: "No one in their right mind would start an organization with the word 'global' in its title today . . . That's so 2005, it feels so dated."[6]

Indeed, 2005 is a signal year in terms of the last upswing of the globalization yo-yo. That year, Thomas Friedman's *The World Is Flat* was published, going on to become the best-selling book about globalization ever. Amid the flat-world hysteria in the run-up to the 2008 global financial crisis, it was easy to forget that less than a decade earlier, globalization expectations had experienced a downswing rather than an upswing. In the late 1990s, the euphoria after the fall of the Berlin Wall ran headlong into the Asian financial crisis.

Business anxiety back then was so high that a leading strategy consulting firm convened a set of thought leaders in early 2001 to examine the implications for companies. I teamed up with one of the firm's partners to frame the discussion for a "global salon." Figure I-1, which is adapted from our presentation at that salon, highlights many of the global issues that business leaders today are thinking about again in the present pessimistic environment.[7] Should strategies switch from the pursuit of scale to local responsiveness? Should firms' geographic presence be narrowed to reduce risk? Should

FIGURE I-1

Globalization: the yo-yo effect

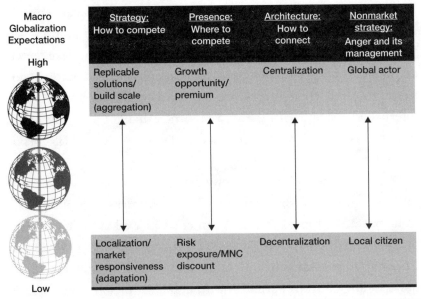

Macro Globalization Expectations	Strategy: How to compete	Presence: Where to compete	Architecture: How to connect	Nonmarket strategy: Anger and its management
High	Replicable solutions/ build scale (aggregation)	Growth opportunity/ premium	Centralization	Global actor
Low	Localization/ market responsiveness (adaptation)	Risk exposure/MNC discount	Decentralization	Local citizen

organizational power be pushed out to region and country leaders? And should multinationals try to act and look like their national counterparts in their dealings with governments and societies around the world?

Our lead example for raising these questions and the answers that were being considered in 2001 was Coca-Cola, judged at the time to possess the world's most valuable brand as well as its broadest geographical footprint. For most of Coke's history, its cross-border strategy and architecture, in particular, fit into the lower gray band spanning the different choices depicted in figure I-1. As James Quincey, who became CEO in 2017, put it, "Coke went global before globalization . . . [T]he way that worked is, 'You are now in charge of Country X. Go away. Good luck. There's only two rules. You can't change the formula and you can't steal the money. Please come back once a year and tell me how it's going.' That was the model for 100 and something years."[8]

But after Roberto Goizueta became CEO in 1981—as globalization was gathering momentum—Coke shifted gears to an approach more aligned with the top gray band in the figure. Goizueta emphasized growth based on Coke's megabrands, expanded its presence from 160 countries to nearly 200, and engaged in an unprecedented amount of centralization by consolidating divisions and putting consumer research, creative services, and TV commercials under Coke's internal ad agency, with the idea of standardizing them. The stock price soared, and *Fortune* rated Coke as the most admired US corporation for several years running.

Douglas Ivester, who took over when Goizueta died unexpectedly in 1997, continued with this strategy—"No left turns, no right turns," as he put it—but ran into the Asian crisis as well as governmental problems, particularly in Europe. Regulators in the EU resisted Coke's attempts—directed out of its headquarters in Atlanta—to acquire Orangina from Pernod Ricard and a set of soft drink brands from Cadbury Schweppes. Delays in tackling contamination problems caused further strain. Coke's market capitalization collapsed from a peak of $220 billion to below $120 billion as analysts marked it down for its global exposure, and Ivester was fired.

Douglas Daft took over in 2000 and yo-yoed back toward localization. With his manifesto of "Think local, act local," thousands of jobs were cut at headquarters and decision-making authority was sent back out to the field. This was how far we took the Coke story at the global salon in early 2001. We ended our presentation with a question: Were these extreme swings, made in response to shifting sentiments about globalization—most recently, the swing from top to bottom in the figure—truly warranted?

With fifteen-plus years of additional history, the answer to that question from Coke's perspective was clearly "no." The problems with unprecedented localization were quick to surface: scale economies suffered, as did the quality of marketing. Country managers were simply unprepared for their expanded set of responsibilities. In 2002, Coke brought marketing oversight back to headquarters—that task itself a challenge because hiring a new team took longer than firing the old one. But growth continued to lag investor expectations, and Daft resigned in 2004.

It fell to Neville Isdell, who took over from Daft, to strike the right balance between these extremes (see chapter 1). What merits particular attention in this context, given the correspondence between Coke's yo-yoing and some of the recommendations being urged on companies today, is how costly this back-and-forth turned out to be for Coke. Despite the company's manifest strengths, it took the better part of a decade and probably tens of billions of dollars to get re-centered.

Coke is, of course, just one case in point, but its experience should not be discounted. Although history may not repeat itself, it sometimes does rhyme. Instead of simply succumbing to shifts in sentiment and yo-yoing between extremes as Coke did, companies should take a long, hard look at globalization before deciding how they are going to deal with it. This book attempts to help you with that task. Part one looks at where globalization has been and where it might go, and part two explores the implications for the globalization-related choices that companies must confront.

Let me expand slightly on that one-sentence book outline, part by part and chapter by chapter. Part one focuses on the challenges of mapping globalization at a time of great turbulence. It deploys a range of empirical approaches: relying on up-to-date data, peering inside the minds of people (specifically, managers) with surveys, using analytics and statistical inference, analyzing stretch scenarios in depth, learning from history, and, most importantly, identifying robust regularities that offer guidance for the future. No math is required of the reader, but I include much data and many analyses of patterns in the data. As the late Daniel Patrick Moynihan put it, while everyone is entitled to their own opinions, everyone is *not* entitled to their own facts. For the same reason, there are lots of endnotes and references to additional readings. Tables are kept to a minimum, though; I rely on maps, other visualizations, strikingly large (estimated) effects, mini-cases—such as Coke—and stories, plain and simple, to help bring the data to life.

The individual chapters in part one focus on different time frames. More specifically, chapter 1 looks at the data on globalization from past to present and concludes it does not (yet) indicate that we are in the grips of a globalization apocalypse. The data does support two laws: the law of semiglobalization, which posits that globalization is neither (nearly) zero nor complete, and the law of distance, which posits that the cross-border interactions that do take place are dampened significantly by distances of various types between countries. Looking at the data and juxtaposing it with estimates from surveys of managers and other groups also highlights the importance of guarding against *globaloney*—the pernicious tendency to overstate how globalized the world actually is. This habit turns out to be costly to business as well as society.

Chapter 2 focuses on the short-to-medium-run future and, in particular, on a way forward in a world that is, as military strategists put it, VUCA (volatile, uncertain, complex, and ambiguous)—and subject to shocks we can't even anticipate. Analysis of historical shocks, most notably the global trade war of the 1930s, during which the value of world trade fell by two-thirds over a three-year period, confirms that the laws of globalization continued to apply. Analysis of recent shocks, most notably Brexit, illustrates how helpful they are when looking ahead. The chapter concludes with a discussion of the broad implications of a VUCA world for business decision making.

Chapter 3 focuses on the longer run—on a success scenario in which there *is* relatively robust growth globally. It looks at one of the indispensable elements of such a scenario: significantly faster growth in emerging economies, particularly in emerging Asia, than in advanced ones. (Because of demographics, it is hard to devise scenarios in which emerging economies *don't* grow faster but there is robust global growth anyway.) This big shift, south by southeast, helps anchor a discussion of several trends likely to manifest themselves over the next decade and beyond. The chapter also paints a broad picture of the differences in business environments in emerging versus advanced economies and in their patterns of international engagement.

And it starts to consider differences in where enterprises from emerging economies and advanced economies are coming from as a way of beginning to predict where these businesses might go.

Part two of this book moves from mapping globalization to managing it at the company level, with the intent of helping managers do more than bounce between the opposite extremes depicted in figure I-1. The four chapters in part two each address one of the four broad dimensions of choice depicted in that figure: strategy, presence, architecture, and nonmarket strategy (SPAN). Since this is a large body of content to cover, the focus is kept squarely on how companies can respond to the evolving challenges of competing across borders and distance. Each chapter offers recommendations that are organized, for mnemonic purposes, into acronyms, as depicted in figure I-2, and elaborated on below.[9] The advice in these chapters extends beyond just keeping one's balance between eternal opposites to lay out a richer palette of possible responses.

FIGURE I-2

Effective globalization

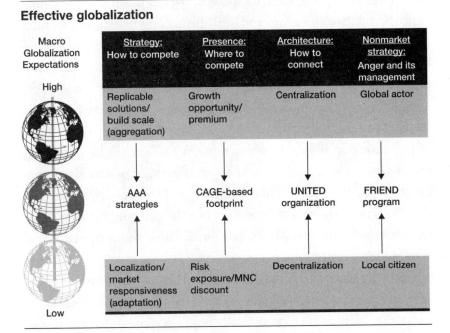

Chapter 4, on strategy, explains why pure adaptation to local conditions, while talked up during downswings, is likely to work out no better for most multinationals than it did for Coca-Cola under Daft. It also discusses why strategies of pure aggregation in the pursuit of scale economies, which Coke came close to embodying by the end of Goizueta's reign, tend to be too extreme as well. And the chapter goes beyond suggesting striking the right balance between adaptation and aggregation, in two ways. First, it specifies more than two dozen levers and sublevers that can improve the trade-off between adaptation and aggregation. Second and even more broadly, it suggests thinking of three AAA strategies—adaptation and aggregation *and* arbitrage—rather than picking a point on the continuum between the first two. Chapter 4 also discusses how emerging-economy enterprises do relatively well at arbitrage and incumbent multinationals from advanced economies at aggregation, and the chapter then looks at the strategic implications for both types of enterprises. In particular, given the rise of "insurgents" from emerging economies, incumbents from advanced economies will often need to pursue a mix of the AAA strategies.

Chapter 5, on presence, tries to avoid overconfidence about global expansion during upswings and funk during downswings by looking at the basic logic of multinational presence. The law of distance as applied to foreign direct investment (FDI) packs a big punch here, and only partly because of the large effects of cultural, administrative, geographic, and economic (CAGE) distance (summarized in chapter 1). The CAGE distance framework supplies the basis for a logic of presence that makes business sense regardless of the prevailing mood about globalization. And by overlaying CAGE-based cross-border analysis with the characteristics of the countries, industries, and firms actually involved, readers can think through the implications for their own companies. Both qualitative and quantitative examples are provided.

Chapter 6, on architecture, expands on questions of how to organize. It begins by reviewing how a firm's strategy should affect its organization: why adaptation typically requires some decentralization, why aggregation requires some centralization (as already suggested by figure I-1), and why arbitrage is often facilitated by a strong, cross-cutting functional axis. As a result, multinationals that employ all three AAA strategies tend to have complex structures. But structure is only part of what is required. They also need to rewire themselves, within and without, including forging new connections at the top. The acronym UNITED denotes a range of ways firms can boost their organizational capacity to bridge borders and distance: a unifying culture, networked innovation, initiatives and task forces, technology enablers, expatriation and mobility, and development programs.

Finally, chapter 7 is about nonmarket strategy, or business engagement with the wider world. Strategists have typically treated nonmarket strategy as an afterthought to market strategy, but nonmarket issues assume increased salience with rising international tension, policy uncertainty, distributional concerns, and anger (especially in the West) about globalization due to factors that range beyond its economic effects. This chapter explains why trying to behave like a local citizen everywhere is unlikely to work any better for multinationals than pure localization would work with respect to the other three components of SPAN. And the discussion of what should be done about the societal challenges facing multinational firms focuses on anger management rather than on trying to get what one wants out of the government, about which corporate public affairs professionals already tend to be pretty sophisticated. Anger appears to be inflamed by an interaction between globaloney and large degrees of partiality—how much people tend to favor others from their own country over foreigners. To counteract this anger, the chapter proposes a FRIEND program involving facts, rhetoric, increases in international informational interactions, education, nonmarket strategy improvements, and distributional fixes. Even if rebuilding societal support for globalization and multinational firms is likely to take a long time, we had better get started.

This focus on anger management in nonmarket strategy exemplifies my intent for this book to address present pressures on globalization with insights that will also stand the test of time. History suggests that sentiments about globalization will continue to yo-yo, but that the laws of semiglobalization and distance will endure—and that recommendations grounded in those laws can help firms manage their way through the turbulence and even profit from it. The global road map keeps changing, but those changes largely conform to predictable patterns. If it were otherwise, I would be much more skeptical about the abilities of today's multinationals to surmount the challenges that they face—and would not have written this book.

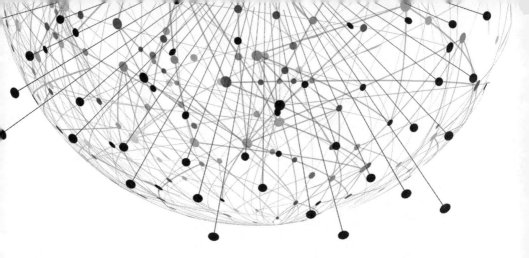

Mapping Globalization

What Is—and Isn't—Changing

Part one maps the present state of globalization and examines how the international environment is changing over time. Chapter 1 debunks popular and dangerous myths that prevent managers from thinking clearly about globalization while introducing a pair of laws on which firms can ground their international strategies. Chapter 2 stress-tests those laws considering the twin shocks of Brexit and the Trump presidency as well as the historical experience of the last global trade war, in the 1930s. Chapter 3 examines how the rise of emerging economies is likely to impact globalization over a longer time horizon.

1

The State of Globalization

How globalized is the world today, and has globalization been increasing or decreasing? Believe it or not, many managers can't answer those basic questions correctly, even though the wrong answers can lead to costly business blunders. In other words, managers' mental maps of globalization tend to be highly distorted.

Some of the distortion doubtless reflects the turbulence of the environment, which can widen the gap between perceptions and reality. Some distortion might reflect media noise. The media are particularly prone to yo-yoing, since no one ever attracted more eyeballs by declaring that "not much has changed." And quite a bit of misinformation reflects powerful biases that operate at the personal (and interpersonal) level and that will be discussed in some detail later in this chapter.

But first, the good news: there *are* stable patterns behind the turbulence, on which firms can build strategies for sustained success. This chapter uses up-to-date data to present two laws of globalization and to debunk dangerous myths. This characterization of the state of globalization sets the stage for the analysis of how various types of shocks might change globalization in the short to medium run (chapter 2) and in the long run (chapter 3). These assessments of globalization over different time frames then underpin the recommendations for what firms should do about globalization (part two).

I begin this chapter by confronting the news headlines about globalization's trajectory with hard data on international flows of trade, capital, information, and people. Because the available evidence does not indicate that globalization has gone into reverse—at least not yet, I turn next to a finer-grained examination of what I refer to as the *depth* and *breadth* of globalization. This assessment provides a clearer view of how globalized the world is today. It also illustrates two regularities that are so powerful they merit recognition as scientific laws: the *law of semiglobalization* and the *law of distance.*[1] I also present data from a multicountry survey that highlights how managers tend to believe that the world is far more globalized than it really is. The chapter therefore concludes with a discussion of the steep costs such exaggerated perceptions or *globaloney* impose upon companies and the world at large.[2]

Globalization in Retreat?

The 2008 global financial crisis shattered the confidence about globalization's prospects that had dominated the public and corporate discourse at least since 2001, when China joined the World Trade Organization (WTO) and memories of the 1997 Asian financial crisis began to fade. In the span of just three weeks in 2015, the *Washington Post* ran one headline declaring, "Globalization at Warp Speed," and then another asking, "The End of Globalization?"[3] Ambiguity reigned.

Then came Brexit. To use the same newspaper as a bellwether, after the June 2016 referendum, the *Washington Post* published an article bearing the headline, "Britain Just Killed Globalization as We Know It."[4] Returning the favor, after Trump's election, the *Guardian* in the United Kingdom starkly proclaimed, "Globalisation Is Dead."[5]

These two newspapers weren't alone in their pessimism. A broader tonal analysis of newspaper stories mentioning globalization reveals a sharply negative turn from 2015 to 2016. On average, negative stories outnumbered positive ones in 2016 by a factor of four to one in the United States and by two to one in the United Kingdom and India.[6]

Pessimism about globalization carried over from the newsstand to the bookstore with titles such as *From Global to Local* appearing in 2017 and *Us vs. Them: The Failure of Globalism* in 2018.[7] Public and business sentiment about globalization was clearly on a downswing. But we've seen this before, and perceptions can veer far away from reality. Do the facts support such a bleak depiction of globalization's trajectory? In light of hard data, the answer is "no."

My colleague Steven Altman and I compile the biennial DHL Global Connectedness Index, which measures international inter-actions across 140 countries accounting for 99 percent of the world's economic output and 95 percent of its population. The most recent edi-tion, released in November 2016, tracked international flows of trade, capital, information, and people from 2005 through 2015.[8] Figure 1-1

FIGURE 1-1

DHL Global Connectedness Index, 2005–2015

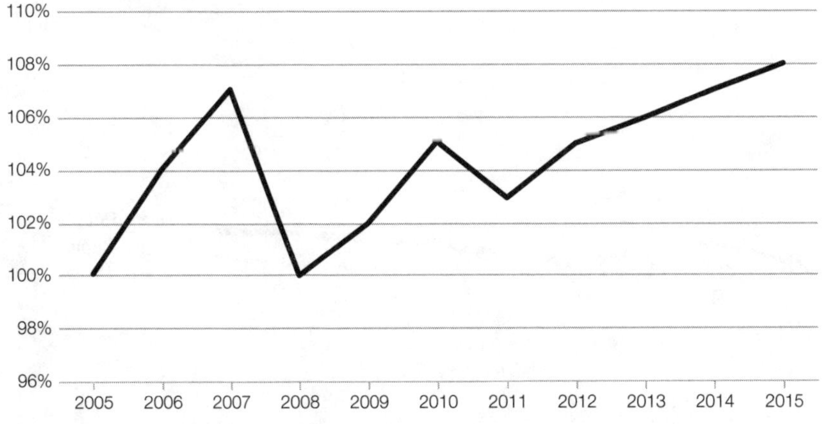

Source: Adapted from Pankaj Ghemawat and Steven A. Altman, *DHL Global Connectedness Index 2016: The State of Globalization in an Age of Ambiguity* (Bonn: Deutsche Post DHL, 2016), figure 1.3.

summarizes the results of the index at the global level demonstrating that although globalization was hit hard during the 2008–2009 financial crisis, it recovered and eventually surpassed its precrisis peak in 2014. And although globalization slowed in 2015, it had not—at least as of the end of the period studied—shifted into reverse.[9]

Figure 1-1 aggregates across the depth and the breadth of globalization. Depth captures how much of flows that could take place either domestically or internationally cross national borders. Breadth focuses on the flows that *are* international and measures whether they are dispersed globally or more concentrated, for example, among neighboring countries.

To focus first on depth, figure 1-2 unpacks trends along the four pillars of the index: trade, capital, information, and people. Trade (measuring both merchandise and services trade) turns out to be the only pillar on a multiyear decline. Capital (based on flows and stocks of FDI and portfolio equity) fell the farthest at the onset of the financial crisis, but has recovered somewhat since 2011. Information (capturing international telephone calls, international internet band-

FIGURE 1-2

DHL Global Connectedness Index depth pillars, 2005–2015

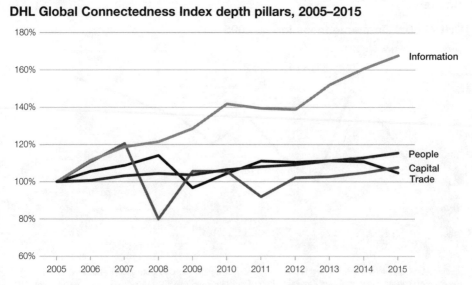

Source: Pankaj Ghemawat and Steven A. Altman, *DHL Global Connectedness Index 2016: The State of Globalization in an Age of Ambiguity* (Bonn: Deutsche Post DHL, 2016), figure 1.5.

width, and trade in printed material) has surged over the last decade, although the increase in its depth is moderated by the explosion in domestic information flows that has also taken place.[10] And while visa and work permit restrictions continue to constrain migration, the steady growth of international tourism has been driving consistent increases in international people flows.

Although the depth of trade and capital flows remained below their precrisis peaks, the depth of globalization as a whole had clearly not gone into retreat through 2015. And even the large drop-off in trade depth was almost entirely a price effect, driven by plunging commodity prices and the growing strength of the US dollar. (The value of merchandise trade fell 13 percent in dollar terms in 2015, but trade volume grew a modest 2.6 percent.)[11]

If the depth of globalization shows no signs of having collapsed, what about its breadth? While breadth can be measured in several ways, given breathless predictions of the "death of distance," the average distance traversed by international flows supplies a convenient metric. If the breadth of interactions was shrinking, one might expect distances to become shorter. In fact, the opposite is true. Figure 1-3

FIGURE 1-3

Average distance traversed by international flows, 2005–2015

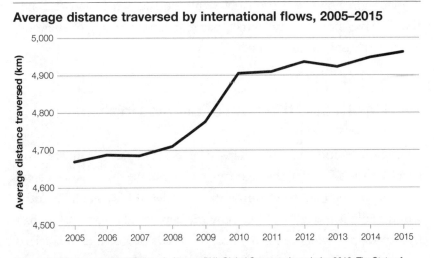

Source: Pankaj Ghemawat and Steven A. Altman, *DHL Global Connectedness Index 2016: The State of Globalization in an Age of Ambiguity* (Bonn: Deutsche Post DHL, 2016), figure 1.4.

plots the average distance covered by the flows included in the DHL Global Connectedness Index and reveals that international flows continued to stretch across greater distances through 2015.[12] This expansion has slowed, however, compared to its brisk pace between 2008 and 2010, a period when the share of flows from emerging markets (which tend to interact over greater distances) was rising swiftly and when firms from crisis-hit countries desperately sought growth far from home.

In short, neither depth nor breadth metrics indicate that globalization declined over the decade in question, although its growth *has* slowed. Devoted gloom-and-doomers might retort that these metrics don't tell the whole story, and that 2016 or 2017 data will reflect a decline. Maybe, but not yet. Limited data from the year of Brexit and Trump points to more of the same, namely, close to flat trade and FDI depth. Trade depth declined *less* in 2016 than in 2015 and preliminary data shows it growing in the first two quarters of 2017.[13] And even though FDI flows in 2015 were inflated by a wave of overseas corporate inversions by US companies (the wave ended in April 2016, when the US Treasury issued new rules cracking down on such transactions), FDI depth surrendered only a fraction of its prior year increase.[14] Data across all the components of the DHL Global Connectedness Index isn't available yet, but factoring in people and information flows will probably reinforce the conclusion that neither "Leave" nor "America First" has managed to stop globalization, let alone throw it into reverse.

Depth and the Law of Semiglobalization

Since globalization has not collapsed (at least not yet—its future prospects are the subject of the next two chapters), we can look for useful patterns in the data to examine in more detail how globalized the world really is today. We'll see how the depth and breadth of globalization supply evidence for my proposed laws of globalization across many types of international activity and over time.[15]

My first law of globalization can be summarized as follows:

> International interactions, while not negligible, are signifi-
> cantly less intense than domestic interactions.

In other words, national borders still present formidable barriers to international interactions, but the flows that do get across them are too significant to allow firms to focus exclusively on domestic opportunities and threats. I call this the *law of semiglobalization* because it highlights how the depth of globalization is significantly above zero but still far smaller than it would be in a perfectly integrated world.

Figure 1-4 provides depth metrics for macro-level trade, capital, information, and people flows, and figure 1-5 reports depth metrics pertaining to the business activity of multinational firms. Across both figures, the measures shown are simple depth ratios. For any type of activity that could happen either within or across national borders, I divide the amount of international activity by the total activity (international plus domestic). Across both figures, the average depth ratio is about 20 percent. Not only is domestic activity much more intense than international activity, domestic activity also almost always far surpasses international activity in absolute terms.[16]

Given the centrality of trade to debates about globalization, the multiple trade metrics reported in figure 1-4 merit more explanation. Gross exports of goods and services as a percentage of gross domestic product (GDP) (28 percent in 2016) is the simplest and most commonly cited measure of trade depth. It is calculated by summing up the shipment values tallied by customs agencies around the world and dividing by total output. But because the same content can cross borders more than once in multicountry supply chains, gross exports depth overstates the proportion of output that is traded. Exports depth based on trade in value added terms removes such double counting and indicates that exports really account for closer to 20 percent of world output rather than nearly 30 percent.[17]

FIGURE 1-4

The law of semiglobalization in trade, capital, information, and people flows

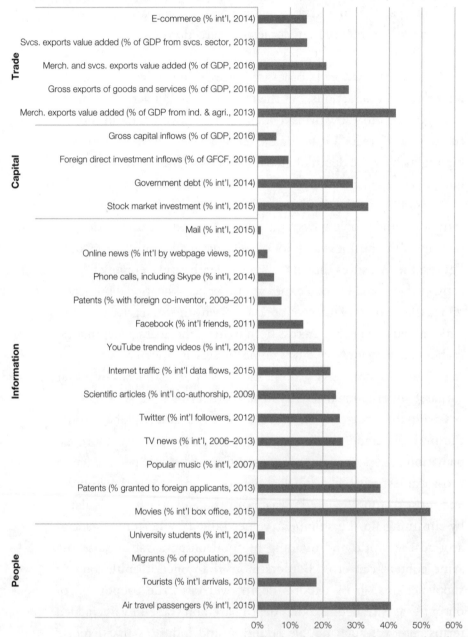

Sources: See chapter 1 endnotes on page 220.

Note: agri. = agriculture; GDP = gross domestic product; GFCF = gross fixed capital formation; ind. = industry; int'l = international; merch. = merchandise; svcs. = services

FIGURE 1-5

The law of semiglobalization at the firm level

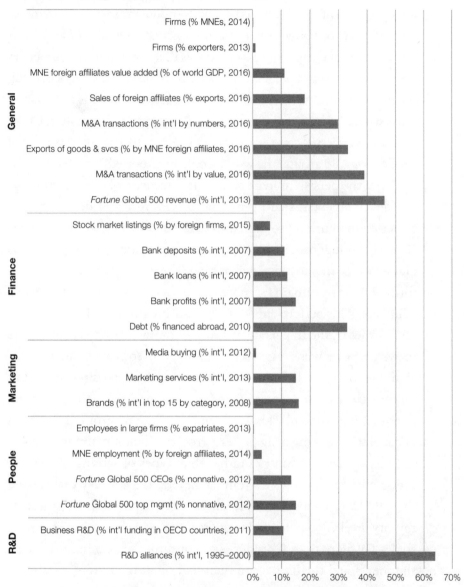

Sources: See chapter 1 endnotes on page 221.

Note: GDP = gross domestic product; int'l = international; M&A = mergers and acquisitions; mgmt = management; MNE = multinational enterprise; OECD = Organisation for Economic Co-operation and Development; R&D = research and development; svcs = services.

Adjusting for multicountry supply chains also highlights how much more intensively goods are traded than services. Exports account for about 40 percent of value added in goods-producing sectors (agriculture and industry) but only 15 percent in services.[18] This way of looking at trade depth also helps address objections that some kinds of output are not tradable. Most of what is impossible to trade is in the service sector, but even in goods-producing sectors alone, actual trade falls well short of what would be expected if borders (and distance) didn't matter. Under such counterfactual conditions, theory suggests that about 92 percent of goods produced around the world would be exported![19]

Given the persistent hype about the internet and other technological developments ushering in a borderless future, I devote special attention in figure 1-4 to measures of the depth of information flows. Despite the supposedly magical immaterial qualities of digital goods and services, and no matter what kind of technology is employed, information flows remain far more intense within rather than between countries. This pattern applies to everything from snail mail to overall internet traffic to particular types of online activity such as page views on news websites, videos trending on YouTube, and relationships on social media. The only depth metric surpassing 50 percent on figure 1-4 is for movies. This ratio will probably fall, as alternatives to Hollywood blockbusters continue gaining ground. China, in particular, is making a big push to grow its domestic film industry.

Looking across countries rather than types of activity, the law of semiglobalization holds even in Singapore, the country that topped the 2016 DHL Global Connectedness Index depth ranking as well as my city-level Globalization Hotspots index.[20] Even though Singapore trades far more than it produces or consumes, if you remove transshipments and the like, more than half of all the output consumed or invested in Singapore comes from inside Singapore itself, even though Singapore constitutes just 0.4 percent of the world economy.[21]

The law of semiglobalization has also held over a long historical period, even as the depth of globalization for many variables has increased, as illustrated for exports and FDI in figure 1-6. In 1820, exports

FIGURE 1-6

Historical exports and FDI stocks depth trends, 1820–2016

Sources: **Exports 1820:** Angus Maddison, *Monitoring the World Economy 1820–1992* (Paris: OECD, 1995).
Exports 1870–1949: Mariko J. Klasing and Petros Milionis, "Quantifying the Evolution of World Trade,
1870–1949," *Journal of International Economics* 92, no. 1 (2014). **Exports 1950–1959:** Penn World Tables
9.0. **Exports 1960–1979:** World Bank *World Development Indicators*. **Exports 1980–2016:** World Trade
Organization, *Statistics Database*, and International Monetary Fund, *World Economic Outlook*. **FDI 1913–1985:**
1994 UNCTAD World Investment Report. **FDI 1990–2016:** UNCTAD, *World Investment Report 2017* (Geneva,
United Nations: 2017).

Note: FDI = foreign direct investment; GDP = gross domestic product.

still added up to less than 3 percent of world GDP. But between the late
nineteenth and early twentieth centuries, exports depth increased from
8 percent to 15 percent, and FDI stocks started to register as significant
as well. After an interwar slump (analyzed further in chapter 2), international flows began to deepen again in the second half of the twentieth century. By the beginning of the twenty-first century, international
flows were mostly well into record territory (with immigrant intensity
and broad capital mobility representing two notable exceptions).

Because of this evolution, most business leaders do appreciate that
international activity has grown too big to ignore. The aspect of the
law of semiglobalization that many have not recognized is that international interactions are still significantly less intense than domestic
ones. And even when people do understand that borders matter, they
tend to underestimate by how much.

Look again at figures 1-4 and 1-5, but this time, cover the actual values and try guessing what they are. Or if you've already studied the figures closely, try quizzing a friend or colleague. Most people— including CEOs, countries' envoys to the WTO, MBA students, and members of the general public—overestimate these metrics by a wide margin. Using a common set of metrics across multiple surveys, I've asked these kinds of questions of tens of thousands of people across several dozen countries. The average respondent over- estimates the depth of globalization by five times! Later in this chap- ter, I present more on why people believe so much globaloney and why it matters.

Managers, in particular, tend to guess no more accurately than other groups. And while they could perhaps be forgiven for not being more clued in about the country-level metrics in figure 1-4, the inaccuracy of their intuition about the firm-level indicators in fig- ure 1-5 is more startling. Multinationals are exceedingly rare—less than one in a thousand firms (0.1 percent) have foreign operations, and only about 1 percent export. Of course, since multinationals are, on average, much larger than their domestic counterparts, their con- tributions to global economic activity *are* larger. The operations of multinational firms outside of their home countries generate about 3 percent of employment and 11 percent of output—but these values are still far shy of the 30 to 40 percent, respectively, that managers typically guess them to be.

I'll discuss how we can use the law of semiglobalization through- out the rest of this book. But for now, note that depth metrics and, by extension, the law of semiglobalization should guide firms about the extent to which business decisions should be based predominantly on domestic versus international considerations. Where depth is low, domestic market conditions, regulations, cultural preferences, and so on, should dominate. Where depth is high, managers have to devote more attention to international flows. In those cases, by extension, my second law of globalization—pertaining to its breadth rather than depth—becomes more salient.

Breadth and the Law of Distance

Now that we've considered the proportion of activity that takes place within versus across national borders, let's examine the smaller subset of flows that *do* cross national borders. Here, the second law of globalization—*the law of distance*—comes into play:

> International interactions are dampened by distance along cultural, administrative, and geographic dimensions and are often affected by economic distance as well.

In other words, distance isn't dead—or dying.

My second law of globalization deliberately echoes Newton's universal law of gravitation in physics. The idea behind gravity models in both physics and business is similar. The interactions between two bodies or places are proportional to their sizes and inversely proportional to the distances between them. But in business, *distances* can mean geographic distance as well as cultural, administrative, and economic distance generated by similarities and differences across countries.

The observation that distance, as well as size, matters in economic interactions prompted a hilarious Twitter exchange in September 2016. Science expert Paul Nightingale and Douglas Carswell, then the UK Independence Party's lone member of the British Parliament, were discussing the principal cause of the earth's tides. Nightingale pointed out that the moon matters more than the sun, even though the sun has twenty-seven million times the mass of the moon. When Carswell refused to accept this observation about the moon's importance, Nightingale referred the politician to Isaac Newton's *Principia*. To which a third party, in keeping with the spirit of the times, added the comment, "I think we've had enough of so-called 'experts' on gravity like Newton."

In defense of the law of distance in the business context, gravity models are regarded as providing some of the most robust results in economics.[22] Distance in particular explains why the rest of the European Union exports as much to the United Kingdom as it does to the United States, which has an economy seven times as large as the United Kingdom's. Distance also explains why the United Kingdom exports more to Ireland than to China, despite China's being about forty times larger than Ireland. That is why gravity models were the backbone of the UK treasury's generally well-regarded analysis of the long-term consequences of Brexit.[23]

For a visual sense of how the law of distance plays out, consider the map of Germany's merchandise exports displayed in figure 1-7, one of many such cartograms that you will encounter in this book. Countries have been resized to make their areas proportional to the value of Germany's exports to them. The one country not sized according to data is Germany because, given the law of semiglobaliza-

FIGURE 1-7

Rooted map with countries sized according to Germany's merchandise exports to them and shaded according to Germany's share of their merchandise imports, 2015

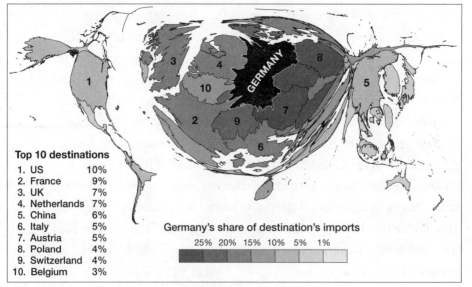

Top 10 destinations

1. US   10%
2. France   9%
3. UK   7%
4. Netherlands   7%
5. China   6%
6. Italy   5%
7. Austria   5%
8. Poland   4%
9. Switzerland   4%
10. Belgium   3%

Germany's share of destination's imports

25% 20% 15% 10% 5% 1%

Source: Data from International Monetary Fund, Direction of Trade Statistics (DOTS).

tion, it would loom disproportionately large if drawn according to the scale of its internal economic activity. Additionally, to blend size- and share-based perspectives, all countries except Germany have been shaded according to Germany's share of their imports. (Similar maps for other countries and other types of international activity are available on my website at www.ghemawat.com/maps.)

Germany was the world's third-largest exporter in 2015, and de- rived 40 percent of its GDP from merchandise exports, significantly more than the largest exporter in absolute terms (China, with 21 percent) or the second-largest (the United States, with 8 percent). Yet while Germany is renowned as a global export powerhouse, two- thirds of its exports went to other countries within Europe, so Europe appears far larger on this map than it does on a normal one. Even within Europe, countries physically close to Germany are enlarged more than countries farther away. Physical distance alone explains close to half of the variation in Germany's share of its trade partners' imports.[24]

In addition to their relation to physical distance, Germany's ex- ports also illustrate other ways that distance affects trade patterns. My CAGE distance framework highlights four dimensions of distance (cultural, administrative, geographic, and economic—see table 1-1). I use the framework here to help explain patterns of international ac- tivity and will apply it to firm decisions about where to operate abroad in chapter 5.[25] Germany's exports to most of its European neighbors are eased by their shared membership in the European Union, an entity that reduces administrative distance. Germany's exports to Switzerland and Austria—among the countries where Germany has the highest share of imports—benefit from a common language and other cultural similarities. Economic similarities and differences also matter, though they are harder to see from the map because they can have both positive and negative impacts, depending on what is being traded.[26]

Economic gravity models can quantify the effects of multiple dimen- sions of distance through analysis of patterns of interactions among *all*

TABLE 1-1

The cultural, administrative, geographic, and economic (CAGE) distance framework at the country level

	Cultural distance	Administrative distance	Geographic distance	Economic distance
Country pairs (bilateral)	• Different languages • Different ethnicities; lack of connective ethnic or social networks • Different religions • Lack of trust • Different values, norms, and dispositions	• Lack of colonial ties • Lack of shared regional trading bloc • Lack of common currency • Political hostility	• Physical distance • Lack of land border • Differences in time zones • Differences in climates and disease environments	• Rich-poor differences • Other differences in cost or quality of natural resources, financial resources, human resources, infrastructure, information, or knowledge
Countries (unilateral or multilateral)	• Insularity • Traditionalism	• Nonmarket or closed economy • Extent of home bias • Lack of membership in international organizations • Weak institutions, corruption	• Landlocked geography • Lack of internal navigability • Geographic size • Geographic remoteness • Weak transportation or communication links	• Economic size • Low per-capita income

Source: Reproduced from Pankaj Ghemawat, *Redefining Global Strategy: Crossing Borders in a World Where Differences Still Matter* (Boston: Harvard Business School Press, 2007), 41 (table 2-1).

countries. The models enable us to extend the example of Germany's trade patterns to the entire world, across all dimensions of the CAGE framework, and to many types of activity beyond trade. Coverage of all these dimensions and activities extends beyond the scope of this book. Here, I'll focus on aggregate trade and FDI across all industries and will discuss industry-level distance effects in chapter 5. Readers interested in similar analyses for a wide variety of other international activities can visit my website at www.ghemawat.com/cage.

Figure 1-8 quantifies the effects of CAGE distance on merchandise trade and FDI stocks based on patterns of international interactions observed across all countries from 2005 to 2015 for trade and from 2005

FIGURE 1-8

The law of distance for merchandise trade and foreign direct investment (FDI) stocks

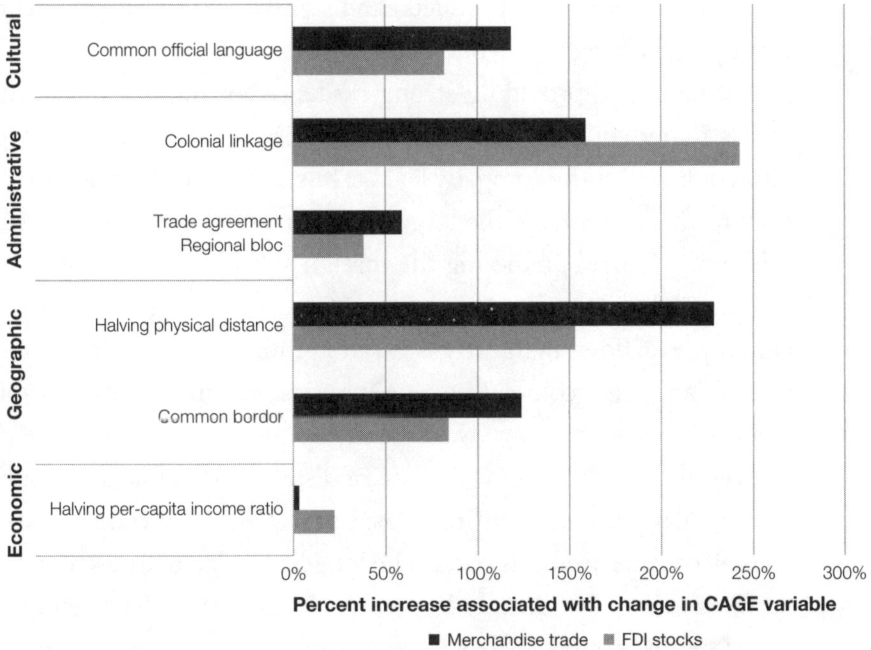

Source: Gravity model estimated using data from International Monetary Fund *Direction of Trade Statistics (DOTS)*; United Nations *Comtrade*; United Nations Conference on Trade and Development (UNCTAD) *Bilateral FDI Statistics*, 2014; International Monetary Fund *Coordinated Direct Investment Survey*; CEPII *GeoDist*; International Monetary Fund *World Economic Outlook Database*; and World Trade Organization *Statistics Database*.

to 2014 for FDI. Halving physical distance more than triples trade (increasing it by 228 percent) and more than doubles FDI (153 percent).[27] A common language roughly doubles both types of activity, as does a common border. And if one country colonized the other at some point in history, the boost to trade and FDI between the two is even larger—despite most of those colonial linkages having ended decades ago. The joint effect of all the commonalities on figure 1-8 is a boost of about sixty-eight times for trade and forty-nine times for FDI.[28]

While economic distance has only a small effect on aggregate trade flows, this isn't because economic distance doesn't affect trade much. It is because the aggregate analysis includes both industries for which trade is spurred by economic differences and others for which trade is dampened by such differences. In an industry-level analysis covering ninety-seven product categories, distance had significant positive effects on forty-four categories (indicating that economic arbitrage predominates for those products) and significant negative effects on twenty (indicating that economic distance dampens trade).[29]

In addition to providing strong evidence for the law of distance across many country- and industry-level activities, gravity models also work well at the company level. Thus, the law of distance applies even to the locations of the largest multinational firms' foreign subsidiaries. A model predicting the foreign subsidiary locations of the *Fortune* Global 500 using the same CAGE distance variables used for country-level flows in figure 1-8 found significant effects for common official language, colonial linkage, physical distance, and per-capita income disparities.

Even more surprisingly, the law of distance shows no signs of becoming less relevant over time, despite large drops in transportation and telecommunications costs. The longest available time-series data pertains to merchandise trade, for which researchers have generally found that distance effects have either remained stable or risen over time.[30] And for simpler evidence of the persistence of the law of distance, consider the average distance traversed by merchandise trade flows since 1950 (figure 1-9). That distance has fluctuated between 4,500 and 5,500 kilometers (between around 2,800 and 3,400 miles)

FIGURE 1-9

Average distance traversed by merchandise trade flows, 1950–2015

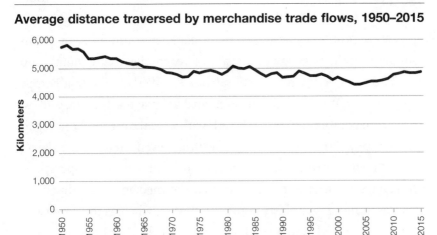

Source: Data from International Monetary Fund *Direction of Trade Statistics (DOTS)*, and CEPII *GeoDist*.

over most of the period analyzed. If cross-country distances and differences didn't matter, one would expect to see that distance rise to about 8,300 kilometers (5,200 miles) (just shy of the average distance between countries).[31]

What might explain the persistence of distance effects? Surprisingly, transport costs account for only a small portion of the total costs of traversing distance—only 4 to 28 percent, according to one study.[32] A literature review finds that "the consensus is that the bulk of trading costs are due to trade-reducing factors such as differences in legal systems, administrative practices, market structures, networks, languages, and monetary regimes."[33] Distance effects have more to do with history and institutions than they do with transportation.

Beyond applying to many types of international activity over a long swath of history, the law of distance also holds up all around the world. Thus, even though the United Kingdom tops the breadth rankings on the DHL Global Connectedness Index, its international activity still conforms to the law of distance. More than half of the UK's exports, imports, and inward FDI stocks involve European partners, as do roughly 40 percent of its outward FDI stocks, outward portfolio equity stocks, and international telephone calls. Of course, this application of the law of distance does raise obvious questions about Brexit, which I address in the next chapter.

As an indication of how the law of distance contradicts intuitions, consider that the majority of my survey respondents consistently support Thomas Friedman's assertion from *The World Is Flat* that companies now operate on "a global, Web-enabled playing field that allows for . . . collaboration on research and work in real time, without regard to geography, distance, or in the near future, even language."[34] Managers also vastly overestimate the breadth of multinationals' operations. US managers, for example, believe that the median US multinational operates in more than thirty countries abroad, whereas the correct answer is three.[35] And even if you focus on the world's five hundred largest firms by revenues, managers across all six countries on my 2017 round of surveys also greatly overestimated their reach.[36] Fewer than one in ten of these firms generate at least one-fifth of their revenue from each of the broad triad regions of North America, Europe, and Asia-Pacific. In contrast, the managers guessed on average that nearly half (44 percent) of these companies do so.[37]

As will be shown throughout this book, the law of distance has many business applications. But for now, note that gravity models and the CAGE framework help explain where firms have their best shot at succeeding abroad and where they should expect the most formidable competition. The distance effect estimates from gravity models also help provide tools for making business decisions (e.g., the CAGE Comparator tool on my website). And they are particularly powerful when customized according to firm and industry characteristics.

Blinded by Biases

People's tendency to overestimate how globalized the world is persists across countries, age groups, genders, levels of education, political party preferences, and every other control variable I've examined.

How could even experienced international executives be so far off base? At play are powerful psychological biases, three categories of which are particularly pertinent: perceptual biases, motivational distortions, and "technotrances."[38]

One of the clearest perceptual biases about globalization is *vividness bias*, the tendency of people to overemphasize the new or unusual. For example, economist Daniel Cohen notes that French people will notice the McDonald's on a street corner but will ignore the thousands of cafés still selling *croque monsieurs*.[39] Then there is the pattern of believing-is-seeing: in the words of the fable writer Jean de la Fontaine, "everyone believes very easily whatever they fear or desire." Furthermore, *projection bias* seems to be a particular problem for senior executives. Just because you may lead a highly global life doesn't mean that this is how most of the world operates. Parag Khanna has estimated that 90 percent of the people around the world never leave the countries where they were born.[40]

Motivational distortions are also rife in business. Globaloney can be useful for a chief financial officer talking up a firm's international prospects to investors. Ditto for a CEO trying to push his or her organization to become more global. And globaloney can also be a useful marketing device, for example, in taglines like "the world's best lasagna" or the World Series in baseball. But executives shouldn't let such public-relations efforts cloud their decision making.

Technotrances, however, may be what really turbocharge globaloney. These states of mind have been with us for a long time, from the age of sail onward. Technotrances involve a fantasy (or nightmare, depending on one's perspective) in which a new technology abolishes borders and distances, regardless of national polities and their laws, cultural differences, or the simple fact that out of sight tends to mean out of mind. While the transformational technology invoked changes over time, the faith that new transportation and telecommunications technologies will drive more globalization has been a constant.

Digitization is what currently seems to drive the most technotrances. The frenzy about its potential reaches its highest when the talk is about social media.[41] But as shown in figure 1-4, only 14 percent of friendships on Facebook cross national borders. Not only is it not much fun, usually, to friend somebody with whom one doesn't share a common language, but there are other cross-border impediments as well. China has its own homegrown alternatives to US social networks, which are banned there, reminding us that administrative policies can trump technological connectivity. And since our online friendships are typically heavily skewed toward people whom we also know offline and who hence typically live close to us, geographic distance comes into the picture as well.

The final argument against both technotrances and globaloney in general is history. Recall from the introduction that no less a Silicon Valley figure than Peter Thiel—PayPal cofounder and Facebook board member—has argued that some combination of technotrances and globaloney is responsible for every major financial crisis going back to 1720.[42]

The Costs of Globaloney

Globaloney is *not* a harmless delusion. It comes at a steep cost for both business and public policy. Starting with business, the Coke example highlighted in the introduction illustrates how globaloney can imperil a corporation. As described earlier, Coke's performance eventually stumbled and its market capitalization collapsed after former CEO Roberto Goizueta pushed the company to an extreme version of standardization and centralization in the 1980s and 1990s. To illustrate how the Coke case was driven by a set of widely held misconceptions about international strategy, consider four (erroneous) propositions that I ran past managers on my 2017 six-country survey:

1. The truly global company should compete in all major markets.

2. Competing the same way everywhere is the highest form of global strategy.

3. The truly global company should have no home base.

4. Globalization offers virtually limitless growth opportunities.

Under Goizueta, Coke succumbed to every one of these myths, even though they all fly in the face of established research. And if you also found yourself nodding as you read them, you're not alone. More than 70 percent of my survey respondents agreed with each of these propositions as well.[43]

Coke had targeted global ubiquity (myth 1) even before Goizueta became CEO. As Robert Woodruff, who ran Coke from the early 1920s to the early 1980s, once put it, "we feel that we have to plant our flag everywhere, even before the Christians arrive."[44] Goizueta's largest shift was his embrace of uniformity (myth 2), summed up by his repeated statement at a 1996 bottler's conference that there was "one system, one future."[45] Goizueta also took statelessness (myth 3) to heart, declaring, "The labels *international* and *domestic* . . . no longer apply. Today, our company, which just happens to be headquartered in the United States, is truly *a global company.*"[46] And he saw globalization as a source of endless growth (myth 4): "At this point in time, people in the United States consume more soft drinks than any other liquid, including ordinary tap water . . . We will see the same wave catching on in market after market until the number one beverage in the world will not be tea or wine or beer. It will be soft drinks. Our soft drinks."[47] Talk of a plan for world domination!

Since all these myths are rooted in globaloney, managers with more exaggerated perceptions of levels of globalization are, unsurprisingly, significantly more likely to believe in them—even after controlling for age, gender, and other factors. When managers overestimate how globalized the world is, they underestimate the need to carefully understand and respond to differences across countries. They invest in products and services that underperform in foreign markets, and they struggle to build and maintain the relationships that underpin sustained success abroad.

Business errors based on globaloney not only harm the firms in-volved, but also foul the general business environment by stoking anger against globalization. How do you think people in countries with deeply rooted tea- and coffee-drinking cultures would view a distant corporation's vision of converting them to cola? When busi-ness leaders show a lack of respect for the uniqueness and even the sovereignty of foreign countries, multinational firms come off as market imperialists. And statistical analysis also affirms that globalo-ney among the public exacerbates fears about globalization. It makes sense that people who overestimate the depth of globalization more than others do also worry more about globalization's allegedly harm-ful consequences.[48]

Once you have cut through the globaloney, what can your business do differently as a result? The answer is *not* hyperlocalization, Coke's disastrous response under CEO Douglas Daft in the early 2000s. Spe-cific business implications are the topic of part 2 of this book, but consider here a few highlights from the Coke example.

Starting with strategy (the focus of chapter 4), CEO Neville Is-dell, who took over in 2004, blended adaptation in response to cross-country differences with aggregation in the pursuit of scale economies and arbitrage-driven cost reductions. Coke now positions itself as a "total beverage company." With regard to presence (chap-ter 5), while Coke didn't scale back the number of countries where it operates, it did move toward more nuanced resource allocation by applying different costs of capital to investments in different mar-kets. And the company reportedly stopped worrying about when (if it all) it would enter North Korea. Architecturally (chapter 6), Isdell brought back the structural distinction between domestic and inter-national that Goizueta had abolished ten years earlier. Isdell also built up linkages across organizational units by instituting, for example, an annual meeting of product development leaders from around the world. Finally, in terms of nonmarket strategy (chapter 7), Coke now spouts less rhetoric about being a stateless company. But it doesn't talk or act as if it can simply hunker down and be a local citizen, either. Under Isdell and particularly his successor, Muhtar Kent, Coke promoted a series of corporate sustainability initiatives that are supposed to extend well beyond compliance with local requirements.

To conclude, this chapter has mapped the present state of globalization and argued for a pair of laws that govern its depth and breadth—debunking a lot of starry-eyed globaloney in the process. We have explored some of the biases that feed globaloney and looked at the tolls it takes on both public policy and business strategy. Some readers may have been surprised by how much emphasis I have placed, even in turbulent times, on *laws* that are expected not to change. There is, nonetheless, a strong strategic rationale for doing so. As Amazon CEO Jeff Bezos, who is certainly no stranger to turbulence, once put it: "It helps to base your strategy on things that won't change. When I'm talking with people outside the company, there's a question that comes up very commonly: 'What's going to change in the next five to ten years?' But I very rarely get asked 'What's not going to change in the next five to ten years?' At Amazon we're always trying to figure that out, because you can really spin up flywheels around those things."[49]

But are the laws of globalization likely to continue to hold in spite of Brump and other shocks that might lie ahead? The next chapter stress-tests the two laws.

Global Generalizations

1. The present wave of disillusionment and anger about globalization isn't entirely new. Technology-driven expectations of the demise of borders and distance have a long history of racing ahead of reality and then reversing.

2. Hard data on the depth and breadth of international flows indicate that—at least as of the end of 2016—globalization had slowed down but not gone into reverse.

3. Contrasting views of globalization from research data, the media, and managers point to an even larger problem: globaloney. Businesspeople (and the public) wildly overestimate how globalized the world is today.

4. Public policy and the business environment suffer because of globaloney. People with more exaggerated views of the levels of globalization also see globalization as more harmful, fueling pressures for protectionism.

5. Globaloney can have even larger direct costs for firms. Many international businesses make blunders when they overestimate the levels of globalization and, by extension, underestimate the cross-country differences and distances that they must address to succeed abroad.

6. Fortunately, globalization is subject to a pair of regularities that are so dependable that they merit recognition as scientific laws.

7. The *law of semiglobalization* (depth) stipulates that international interactions, while not negligible, are significantly less intense than domestic interactions.

8. The *law of distance* (breadth) stipulates that international interactions are dampened by distance along cultural, administrative, and geographic dimensions and are often affected by economic distance as well.

9. These two laws apply across a wide array of macrolevel trade, capital, information, and people flows and have done so for decades.

10. The laws of globalization provide a stable foundation on which strategies can be constructed even in the midst of an antiglobalization backlash.

2

Globalization and Shocks

The previous chapter established that globalization is neither as advanced as many presume nor so negligible that prudent managers can limit their attention to within-country conditions. The law of semiglobalization affirmed that national borders still matter, while the law of distance emphasized that international activity continues to be constrained by cultural, administrative, geographic, and, often, economic distance. We also saw that recognizing those patterns can help businesses avoid costly missteps. But the discussion was based, as were the two laws, on the data to date. What might yet happen as a result of recent shocks, like the Brexit and Trump votes, or ones yet to come?

The standard approach to answering such a question is to specify likely policy changes and assess their implications. But such an approach has several problems. First, key policy details of both Brexit and the Trump presidency remain unclear. Second, waiting for or investing in more information doesn't suffice, because it delays firms' responses without necessarily implying quick learning. And third, even agility in responding to new information has its limits when your firm is receiving lots of signals, often pointing in many different directions. In military strategy-speak, we are, at least for the short to medium run, stuck in a VUCA (volatile, uncertain, complex, ambiguous) world.

How should business leaders approach such turbulence? In chapter 1, I quoted Jeff Bezos on the strategic value of grounding decisions in realities that one is confident will *not* change. If executives can be sure that the laws of globalization will continue to hold, then these laws can guide a firm's strategic commitments in a turbulent environment.

This chapter therefore focuses on stress-testing the laws of globalization. First, I examine President Trump's still-evolving policies related to globalization. Then, given the not insignificant risk of a global trade war, I look back to the last time such a war broke out—in the 1930s—and derive a set of lessons for the present. Next, I consider shocks at the regional rather than global level by looking at the eurozone in the aftermath of the 2008 global financial crisis. Then I describe in more detail the likely effects of Brexit and how they vary across industries and companies. I conclude with some broader lessons for strategy in a VUCA world.

The Trumping of Globalization

Trump's policies, though constantly evolving, are isolationist in rhetoric ("America First") if not in reality. Might they end up breaking the two laws of globalization? Consider the two types of interactions, trade and migration, about which Trump has had the most to say and which are most likely to see wrenching changes. If the laws of globalization are likely to survive these shocks, they would pass a pretty convincing stress test.

Pre-Trump

Before the Trump administration, the United States obviously conformed to both laws. To start with semiglobalization, flows across

US borders (especially people and trade flows) proved large enough to provoke a backlash, yet still fell far short of what one would expect if borders had ceased to matter. In terms of trade, gross imports and exports accounted for 15 percent and 12 percent, respectively, of US GDP in 2015, far below a zero-border effect benchmark of 76 percent (100 percent minus the US share of world GDP). The United States imports *less* relative to the size of its economy than do all but five other countries with data on this metric (Sudan, Argentina, Nigeria, Brazil and Iran). And despite the cliché that everything consumed in the United States is made in China, less than 3 percent of money spent in the United States goes to Chinese imports—and a good portion of the price of Chinese products sold in the United States actually goes to domestic companies transporting, selling, and marketing those goods. Figure 2-1 maps the origins of goods and services purchased in the United States in 2014. The United States itself dwarfs China and every other country.

FIGURE 2-1

Origins of goods and services purchased in United States, 2014

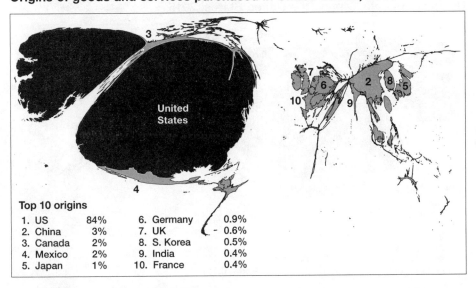

Top 10 origins

1. US	84%	6. Germany	0.9%
2. China	3%	7. UK	0.6%
3. Canada	2%	8. S. Korea	0.5%
4. Mexico	2%	9. India	0.4%
5. Japan	1%	10. France	0.4%

Source: Data from International Monetary Fund *Direction of Trade Statistics (DOTS), World Economic Outlook Database,* and United Nations *Comtrade Database.*

On the migration front, first-generation immigrants constitute 14 percent of the US population (figure 2-2), versus a benchmark without any border effects of 96 percent. But across three separate surveys, Americans' guesses of this percentage ranged from 32 to 42 percent.[1] And simply telling them about the actual intensity of immigration cut the proportion of Americans who believed that there were too many immigrants in the United States by almost one-half![2]

Turning to the law of distance, US international flows have long been disproportionately weighted toward the country's own region. Thus, Canada accounted for 19 percent of US merchandise exports in 2015, and Mexico for 16 percent, even though their combined share of non-US world GDP was only 5 percent. Canada, in particular, is the single largest US export destination and figures in the top five US partners for all but two of the fifteen directional flows included in the DHL Global Connectedness Index, even though it is only the world's

FIGURE 2-2

Origins of people living in the United States, 2015

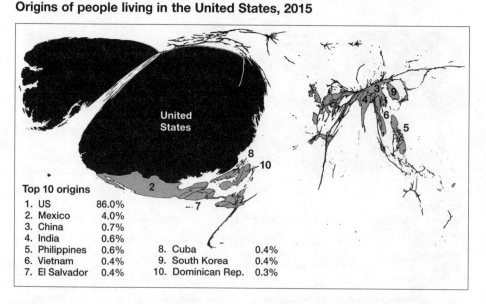

Source: Data from United Nations *International Migrant Stock 2015* and *World Population Prospects*.

tenth-largest economy. The United Kingdom also figures among the top five partners for all but four of the flows, illustrating the non-geographic dimensions of the law of distance (especially a common language and the erstwhile colony-colonizer link). And Mexico, the other North American Free Trade Agreement (NAFTA) neighbor of the United States, makes it into the top five partners more often than China does, although China is ten times Mexico's size. Mexico-US interactions also dwarf those of *all* other country pairs in regard to migrant stocks (Mexico to the US) and phone calls (US to Mexico).

Promises and Policies

Trump's plans for trade on the campaign trail, as laid out by Wilbur Ross and Peter Navarro (both subsequently appointed to key positions in his administration), involved not only staying within the laws of globalization but, at least as far as two-way trade is concerned, strictly staying put. The depth of (two-way) trade globalization was supposed to stay constant under the announced plans: the avowed objective was to cut US imports and boost US exports by equal amounts to eliminate the US trade deficit.[3] And given the objective of achieving bilateral balance with each of the six countries with which the United States runs the largest trade deficits—four of which also happen to be among its six largest trading partners—the breadth of two-way trade would also remain entirely unchanged, as would any estimates of distance effects.

The rhetoric about the flow of people on the campaign trail was even more strident and was backed up by postelection executive orders affecting undocumented immigrants, Muslims, and other groups. Such talk and action seem to have made the United States less attractive as well as less accessible for inflows of people of all types—tourists and students as well as migrants—and may increase outflows, especially with forced deportations. But the changes are unlikely to reduce the flows of students or tourists to a trickle, let alone to make immigrant stocks inconsequentially small. Recall that first-generation immigrants made up 14 percent of the US population in 2015. If the United States were to deport two or three million undocumented immigrants, as Trump promised during the campaign, the expulsion would be a profound human tragedy. But the foreign-born proportion of the population would still round to 14 percent. And even deporting all eleven million undocumented immigrants estimated to be in the United States would reduce the proportion to "only" 11 percent. Also unlikely to change is Mexico's status as the leading origin country: in 2015, about 28 percent of first-generation immigrants in the United States were from Mexico, more than five times as many as from the second-largest origin, China, despite the tenfold difference in populations.

The first two hundred days of the Trump administration brought little additional clarity to Trump's campaign pledges. According to the *Washington Post* "Trump Promise Tracker," of eighteen immigration and trade-related promises made by candidate Trump, two had been kept: the withdrawal from the Trans-Pacific Partnership (TPP) and initiating a renegotiation of NAFTA. Three promises had been broken (including the promise to immediately label China as a currency manipulator). Four had seen some kind of initiative launched, including building "The Wall" and canceling federal funding for "sanctuary cities." Nine promises still could not be rated at all.[4]

And while this characterization does capture a considerable level of temporization, it doesn't quite get at the amount of vacillation on view, which significantly complicates attempts to predict what the Trump administration will actually do. For example, during one afternoon in the administration's first week, a 20 percent border adjustment tax that would apply to all US imports was brought up, then narrowed to apply only to imports from Mexico, and finally characterized as just one idea in a "buffet of options." Not a promising basis for making predictions—the most obvious alternative to relying on the two laws of globalization (assuming they survive this chapter's stress-tests).

Potentially Catastrophic Effects

The preceding discussion suggested that at the aggregate, country level, little is likely to change under the Trump administration. Two caveats are worth adding. First, Mexico is particularly likely to be a punching bag because of its heavy reliance on the US market, the possibility of flipping investments and jobs back across the US border, and Mexico's role as a sender of immigrants—both documented and undocumented. (Canada is vulnerable as well, but seems likely to fare better, at least as of late 2017. Although Canada trades more with the United States than does Mexico, its trade surplus with the United States is less than one-fifth as large, and Canada is not a major source of immigrants.)

The second, bigger caveat—a potential catastrophe, really—has to do with the possibility that Trump just might provoke a global trade war. Many observers agree that this is a distinct possibility. Trump's election, in November 2016, led to a sevenfold spike in Google searches for "trade war," and after the day of three distinct trade policies in late January 2017, the multiple increased to tenfold.[5] My own multinational survey indicates that as of the spring of 2017, business executives pegged the probability of a global trade war or some other major breakdown of globalization over the next five years at about one-third. Considering this large perceived probability, let's delve further into the possibility of a trade war and examine whether the laws of globalization would continue to apply under such a scenario.

A Global Trade War?

What might happen in the event of a global trade war? Observers have floated several forecasts, of which the one issued by Moody's Analytics seems representative. It projected that if the United States imposes tariffs on China and Mexico of 45 percent and 20 percent, respectively—as proposed at one point by candidate Trump—and the two countries retaliate in kind, those shifts, along with the effects of a stronger dollar driven by other parts of the Trump agenda, would shrink US exports by $85 billion in 2019.[6] That is only about 4 percent of total US exports in 2015—and by extension just a rounding error in terms of US export intensity.

While this analysis suggests that the laws of globalization are likely to continue to apply, I am not entirely reassured. The estimated drop in exports suggests a "cone of uncertainty" that seems too narrow. And the assumption that export levels will eventually return to where they were trending before the onset of a trade war may be too sanguine. Note that the global financial crisis has left US output levels still 12 percent below the precrisis trend—roughly a decade after the crisis struck.[7] To counteract the well-known tendency to focus on scenarios that are insufficiently different from each other as well as from the present, let us look further backward than forward—as futurists advise—and draw some lessons from a truly extreme episode, the global trade war in the 1930s.

The early 1930s marked the largest reversal of globalization in history. And that period resembles the present in several respects. Globalization is again in the doldrums.[8] The tensions with the United States engendered by the recent rise of China echo those between the UK and Germany that were a key driver of World War I and the difficulties, including globalization-related ones, which the world experienced in its wake.[9] Both periods also feature rising levels of income inequality and associated fear, anger, and even racism. Historian Geoffrey Jones has pointed out that between 1916 and 1923, the formerly cosmopolitan and multiethnic Ottoman Empire (Turkey) committed genocide against Greeks and Armenians and that by 1921, the Ku Klux Klan—moribund since the 1870s—had five million active US members crusading against African Americans, Jews, and Catholics.

Two obvious differences should also be acknowledged. The Smoot-Hawley Tariff Act of 1930, which directly triggered the collapse of world trade in the early 1930s, represented a general increase in US import tariffs, whereas the Trump administration is talking about targeting only those countries with which the United States runs a large trade deficit. But in an era of multicountry supply chains, not to mention the retaliation threatened by countries such as China, it is easy to imagine targeted moves metastasizing into a global trade war.

The other difference stokes concerns instead of soothing them. At the end of the 1920s, trade intensity was less than one-third as high as it is today: exports amounted to less than 10 percent of world GDP. For this reason, most historians regard the collapse of world trade as having played only a limited role in the Great Depression that followed. Obviously, the impact of a given percentage drop in trade would be much larger this time around.

So, since the similarities between the two situations are strong and the differences do not (entirely) dispel concerns, what can the global trade war in the 1930s teach us today? Two sets of lessons, concerning the depth and breadth of trade, stand out—and support the two laws of globalization.

The Depth of Trade

The trade collapse that began in 1929 was truly staggering as a cycle of retaliations followed the US imposition of the Smoot-Hawley act. The value of world merchandise trade declined month after month until March 1933, as shown in Charles Kindleberger's famous cobweb diagram (figure 2-3). By early 1933, trade flows had dropped by two-thirds relative to where they stood at the beginning of 1929.

But although trade had plummeted, it did not perish. Even in the wake of the collapse, trade flows continued to be significant and choices about where and how to compete became even more important, thanks to pricing pressures. These choices carried special weight because the two-thirds drop-off in value reflected more of a fall in prices than in quantities, which had dropped by less than 30 percent.[10]

FIGURE 2-3

Charles Kindleberger's contracting spiral of world trade, January 1929–March 1933

Total imports of seventy-five countries; monthly values in terms of millions of old US gold dollars.

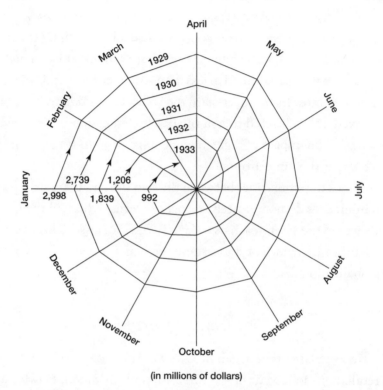

(in millions of dollars)

Source: *The World in Depression, 1929–1939*, by Charles P. Kindleberger, © 1973, 2013 by Charles Kindleberger. Published by the University of California Press. Figure 8: "The contracting spiral of world trade, January 1929 to March 1933," page 172.

The pricing pressures were, however, unevenly distributed. Although the value of commodities and manufactured goods traded suffered similar declines in the 1930s, the drop-off in commodities mostly reflected price effects, and the reduction in manufacturing trade reflected much larger declines in quantities (43 percent versus 7 percent for commodities between 1929 and 1932).[11] The shift in economic output toward manufactured goods—differentiated products that lacked well-defined reference prices; could not be shipped in bulk; and often required substantial local adaptation, marketing, and aftersales support—had already constrained trade growth *before* Smoot-Hawley.[12] In the United States, for example, export intensity decreased from 6 percent in 1921 to 4 percent by 1930.[13] And afterwards, trade in manufactured goods relative to total trade didn't take off again until the 1950s.

What might a two-thirds cut in trade—even though nobody is (yet) predicting a drop-off that large—imply today? It would be devastating, but there would still be more trade relative to global output than at the height of the first wave of globalization before World War I. In 2016, gross world exports added up to 28 percent of world GDP, down from a peak of 32 percent in 2008 but more than triple the 1929 level of about 9 percent. So the law of semiglobalization would probably continue to apply even in the event of a major trade war: companies and countries would still have to devote substantial attention to export market opportunities as well as competition from imports.

The other notable present-day implication is that services might be the contemporary analogue to manufacturing a century ago. They account for a large—and increasing—share of economic activity: more than 80 percent of private-sector jobs in the United States, for example, are in services.[14] But services trade is still less intense than trade in goods, as discussed in chapter 1. And while information technology (IT) has enabled significant offshoring of back-office services, there have also been setbacks, most notably the end of the WTO's efforts in its Doha Development Round to promote services trade through both investment and trade agreements. Recent developments make it even harder to be optimistic about the depth of services trade in the near term.

The Breadth of Trade

A second set of historical lessons pertains to the breadth of trade. The global trade war did not change the breadth of trade much, despite the big drop in the depth of trade. In particular, my regression analyses of world trade in 1935 versus 1928 show that various sorts of distance continued to dampen trade flows, to a similar extent in both years. The relationship between trade flows and geographic distance barely budged: the elasticity of the former with respect to the latter consistently approximated –1.[15] And the joint effects of a common language and colonial ties remained as powerful as before. All else equal, country pairs with these ties continued to trade about five times as much with one another as did pairs without such ties. Consequently, the identities of the largest trading partners of countries (or groups of countries) remained largely unchanged. Three-quarters of the countries or groups' top partners did not change at all, and none of the top partners in 1928 fell below second place in 1935.

That said, there *were* some variations across countries. Exports dropped more than proportionally in North America—where the United States had kicked off the trade war (see figure 2-4). Small

FIGURE 2-4

Origins of world exports, 1928 versus 1935

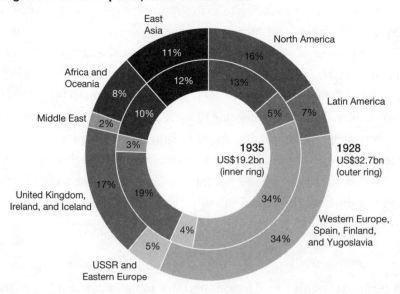

Source: United Nations Statistics Division.

Note: Export value of "Other Sterling Area," as reported by the United Nations Statistics Division, is redistributed to appropriate regions using the 1950 GDP of available countries from Angus Maddison, "Historical Statistics of the World Economy: 1–2008 AD," 2010.

countries and large countries suffered similar percentage hits to trade values, but since the smaller countries had higher trade intensities, these represented a larger share of their GDPs—roughly twice as much for the smaller countries for which data is available as for the bigger ones. And recovery involved a raft of accords to reduce tariffs preferentially. Between 1934 and 1937, for instance, the United States struck bilateral tariff-reduction agreements with seventeen countries, the majority of them in the Western Hemisphere.[16]

Another relevant policy implication is that even if the United States targets Mexico for tariffs, Mexico, as well as Canada, are likely to remain among the largest US trading partners—and very dependent on the United States for their exports—irrespective of what happens in the US-initiated talks to renegotiate NAFTA. Thus, more than a hundred years ago, the United States already accounted for 55 to 60 percent of Mexico's imports and 65 to 75 percent of its exports—and US businesses had invested more in Mexico than in any other country.[17] As Mexican foreign minister Luis Videgaray remarked in fall 2017, "If the negotiation does not go well, it would not be the end of trade between Mexico and the United States . . . There would be no leap into the abyss."[18] And economist Tyler Cowen has even suggested, given the findings from gravity models: "American trade with China may well be more fragile than American trade with Mexico . . . [despite] the recent rhetorical spats with Mexico, however rocky the latter may have seemed."[19]

I wouldn't go quite that far. What is said—and done—matters. Mexico is reportedly thinking of retaliation if hit with US tariffs, including, for the first time, playing the China card. The conclusion that I draw is that if a global trade war does break out, deepening isolationism would be the wrong response at the country level. Rather, countries should use whatever linkages and leverage are available to mitigate its effects. In this respect, apart from the general inadvisability of initiating a trade war, the apparent focus of the current US administration on beating up its natural trading partners in NAFTA just because it can (the United States accounts for 81 percent of merchandise exports from Mexico and 77 percent of those from Canada) looks particularly shortsighted. In light of both current trade patterns and gravity models of future potential, the US zone of trade dominance—the areas where the United States trades more than the European Union and China do—is mostly confined to the Americas north of the equator. And Mexico and Canada account for more than 70 percent of the non-US GDP in this zone. They are the United States' largest natural markets, because of their proximity as well as their size.

I will next push further on this theme of natural markets or regions and their implications at the industry and company levels by focusing on two shocks that happened at the regional rather than the global level. These two events took place in the world's most internally integrated region, Europe. The first is the eurozone crisis that peaked in 2011–2012, and the other is the still-evolving case of Brexit.

Eurozone Exigencies

The global financial crisis of 2008 was followed by the eurozone crisis, of which the most visible manifestation was Greece's teetering on the verge of defaulting on sovereign obligations. Greece got attention in Europe and beyond, mostly because of doubts the episode raised about the future of the euro as a common currency. Deserving of more attention than it received, however, is the financial deglobalization the eurozone experienced, without the demise of the euro. Analysis of this trend will help broaden the analysis of shocks beyond trade to capital flows. Europe is particularly salient in this regard because rising capital flows there, especially after the introduction of the euro, contributed more than half of the precrisis run-up in global gross capital flows, and their diminution constituted nearly three-quarters of the postcrisis collapse in global gross capital flows.[20]

Figure 2-5 tracks bank lending within the European Union since 2000. It focuses on loans because it was debt—rather than the more

FIGURE 2-5

Intra–European Union cross-border debt claims by domestic banks, 2000–2016

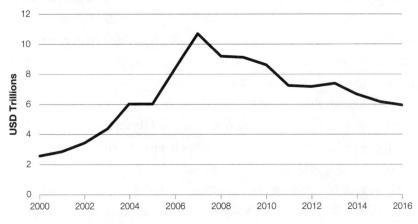

Source: Data from Bank for International Settlements *Consolidated Banking Statistics.*

stable equity flows covered in the DHL Global Connectedness Index—that drove the rise and fall of global gross capital flows.[21] The 45 percent decline in intra-EU bank loans depicted in the figure is indeed large—not that much smaller in percentage terms than the drop-off in world trade during the global trade war in the 1930s.[22] But despite this large decrease in depth, the breadth of such lending remained relatively unchanged. (The same basic pattern of a large drop in depth but steady breadth also applied to EU members' FDI flows over this period.)

One indicator of such stability is provided by estimated distance effects, as in the case of the trade war in the 1930s. The same type of regression analysis conducted for that episode was applied in this context to bank lending from 2000 to 2016. The regression showed that the estimated effects of distance generally remained quite stable for European lenders with respect to both intra-EU and worldwide lending. The only exception to this pattern pertained to economic distance and reflected how lenders became more risk-averse. Both worldwide and within the European Union, banks' propensity to lend to countries with very different per-capita incomes declined during the crisis period.

Another indicator of stability comes from how little the leading sources (and destinations) of funds in the banking analysis changed, despite the large decline in cross-border bank lending. Thus, between 2007 and 2012, there was a very high correlation (0.92) between the ranks of countries where EU-based banks had their largest intra-EU loan exposures. For 64 percent of reporting countries, the same country was the top destination in both years.

Note the implication of this analysis: parametric estimates of distance effects from before the onset of the eurozone crisis could be used to predict the distribution of such interactions today. On average, distance and size effects, along with country characteristics, explain roughly three-quarters of the variation in patterns of international bank lending. These figures affirm not just the applicability of the law of distance to a range of flows but also its relative stability.

Brexit and Beyond

In spring 2017, UK prime minister Theresa May invoked Article 50, triggering a two-year countdown to withdrawal from the European Union. But by late 2017, the terms of separation remained murky. And it is hard to predict how a bargaining game—one involving strong emotions as well as economics—will play out. But the negotiation of the terms of separation—whether Brexit will actually be soft, involving some degree of preferential access for the United Kingdom to markets in the European Union, or hard, involving terms no better than those available to any other member of the WTO—may stretch into 2019. And to truly see the effects of the eventual terms of separation, we will have to wait until 2020 or beyond. But these timing considerations don't mean that we completely lack visibility into the post-Brexit future.

The law of semiglobalization reminds us that while the United Kingdom's cross-border interactions are generally deeper than those of the United States, they still fall far short of the levels one would expect if borders (in this case, even intra-EU borders) had ceased to matter. UK gross exports of goods and services were 28 percent of GDP in 2015, and imports 29 percent, as compared to a zero-border-effect benchmark of 96 percent (100 percent minus the UK share of world GDP). And although Brexit *is* supposed to reduce some types of cross-border interactions, greater insularity is not the same as total isolation. Even with "little Englanders" in charge, total isolation looks entirely implausible. But that is perhaps obvious, given the earlier discussion of the United States under Trump. The less obvious implications, flowing from the law of distance, concern the breadth or distribution of the United Kingdom's international interactions—and directly contradict some of the promises made by Brexiteers.

The United Kingdom's Natural Markets

According to gravity models and the distance effect estimates they produce, the rest of the European Union clearly is and will be the United Kingdom's largest natural trading partner. To give this broad assertion more specific form, think of the claim, made repeatedly by the UK Independence Party (UKIP) and other pro-Brexiteers, that the United Kingdom's "real friends" (in politician Nigel Farage's words) are better targets for British commercial policy than is the European Union.[23] Or as UKIP's spokesperson for the Commonwealth poetically put it, "outside the EU, the world is our oyster, and the Commonwealth remains that precious pearl within."[24]

How likely is the United Kingdom to gain more from a free hand in negotiating with the Commonwealth—former British Empire states such as Canada, Australia, India, and South Africa—than it would lose from reduced access to the European Union? The GDP of the rest of the Commonwealth (i.e., excluding the UK) is only 55 percent as large as that of the rest of the European Union. So, size alone gives the European Union a large advantage over the Commonwealth in terms of market potential (see the first panel in figure 2-6). The middle panel adjusts for the effects of physical distance. The center of economic

FIGURE 2-6

UK's relative market potential in the rest of the European Union versus the rest of the Commonwealth

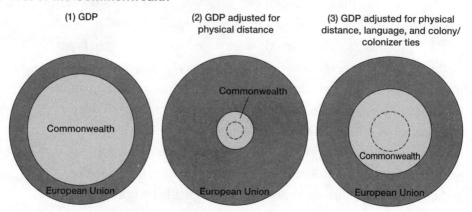

(1) GDP

(2) GDP adjusted for physical distance

(3) GDP adjusted for physical distance, language, and colony/colonizer ties

Note: Dashed line represents market potential adjusted for the most recent estimates of the distance effect.

mass of the rest of the Commonwealth is 8.4 times as far away from the United Kingdom as is the rest of the European Union. Assuming that halving distance doubles trade, the market potential of the Commonwealth for the UK is only 6.5 percent (55 percent divided by 8.4) as large as that of the European Union (the larger interior circle in the second panel in figure 2-6). But as we saw in the previous chapter, global gravity models of trade point to physical distance having an even larger effect—as indicated by the central tendency across hundreds of studies over decades.[25] My latest estimate using all the countries for which data is available indicates that halving distance boosts trade by 228 percent. This estimate of the distance effect reduces the relative market potential estimate for the Commonwealth versus the European Union to less than 2 percent—the smallest circle in the second panel in figure 2-6, the one that is delineated by a dashed line.

Of course, the comparison in the second panel ignores the cultural and administrative respects in which the Commonwealth might be intrinsically closer to the United Kingdom than the European Union is. The United Kingdom has a common official language (English) with 91 percent of the rest of the Commonwealth (on a GDP-weighted basis) and a colony-colonizer link with 99 percent, versus only 2 percent on both of those factors with the rest of the European Union. According to my estimates, all else being equal, a common language normally boosts trade to 2.2 times what it would be without a common language. I have also estimated that a colony-colonizer link has a multiplier effect of 2.5. Thus, the joint effect of sharing a language and sharing a colony-colonizer link is 5.5 times the trade relative to what it would be between countries with neither of these similarities.[26] These effects do boost the United Kingdom's natural market potential in the Commonwealth relative to the European Union (panel 3 of figure 2-6). But despite this boost, the predicted market opportunity in the rest of the European Union remains several times larger. (Again, the dashed line delineates the more conservative estimate.)

This conclusion holds across a range of sensitivities and is bolstered by some additional considerations. The joint effect of a common language and a colony-colonizer link would have to be much larger than in any previous study of which I am aware to reverse the conclusion of a larger natural market in the European Union. Additionally, this conclusion holds well beyond the realm of merchandise trade. Services trade and, by extension, FDI are especially important in the case of the United Kingdom. Among the world's thirty largest economies, the United Kingdom ranks first in the proportion of its GDP generated by the services sector (80 percent in 2015).[27] Physical distance constrains services trade and FDI somewhat less than it constrains merchandise trade, and the colony-colonizer boost for services trade and FDI is larger than for merchandise. Nonetheless, putting all the effects together, the United Kingdom again has far larger market opportunities in the rest of the European Union than in the rest of the Commonwealth.

The nature of this analysis (a long-run snapshot) also skips over some of the awkward dynamics of actually negotiating trade agreements with the fifty-two other countries in the Commonwealth—at a time when Britain has very few experienced trade negotiators (as of mid-2016, roughly 0.5 per Commonwealth country!).[28] Doubts can also be raised about the proposition that the United Kingdom on its own might achieve better terms with the Commonwealth countries than those currently enjoyed via the European Union. The European Union is an economic heavyweight, whereas Britain is not: Britain accounts for only 16 percent of EU GDP. And one pessimistic perspective on the idea (hope?) of real friendship trumping all else is provided by the generally disappointing results of Prime Minister May's visit to India in November 2016. The British wanted more trade and investment ties, but India's Prime Minister Narendra Modi explicitly linked that to relaxation of British visa conditions for Indians intent on studying in the United Kingdom.[29] Like the European Union, India has problems with British insistence on stringent controls over people inflows.

That said, how much Britain will trade with the European Union after it withdraws from the EU *does* depend on the negotiated terms of separation. Consider the consequences of another case of Brexit that wasn't very well thought out: the United Kingdom's withdrawal from India, accompanied by its partitioning into India and Pakistan. Pakistan now accounts for 0.8 percent of India's exports, twice Pakistan's share of world GDP but less than one-tenth of what gravity modeling would predict. Of course, India-Pakistan is an extreme case (and for that reason, perhaps the one cited most often by the few economists who don't believe in gravity models): the two countries have fought, depending on how you count, three or four wars since independence. Nobody is yet predicting a shooting war between Britain and other EU members, but the discussions between them have not always been friendly. For that reason as well as purely technical ones, there will most likely be a deterioration of trading relationships with Britain's largest natural market; the only question is to what extent.[30]

Industry Implications

Given this prediction, the natural next question is which industries and companies are likely to be hurt the most by Brexit and therefore face the greatest need to reconsider their current operating models.

In this context, the biggest change likely to be unleashed by Brexit is the greater administrative distance between the United Kingdom and its former partners in the European Union. Industries with great sensitivity to administrative distance are likely to be affected the most—unless, of course, the provisions under which UK-based operations can access EU markets happen to be eased the most for these industries (and at least from the perspective of EU concessions, such provisions look implausible right now).

Industries with high sensitivity to administrative distance include those that:[31]

- Are subject to high levels of regulation
- Produce staples or "entitlement" goods or services (e.g. health care)
- Are large employers or suppliers to the government
- Include national champions
- Are construed as vital to national security
- Control natural resources
- Require large, irreversible, geographically specific investments

No wonder financial services firms with extensive cross-border operations, for which the EU "financial passport" is very important, are rethinking the extent to which their European personnel are based in the United Kingdom. For example, Goldman Sachs announced that it will be shifting jobs away from London while adding several hundred in Europe—during just the first stage of Brexit.[32] And airlines and media companies are, for similar reasons, highly alarmed.

Another marker of industry sensitivity to Brexit is large scale economies that need to be amortized over (international) regional markets, rather than just within national markets. For example, BMW has discussed whether to move the manufacture of the Mini outside the United Kingdom despite the very British image of that brand.[33] Industries that are highly dependent on either exporting or importing will also obviously be especially sensitive to Brexit. While exports tend to get more attention, the European Union is an even more important source for UK imports than it is a destination for UK exports. Finally, belonging to the services sector—a particularly important sector to Britain but one in which overcoming barriers often requires investment treaties as well as trade agreements—also makes an industry sensitive to Brexit.

Company Implications

At the company level, some additional attributes seem likely to be associated with high degrees of exposure to Brexit. Companies that depend much more on exports or imports than their competitors do are likely to be the hardest hit. In the US context, consider the asymmetric responses of New Balance and Nike to Trump's scrapping of the TPP. New Balance, which had stayed focused on local manufacture, supported Trump's move, whereas Nike, which had built up international supply chains, did not.[34]

Small firms that aren't yet exporters or importers are also less likely to start trading abroad, since such firms typically look nearby for their first international transactions. And at the other end of the size spectrum, companies that use Britain, particularly London, as their regional headquarters for serving all of Europe (e.g., many US multinationals) are likely to need to reconsider basing that role there. Similarly, other companies that use London as their global headquarters, especially if most of their business lies outside the United Kingdom (e.g., Vodafone, which derives some 85 percent of its revenues from abroad), may need to reconsider what they do in the UK.[35] The British companies that may have private reasons to cheer are those that are focused on the UK and that are trying to hold off regional or even global competitors at home.

As this discussion has reminded us, any assessments or business decisions need to be made with granularity. Not all companies within the same industry, let alone all industries, will be affected in the same way. Similarly, in terms of what is to be done, again, the appropriate response will be predicated on the specifics of a company's situation. But given the separate tracks down which the United Kingdom and the European Union seem to be moving, there is now more cause to consider making changes to your strategy than there was in the immediate aftermath of the Brexit vote, when it was still unclear whether Article 50 would ever be invoked, let alone when.

Dealing with a VUCA World

The discussion of the industry- and company-level implications of Brexit brings up the broader issue of how to deal with a VUCA world.[36] This chapter has already suggested one response: relying on the laws of globalization (and associated parameter estimates) to point the way forward. But a wide variety of other responses to VUCA conditions, at least in the short to medium run, could also enhance benefits and opportunities or could reduce costs and risks.[37]

One such response is to time strategic moves to take advantage of volatility or fluctuations. Thus, after the Brexit vote in June 2016 and a flash crash in October forced the British pound down to its lowest level against the dollar in thirty years, Rupert Murdoch's 21st Century Fox unit bid (for the second time) for the 61 percent of Britain's Sky Television that it didn't already own.[38]

Another response, which can help support the first one, involves keeping buffers or excess capacity—ranging from physical to financial—to deal with volatility. For instance, the record amounts of cash that companies have on hand enable them to move more quickly on acquisitions. But while large amounts of excess capacity may broaden opportunity sets, they also carry opportunity costs, not to mention risks.

Yet another set of responses has to do with more effective adaptation over time. Flexible budgeting is a good example of quicker variation of key managerial parameters than is permitted by typical budgeting cycles. But since such variation creates complexity, business leaders also have to think about levers for improving the trade-offs between variation and standardization. For instance, a company could focus on a particular segment because its growth, at least, is predictable. Thus, a recent Boston Consulting Group report suggests targeting "new borderless markets of connected consumers and businesses."[39] Externalization, as in joint ventures or franchisee relationships, can reduce the burden of local adaptation by shifting it onto partners—and can also help provide a local face in case of protectionism. Then there is the possibility of design, such as Zara's quick-response model. This business model lets the company see which clothing items are selling and quickly adjust production, as opposed to trying (like everybody else) to predict what will sell. And even more broadly, one might think of generalized innovation or reconfiguration possibilities, such as the platform that Amazon has built for launching new businesses.

Variation, focus, externalization, design, and innovation are elaborated on further in chapter 4, as five levers for adaptation. Although that chapter emphasizes responses to differences across countries rather than over time, the ideas advanced there, if plugged into the present context, could help firms adapt more effectively over time.

In addition to that grab bag of ideas, several other observations are also worth making:

- Don't simply succumb to uncertainty or VUCA-dom. People are often too prone to focusing on extreme possibilities—to assuming that uncertainty is zero or that it overpowers all attempts at analysis—as opposed to intermediate levels of uncertainty that *can* and should be analyzed.[40]

- Predictive abilities can be improved as well, even for major geopolitical events. The laws of globalization, and particularly the notion that breadth may remain stable even as depth drops, offered useful insights on what might happen with Brump. And Philip Tetlock's recent work on superforecasting highlights the importance of staying open to new data, being willing to revise your assumptions over time, thinking in terms of probabilities, and teaming up rather than thinking alone—themes coincident or generally compatible with the ones developed in this book.[41]

- Do look at a deglobalization scenario, as in one involving reduced but nonzero globalization. This chapter focused on scenarios in which depth decreased at a global or regional level but breadth remained about the same. However, it is easy to imagine picking other scenarios, such as ones that affect particular countries as sources of supply or demand. Thus, luxury-goods manufacturers made hay as China grew into the largest market in the world, but they stumbled when it began cracking down on domestic gift-giving and "gray channel" imports in 2012. (The Chinese bought most of their luxury products overseas to avoid domestic tariffs and taxes.) The manufacturers have all moved to deepen their presence in mainland China, but some of them could have been better prepared to do so.

- Avoid reacting to every new development. As futurist Paul Saffo notes, "the incoming future will wash up plenty more indicators on your beach, sooner than you think." Saffo's conclusion: "Bottom line? Be skeptical about apparent changes, and avoid making an immediate forecast—or at least don't take any one forecast too seriously."[42] Instead, preset some triggers for continuing or changing direction, as venture capitalists do.

- Other things being equal, a VUCA world privileges relatively reversible or low-regrets moves over irreversible ones. Thus, US companies thinking of investing in Mexican supply chains might not want to do so right now, whereas firms that have already invested probably shouldn't pull up stakes just yet, although they *should* make backup plans.

Finally, while responses to a VUCA world naturally tend to emphasize short- to medium-term considerations, companies must also ensure they are still building toward long-term success. The global luxury brands in China seem to be on track to achieve this. Rather than giving up, they recommitted themselves and made major strategic changes to make sure they could sustain their presence until the market started to rebound (as it did in 2016). Many increased their focus on e-commerce and social media. They also adjusted their pricing and sales strategies as tighter border controls, tariff adjustments, exchange rate movements, and terrorist attacks in Europe prompted more customers to buy inside China rather than while traveling abroad. Some luxury houses invested in local Chinese brands and product offerings. And astute managers also observed how high-end Chinese brands responded to the anticorruption crackdown to see what lessons they could learn.

If the global luxury brands in China now look like a success case for bridging short- and long-term strategies, Norwegian Air Shuttle's position looks far more precarious. Norwegian had grown rapidly to become Europe's third-largest low-cost airline, and it pioneered low-cost flights across the Atlantic on a new generation of narrow-body aircraft in 2017. One of the keys to Norwegian's strategy was to move fast on ordering new airplanes. Norwegian's CEO, Bjørn Kjos, described his approach versus Ryanair, Europe's largest low-cost airline, as follows: "I know Ryanair is just waiting to get underway with their long-distance efforts . . . But we have taken all the planes—and—I heard that when I asked [Ryanair CEO] Michael O'Leary how it's going: 'Bjørn, godammit, you've taken all the aircraft!'"[43] O'Leary, however, had a very different perspective. He argued in September 2017 that Norwegian is "not long for this world" because the rival airline had overextended itself and was short of cash.[44] Norwegian's bold strategy may ultimately prove a success, but its limited use of buffers is particularly dangerous in a VUCA environment.

Global Generalizations

1. Ambiguity about the policy changes that will result from Brexit and Trump favors relying on the laws of globalization—if the laws can be expected to hold in spite of these shocks.

2. Before Trump, the United States clearly conformed to the laws of globalization. Worries about imports featured

heavily in the presidential campaign, but only five countries import less relative to the sizes of their economies than the United States does.

3. The Trump administration's avowed intent of eliminating the US trade deficit by raising exports and reducing imports in equal amounts with key partner countries would leave the depth and breadth of US trade flows unchanged.

4. President Trump's rhetoric, however, is strongly antitrade, and fears of a trade war spiked after his election. The last time a global trade war broke out, in the 1930s, the value of world trade dropped by two-thirds. A similar drop today would be devastating, but trade depth would still remain significant.

5. Even as trade depth plummeted in the 1930s, its breadth remained stable as did estimates of how trade was dampened by multiple dimensions of distance. Similarly, the effects of most types of distance on European countries' international bank lending barely budged as cross-border lending collapsed during the eurozone crisis.

6. In case a trade war does break out, countries can minimize the damage by strengthening relationships with their natural trade partners. Canada and Mexico are the largest natural markets for the United States; all three countries would suffer greatly if relationships break down in North America.

7. Even after Brexit, the European Union—not the Commonwealth—will remain Britain's largest natural market. The European Union's larger size and geographic proximity more than offset the United Kingdom's cultural and historical ties to the Commonwealth.

8. The companies that will be affected the most by Brexit are those in highly regulated industries, those that depend on international scale economies or supply chains, smaller companies, and companies in the service sector.

9. The shocks analyzed in this chapter illustrate the challenges posed by a VUCA world. Firms can improve their ability to manage through such turbulence by not getting overwhelmed by the uncertainty and by adopting better forecasting methods, using scenarios, avoiding too much reactivity, and privileging reversible moves.

10. The laws of globalization survive the stress tests related to Trump's policy promises, a prospective analysis of Brexit, and historical analyses of the 1930s trade war and the eurozone crisis. These laws provide a stable frame of reference to ground international strategies in a turbulent environment.

3

Globalization in the Long Run

Chapter 1 focused on evidence of globalization up to the present and concluded that we are not (yet) in the grips of a globalization apocalypse. As I also explained, the evidence supports two laws of globalization: the law of semiglobalization and the law of distance. Chapter 2 examined shocks to globalization, most notably the possibility of a global trade war, which it calibrated by going back to the global trade war of the 1930s. The laws of globalization, which continued to apply during that episode, underpin lessons that seem useful under today's turbulent conditions. This chapter shifts the focus of the analysis further forward, to the long run.

Of course, purporting to analyze the long run when we have so much trouble making predictions about the short to medium run may raise eyebrows. But remember that although weather forecasts tend to lose their accuracy two weeks out, we can predict with reasonable confidence whether the world will be warmer or colder in a hundred years. In the short run, random events often overwhelm the overarching trend, but in the long run, their effects tend to wash out.[1] Or if you don't believe in global warming, think of the yo-yo effect in the context of dieting: without knowing where a person will be in his or her weight loss-gain cycle, we can predict an average weight gain of a pound or two per year through middle age.

In the context of globalization, we *don't* have as clear a sense of whether levels of globalization are likely to be higher or lower in the long run. Although globalization has tended to increase over several centuries, it did suffer a reversal between the two world wars—for longer than the five- or even twenty-year time frames often treated as the long run in the business world.[2] Over the coming decades, we can imagine a range of outcomes for globalization, from its success to its collapse. How should we direct our attention across the vast field of possibilities?

Peter Thiel has proposed a thought experiment that, while keyed to his belief that globalization tends toward extremes (which is inconsistent with the law of semiglobalization), has heuristic value: "Assume that, in the event of successful globalization, a given business would be worth $100/share, but that there is only an intermediate chance (say 1:10) of successful globalization. The other case is too terrible to consider. Theoretically, the share should be worth $10, but in every world where investors survive, it will be worth $100. Would it make sense to pay more than $10, and indeed any price up to $100?"[3]

The implicit lesson carries over from investors to managers pondering global success versus failure in their long-run analyses. Since it is hard to armor a business against Armageddon and since globalization's odds *are* better than those in Thiel's thought experiment, a focus on success scenarios—on how to help make them happen as well as profit from them—is generally more worthwhile. This does not obviate the need to consider deglobalization scenarios in the short to medium run, as advised in the previous chapter. But if you have already done so, you will probably gain little by also focusing on failure in the long run.[4]

Further structure for how to think about the long run is suggested by the observation that if there is to be healthy economic growth and further globalization, the emerging economies of the Global South—particularly those in Asia—will have to grow significantly faster than the advanced economies. (Because of demographics, it is hard to devise scenarios in which emerging economies *don't* grow faster, but there is robust global growth anyway.[5]) This big shift, the south-by-southeast movement of economic activity, serves as the tent pole for what I like to think of as the SMART predictions covered in this chapter:

- South by southeast

- Modest trade growth

- Accelerated globalization along other dimensions

- Regionalization and multipolarity

- Trading places? (US-China rivalry)

These five predictions need not come to pass, but they are likely elements of plausible long-run success scenarios. And companies *should* take a long-run perspective, given how much time they need to fundamentally change their strategies, adjust their global presence, reorganize, and so forth—the kinds of business decisions discussed in part two.

South by Southeast

Since the millennium, the engine of economic growth has shifted from the advanced economies of Europe and North America toward the emerging and developing economies, particularly those in Asia. As shown in figure 3-1, growth rates in the developing world just slightly outpaced those in the developed world over the last two decades of the twentieth century. But beginning in the early 2000s, emerging and developing countries began to achieve much higher overall growth, producing dramatic effects that are already visible today. And there are several reasons to think that this difference in growth rates will persist.

Before elaborating, I should clarify which countries are considered emerging. Antoine van Agtmael coined the term *emerging markets* while he was working for the World Bank back in 1981.[6] Realizing that

FIGURE 3-1

GDP growth rate of advanced versus emerging and developing economies, 1980–2022 (projected)

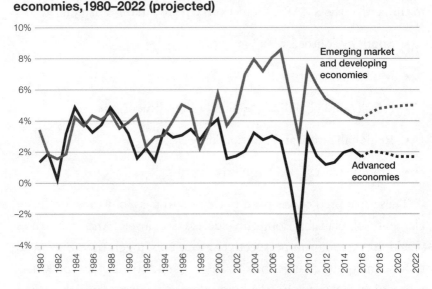

Source: International Monetary Fund, *World Economic Outlook Database*, April 2017.

poor countries needed more marketing appeal to attract investors, van Agtmael came up with his more "uplifting term"—which I use interchangeably here with *emerging economies* as well as another neologism, *the Global South*. Note that van Agtmael's focus on poor countries implied a narrower meaning for *emerging markets* than how some people use the term today: to denote all places that are growing fast. Using this catch-all definition, for example, McKinsey's managing partner, Dominic Barton, told the *New York Times*, "I think we should be considering the United States as an emerging market . . . It's really a high-growth market . . . Frankly, we should be opening up more offices in the United States than in China and India."[7] My prediction that emerging markets will grow relatively fast would be safer with such usage—a tautology, in fact—but would be devoid of any meaningful content. Instead, I stay closer to the original meaning of the term and employ the International Monetary Fund (IMF) classification system, which divides its members into "advanced" and "emerging and developing" economies. While the IMF does not publish its current criteria, it has historically considered countries' per capita incomes, financial market sophistication, and the sectoral composition of their economies.[8]

The *emerging* tag preceded the actual emergence of such economies. Their share of world GDP (at market exchange rates) actually bottomed out in 1992, at 16 percent (figure 3-2). But since 2000, they have accounted for 62 percent of global growth, boosting their share of world GDP to 39 percent by 2016. (The figures look even more dramatic when currencies are valued at purchasing power parity rather than market exchange rates: 78 percent of global growth and 58 percent share of world GDP.) Despite all the talk of an economic slowdown in emerging markets, with most of the advanced economies performing anemically even before Brump, the emerging econ-

FIGURE 3-2

Emerging and developing economies' percentage of world GDP at market exchange rates and PPP-adjusted rates, 1980–2022 (projected)

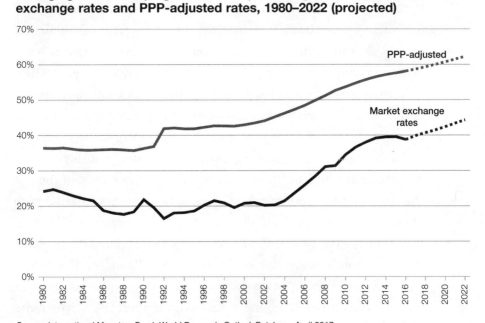

Source: International Monetary Fund, *World Economic Outlook Database*, April 2017.

Note: PPP = purchasing power parity.

omies' growth advantage shows no signs of disappearing. Projections from economic forecasting company Oxford Economics imply that by 2050, emerging markets' share of GDP will be 67 percent.[9] Of course, these are aggregate statistics, and there is a great deal of disparity among the more than 150 countries classified as emerging and developing; among these, growing economies prevail, but some economies are experiencing sluggish growth or are even shrinking.

While there are some success stories in Latin America, Western Asia, emerging Europe, and Africa, the largest overall gains have been in East and South Asia. China and India alone accounted for more than a quarter of global growth over the past decade (at market exchange rates). China is now the world's largest economy if measured at purchasing power parity and is second only to the United States at market exchange rates.

The rising share of output generated in Asia has already caused the planet's economic center of gravity to shift eastward. It moved from south of the Azores islands in 1980 to Algeria by the early 2000s. It now hovers over Iran, and some of the forecasts discussed below imply that it could be in Tibet by 2050.[10] One advantage of visualizing the big shift in terms of a moving center of gravity is that it helps avoid equating the declining share of activity in advanced economies with their absolute decline. Note that per-capita GDP (in constant currency) in the advanced economies was 17 percent greater in 2016 than in 2000 (versus 86 percent greater in the emerging economies).

All that said, these headline growth numbers are probably less important to business decision makers than are the effects of the big shift to emerging economies on the industries or sectors of particular interest to them. Figure 3-3 shows how emerging economies' shares of production (vertical axis) and consumption (horizontal axis) have evolved across a dozen industries since the millennium. Consistent with the law of semiglobalization, which implies that most production and consumption will take place within a single country, most of the industries shown in the figure cluster along the diagonal line (which represents equal emerging-economy shares of production

FIGURE 3-3

Industry-level shifts of production and consumption to emerging economies

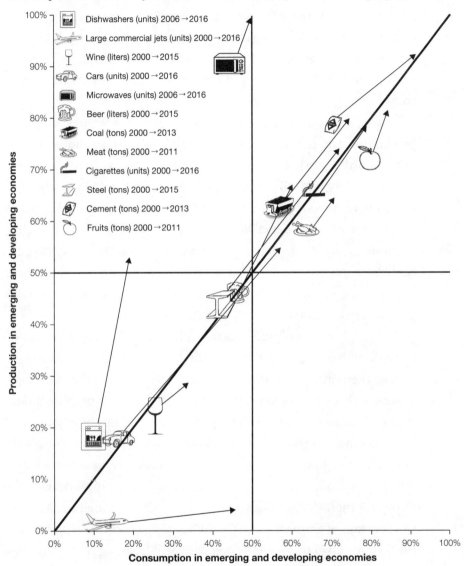

Sources: Based on data from Euromonitor *Passport*, except for the following: large commercial jets (Boeing, Air Transport World, and Bloomberg), wine (Euromonitor, trade data and analysis as reported by the Wine Institute), cars ("Organisation Internationale des Constructeurs d'Automobiles [OICA]), cars ("Organisation Internationale des Constructeurs d'Automobiles [OICA]"), beer (Euromonitor and Kirin), coal (US Energy Information Administration [EIA] *International Energy Statistics*), steel (World Steel Association), and cement (Portland Cement Association, Deutsche Bank, and United Nations *Commodity Production Statistics*).

Note: The icons at the end of the arrows on the chart represent the first year's data. The point of the arrow represents the most recent year's data.

and consumption). An exception, with large exports from emerging economies to advanced ones, is microwave ovens—well above the diagonal line. About 99 percent were produced in emerging economies in 2016, but only 50 percent were sold there. The opposite pattern holds for large commercial jet aircraft—well below the diagonal line—with only 3 percent of production but 47 percent of sales occurring in emerging economies.

Taking a dynamic perspective, emerging economies' share of production and consumption increased in all twelve industries. In other words, there was general movement toward the top right corner of the graph. But the rate of movement varied greatly. The automotive industry exhibited the largest shift: in 2000, less than 20 percent of its production and consumption was in emerging economies; by 2016, that figure had increased to about 60 percent. By contrast, the share of meat production and consumption in emerging economies only increased by six to seven percentage points between 2000 and 2011.

Again, China has played a sizable role in this shift. In 2016, out of thirty-four major industries, China was the largest consumer for eighteen of these industries and the second-largest for another fourteen. Compare this with 2000, when China led in only five of those industries and ranked second in eleven.[11] Change may be coming even in large commercial jet aircraft: Airbus already has two assembly plants in China, and Boeing will open a new plant there in 2018—its first outside the United States.[12] And China is on the way to developing its own domestic capabilities, with state-owned Commercial Aircraft Corporation of China, Ltd. (COMAC) having successfully test-flown the C919 in 2017 (although the company still faces regulatory hurdles before the airplane can operate commercially).[13]

Returning to the macro level and looking forward, the emerging share of the world economy does indeed look set to continue its increase. While the salience of China as a growth pole is likely to diminish (more on that below), there are several reasons to think that emerging economies in general and emerging Asia in particular will continue to grow faster than advanced economies:

- Looking backward, the big south-by-southeast shift has proven to be a stable megatrend. John Naisbitt identified a set of mega-trends in 1982 and updated them with Patricia Aburdene in 1990.[14] Most of the trends were quickly pronounced vacuous or invalid, dead on or before arrival.[15] But some rare exceptions turned out to be valid predictions. In his earlier book, Naisbitt foresaw the change from "national economy to global economy." He also described the "rise of the Pacific rim" in the latter book. Both these megatrends coincide roughly with the major thrust of the argument in this chapter.

- Prominently cited long-term forecasts—from Oxford Economics, the Economist Intelligence Unit, McKinsey, and the Organisation for Economic Co-operation and Development (OECD)—point to a concentration of economic growth in emerging economies, and in emerging Asia in particular. We can see in figure 3-4 the evolving shares of GDP at market exchange rates held by each country in 1992 (when the share of emerging economies bottomed out), in 2016, and projected for 2050.

- These GDP forecasts are consistent with demographic trends, which we generally can predict more confidently. The United Nations Population Division forecasts that the emerging world will account for 97 percent of population growth between 2016 and 2050, although the bulk of this growth is projected to occur in Africa, where per-capita incomes are not expected to rise as much as in Asia. And when we look at demographics in the currently developed world, Japan's population is projected to drop from 126 million to 107 million, and Europe is expected to experience a crunch from its soaring dependency ratios.[16] Of the large developed economies, the demographic

FIGURE 3-4

Maps with countries sized according to GDP at market exchange rates

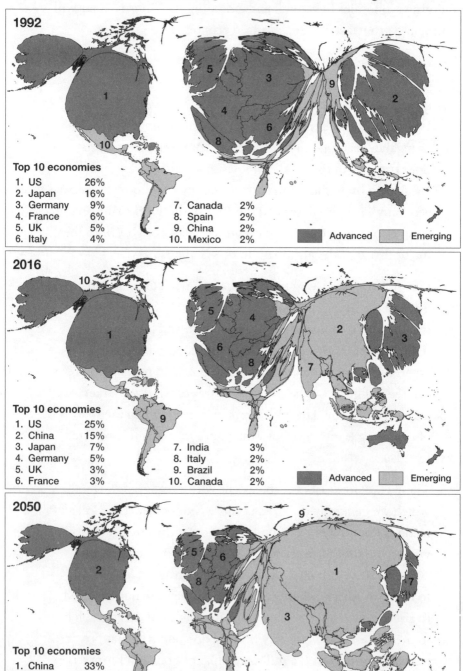

1992

Top 10 economies

1. US	26%			
2. Japan	16%			
3. Germany	9%	7. Canada	2%	
4. France	6%	8. Spain	2%	
5. UK	5%	9. China	2%	
6. Italy	4%	10. Mexico	2%	

Advanced   Emerging

2016

Top 10 economies

1. US	25%		
2. China	15%		
3. Japan	7%	7. India	3%
4. Germany	5%	8. Italy	2%
5. UK	3%	9. Brazil	2%
6. France	3%	10. Canada	2%

Advanced   Emerging

2050

Top 10 economies

1. China	33%		
2. US	14%		
3. India	9%	7. Japan	2%
4. Indonesia	4%	8. France	2%
5. UK	2%	9. Russia	2%
6. Germany	2%	10. Australia	1%

Advanced   Emerging

Source: Data from Oxford Economics.

picture looks relatively healthy only for the United States, and even that picture is subject to caveats about the effects of possible restrictions on immigration. Of course, some large developing countries, such as Brazil, China, and Russia, will face demographic challenges as well.

This discussion suggests that the big shift toward emerging economies is not only an indispensable element of a global success scenario, but also a plausible one. With this shift clearly in mind, we can better tackle the remaining SMART predictions.

Modest Trade Growth

While scholars generally agree that globalization is a multifaceted phenomenon, it is often conflated in practice with trade.[17] There are several reasons for this focus on trade-as-globalization. Well into the twentieth century, most international business activity, including FDI, revolved around trade in commodities: people flows were generally more localized, and information flows were much feebler. After an interwar meltdown, trade again led the way in the postwar period. It first surged in the 1960s and, between 1990 and 2010, grew twice as fast as GDP did. By contrast, FDI didn't really take off until the 1980s (see figure 1-6 in chapter 1) and first-generation immigrants have amounted to roughly three percent of world population for over a century.[18] Additionally, we have better data for (merchandise) trade than we do for other dimensions of globalization.

For these historical reasons, as well as trade's recent weakness compared to other types of international interactions, much of the recent discussion of whether we have reached peak globalization really asks whether trade has peaked as a percentage of GDP. Those who assert that trade has peaked often point to potentially adverse technological changes, particularly automation. Thus, a Baxter robot, purchased at $25,000 (the prices are declining rapidly) and amortized over three years, works out to a cost of less than $4 per hour even allowing time for it to "rest" (maintenance). These costs put the automaton close to Chinese labor costs.[19] Declining prices for robots could cap the job growth potential from manufacturing in emerging economies. 3-D printing could do the same, although it is further from being cost-effective. Other pessimists prefer to focus on policy changes in response to more protectionist sentiments among the Western public, the damage that has already been done to international agreements and institutions, and so on. But we need more than such lists to argue that the centuries-old trend of increasing trade intensity—which, if anything, has gathered momentum in the last half-century and, arithmetically, still has a long way to go—is at a point of reversal.

In the short run, one might expect a bump up in merchandise trade because of commodity prices—whose sharp decline was behind the drop-off in trade intensity in 2015—reverting to more-average levels. But that may strike readers as nothing more than a dead-cat bounce. For the longer run, an observation by Roberto Azevêdo, the director general of the WTO, offers a useful reference point: "So, as much as the 'new normal' is not 'normal', actually the 'old normal' was not 'normal' either."[20] To amplify, trade won't grow twice as fast as GDP again on a sustained basis but may well start growing a bit faster again, as it appears to have done in 2017, which would result in rising trade intensity. The observation that trade cannot continue growing twice as fast as GDP should be relatively uncontroversial. Since trade is part of GDP and already a fairly large part, it cannot, mathematically, continue to grow twice as fast as GDP indefinitely. And as for trade starting to grow faster than GDP again rather than slower, I am more convinced, given the historical context, by Azevêdo than by peak traders who assert that another acceleration cannot happen.

How fast trade actually grows relative to GDP is likely to depend on further progress in services trade. While services generate more than two-thirds of global GDP, trade accounts (as noted in chapter 1) for only 15 percent of the value added in the service sector, compared with about 40 percent in goods-producing sectors (manufacturing, agriculture, and natural resource extraction). Some services are inherently untradable (e.g., haircuts, for now), and for others, the principal barriers to trade have to do with the regulatory environment rather than the kinds of tariff and nontariff barriers familiar from manufacturing. And because of the failure of the services component of the WTO's Doha Round, these barriers have proven resistant to multilateral deal making.[21]

On the other hand, there are—what else?—technological reasons to be optimistic about trade in services, or so some argue. Thus, Richard Baldwin's *The Great Convergence* focuses on a new era of globalization fueled by the virtual movement of people through "telepresence" and "telerobotics."[22] The appeal, of course, is that of sourcing labor services from overseas without having any labor move across national borders. But again, in line with the earlier discussion of technotrances, I would warn against focusing on technology *über alles*. There may be psychological barriers in that purely telematic interactions do sound a bit cold, or political reactions if telemigration significantly displaces local jobs.

In terms of the geographic breakdown of trade, forecasts indicate that emerging Asia will account for 34 percent of global trade growth between 2016 and 2025, down from 54 percent between 2007 and 2016. Although emerging economies have powered almost all of the trade expansion in the wake of the global financial crisis, they have already achieved the same trade intensity, on average, as advanced economies (figure 3-5). In fact, since the trade line in the figure is rising slightly, emerging-economy trade intensity relative to advanced-economy trade intensity has actually decreased a little bit since 2005. The major reason is China's rebalancing away from exports, which used to be 33 percent of Chinese GDP and are now down to 21 percent.[23] In summary, since emerging economies do not lag on trade intensity, there is no reason to expect trade to increase as a share of their national income as they get richer, unlike the other dimensions of globalization discussed next.

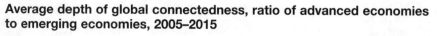

FIGURE 3-5

Average depth of global connectedness, ratio of advanced economies to emerging economies, 2005–2015

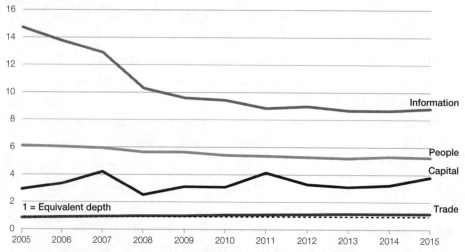

Source: Pankaj Ghemawat and Steven A. Altman, *DHL Global Connectedness Index 2016: The State of Globalization in an Age of Ambiguity* (Bonn: Deutsche Post DHL, 2016), figure 1-6.

Accelerated Globalization Along Other Dimensions

Globalization is about much more than just trade, and trends on other dimensions do not support the notion that globalization has peaked. As figure 1-2 in chapter 1 showed, significant increases in the intensity of cross-border information flows and smaller but steady increases in cross-border people flows have increased levels of globalization. Thus, despite weakness on the trade and capital fronts, the aggregate level of globalization, as tracked in the 2016 DHL Global Connectedness Index, reached a record high.

Particularly interesting about the nontrade metrics in figure 3-5 is how far the emerging economies lag the advanced ones in terms of the internationalization of capital (1 to 4), people (1 to 6), and information flows (1 to 9). If, because of the big shift, emerging economies grow to be more like today's advanced economies, their development should imply more rapid globalization along nontrade dimensions. Acceleration along other dimensions is so much the opposite of trade-led globalization that one might even label it *alt-globalization*.

If that label seems too fanciful, remember that recent increases in globalization have been driven by people and, particularly, information flows. Think of some of the present manifestations. Tourism flows are exploding (outbound tourism from China accounts for 23 percent of the increase over the last decade, with much more to come). Digitization helps people connect more effectively across space. And global megahits abound in popular culture. But even with capital flows, the potential remains large.

The prediction that emerging economies could power the growth of globalization beyond trade also gains support from complementarities across types of flows. Services trade (on which emerging economies also lag behind advanced economies—their overall parity on trade is driven by merchandise trade) tends to be closely linked to capital flows. Hence the stylized fact that reducing barriers to services trade requires more bilateral investment treaties. And digitization also affects services more than merchandise, highlighting the complementarities among trade, capital, and information flows. The fact that sectors with more trade also have more international mergers and acquisitions provides another type of evidence for complementarities that could power faster growth than one would anticipate looking at each type of flow on its own.[24]

For some additional indications, consider the results of my attempts to compile data on emerging economies' shares of world totals in seventy-five economic categories. The category in which emerging economies have the highest share of the world total is population, and the others among the top five, except for mobile-phone subscriptions, are also people-related.[25] In addition to top universities and company-level measures of top brand values and top spenders on R&D, the bottom five categories include two related to portfolio

equity (asset stocks and liabilities flows). The other two portfolio equity measures (asset flows and liabilities stocks) also show up in the
bottom ten. So if we do expect emerging economies to grow faster
than advanced economies, their shares of world totals in portfolio
equity categories are likely to increase disproportionately.

For an example of the big implications, consider some Swiss pension funds the leaders of which I was speaking to under the auspices
of a Swiss private bank. I had assumed that when you run a pension
fund, you have to pay some attention to the long-run forecasts for
the world economy. So I was surprised to learn that Swiss pension
funds' assets in emerging economies typically amounted to less than
5 percent of the total. Geert Bekaert and Campbell Harvey suggest
that a reasonable asset weighting for a diversified portfolio generally
lies somewhere between share of market capitalization and share
of GDP.[26] For emerging economies as a group, these figures came to
about 20 percent and 40 percent, respectively, in 2016. The broader
implication, again, is that if growth is concentrated in emerging
economies, chances are that the equity markets in these countries
are going to become even more important than is indicated by their
relative GDP growth (on which, out of the seventy-five categories,
emerging economies already ranked in the middle).[27]

Alt-globalization will, of course, throw up its own challenges, and
the management of those challenges, as well as ongoing cross-border
interactions, is likely to take on greater importance in the years
ahead. Trade, particularly in the congealed form of merchandise
and especially in commodities, can be thought of as relatively simple
in this respect. Other forms of globalization tend to involve more
people-to-people interaction across borders. This is obviously true of
cross-border movements of people, but also applies to many kinds of
informational interactions such as on social media. Given partiality
or home bias (as discussed in chapter 7), such interactions often need
to be managed if they are to work well instead of simply stirring up ill
will. And although portfolio equity investments don't require direct
personal contact, they do tend to be sensitive to ill will.

Even more broadly, globalization that is less dominated by trade will have implications that range from the multilateral (the WTO will need to rethink what it does) to the personal (you will need to rethink how cosmopolitan you want to be). More discussion of the implications at these macro- and micro-levels can be found in my 2011 book, *World 3.0*.[28] The rest of this book, though, will concentrate on the implications for businesses.

Regionalization and Multipolarity

Long-term trends—particularly the growth projections covered earlier in this chapter—suggest that it is becoming increasingly important to think about the world in terms of regional groupings. The projections do not indicate that any single country will be able to drive growth by itself. Multipolarity is already visible in the data, and it's going to become an even greater feature of the landscape. It's useful to think of multipolarity at various levels of aggregation. A three-pole map of trade leadership shows that the European Union, China, and the United States each have a zone where they are the largest trading partner for a set of countries (figure 3-6, top panel). While China's rising influence in Africa has been striking, the European Union remains the top trading partner for much of the African continent. A seven-pole map showing China, the United States, the European Union, and the rest of the BRICS countries (Brazil, Russia, India, and South Africa) demonstrates the existence of mostly contiguous zones of leadership for this wider set of poles as well (bottom panel). And one can push granularity even further. In the diplomatic crisis facing Qatar in 2017, the key poles were regional rather than global: Saudi Arabia, Iran, and Turkey. These varying levels of granularity illustrate how the world you see depends on what level of aggregation or resolution you decide to use.

In the south-by-southeast trend, the two regions that will see the most overall growth are East Asia/Pacific (part of the zone of

FIGURE 3-6

Multipolar maps of countries' top trading partners, 2015

Three-pole map: United States, European Union, and China

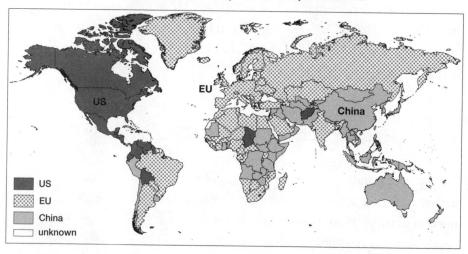

Seven-pole map: United States, European Union, and BRICS (Brazil, Russian Federation, India, China, and South Africa)

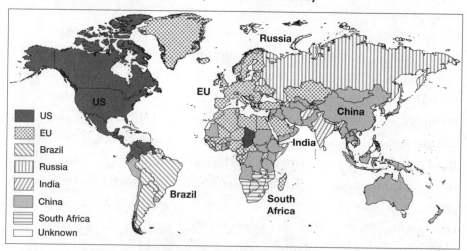

Source: Data from United Nations Comtrade and International Monetary Fund Direction of Trade Statistics (DOTS).

Chinese leadership) and South Asia, anchored in India (figure 3-7). China, however, is slowing down. India is much smaller (economically) than China and not growing that much faster. It would have to grow at 10 percent for eighteen years to get to the position that China holds today. And ASEAN (Association of Southeast Asian Nations) countries represent another, somewhat smaller growth pole. The existence of these three growth poles within the same broad region raises the likelihood that an increasing share of southeast trade may be intraregional rather than interregional.

Note that while such growth poles can be identified in Asia and elsewhere, they pale in comparison with their predecessors. Previous periods of rapid growth in globalization were typically associated with a growth monopole: a single country or region that accounted for 20 percent-plus of global growth. European maritime powers played that role in the first wave of globalization in the decades before World War I. The United States played the leading role between 1950 and 1970, and China did so between 1990 and 2010.[29] No comparable monopoles are evident today, reinforcing the case for multipolarity. Figure 3-7 also shows that while the highest-growth countries (in terms of percentage change) are in Asia and Africa, there will still be substantial growth (in absolute terms) in advanced countries. Even with much higher growth rates in Africa and Asia, advanced economies are projected to be responsible for 36 percent of the absolute growth of world GDP in the next five years, and 27 percent of the growth from 2017 to 2050.

It is worth adding that while most sub-Saharan countries have high projected growth rates, the population explosion also forecast for that region implies that GDP per capita there will remain alarmingly low. According to projections from Oxford Economics, GDP per capita in sub-Saharan Africa will still be less than $3,500 (in today's dollars) as far out as 2050. And the region will also fall further behind in relative terms: sub-Saharan GDP per capita stood at 30 percent of Asia's level in 2017. The ratio is projected to drop to 26 percent by 2022, and to 20 percent by 2050.

FIGURE 3-7

Maps with countries sized according to projected absolute GDP growth and shaded according to projected GDP growth rate (percent change)

2017–2022 (projected)

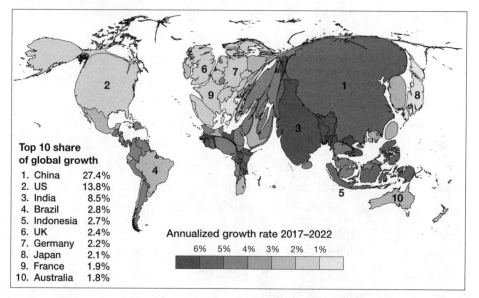

Top 10 share
of global growth

 1. China   27.4%
 2. US   13.8%
 3. India   8.5%
 4. Brazil   2.8%
 5. Indonesia   2.7%
 6. UK   2.4%
 7. Germany   2.2%
 8. Japan   2.1%
 9. France   1.9%
10. Australia   1.8%

Annualized growth rate 2017–2022

6%   5%   4%   3%   2%   1%

2017–2050 (projected)

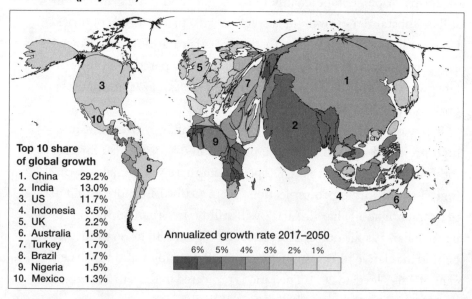

Top 10 share
of global growth

 1. China   29.2%
 2. India   13.0%
 3. US   11.7%
 4. Indonesia   3.5%
 5. UK   2.2%
 6. Australia   1.8%
 7. Turkey   1.7%
 8. Brazil   1.7%
 9. Nigeria   1.5%
10. Mexico   1.3%

Annualized growth rate 2017–2050

6%   5%   4%   3%   2%   1%

Source: Data from Oxford Economics.

We could even push beyond the idea of multipolarity and think about a mosaic rather than a world represented with a few broad shades or patterns. From this standpoint, emerging economies are far more heterogeneous as a category than advanced economies, so they require a far more variegated approach. Within Africa, for example, there is enormous variation in terms of progress (or lack thereof) toward development goals. So the current challenge of dealing with the big shift suggests a less monolithic approach than was taken when China was the key growth pole. But instead of simply stressing that every emerging country is different, businesses can rely on the law of distance and the CAGE distance framework—taken down to the industry level—to elucidate relevant patterns of similarities and differences.

Trading Places?

Even within the multipolar context just described, a key question that continues to be asked concerns the relative strength of the two largest poles, the United States and China. China is already the world's largest exporter, by far. According to the IMF, China surpassed the United States in terms of GDP adjusted for purchasing power parity in 2014. It is also on track to supplant the United States as the world's largest economy at market exchange rates, with projections ranging from 2024 (Oxford Economics and IHS Markit) to 2037 (Economist Intelligence Unit). Whether its ascent to leadership along these dimensions will lead to a shift from a mostly liberal world trading and globalization regime underpinned by the United States and the European Union to a potentially quite different one in which China has more influence—in a nutshell, whether the United States and China are trading places—is a question of great consequence, irrespective of one's business.

To answer these questions in light of what has already happened, several other aspects of the situation need to be recognized, as elaborated in this section. China's centrality in merchandise trade is not matched along any other dimension of globalization measured in the DHL Global Connectedness Index. For that reason, its rise to global hegemon in place of the United States still seems unlikely—although there is some uncertainty around that prediction due to policy initiatives under way in China as well as in the West. And either way, we are likely to see, at the very least, significant tensions between the United States and China.

Who Is More Central?

To compare the current positions of the US and China, I will focus on two of the many measures developed by social scientists to quantify centrality to network structure: *betweenness centrality* and *PageRank*. Betweenness centrality is typically used to analyze the importance of a given node to a network. In essence, it asks the question "If this node were taken offline, how much would it disturb the network?" By contrast, PageRank was designed to measure the importance of websites. The *Page* in *PageRank* refers to Larry Page, a cofounder of Google. The PageRank algorithm made Google the top search engine by sorting sites on the basis of how many sites link to them and by how important those sites are. The top result is the site that has the most endorsements from other highly endorsed sites.

To understand the difference between the two measures, think of how people pass through airports. London's Heathrow Airport ranks first on betweenness centrality, and it is easy to see why: London connects a great many places that are not well connected by other means. For example, trips from North America to Africa or Asia often involve layovers in Europe, and London serves more routes than any other European hub does. As a result, scenarios such as the 2010 eruption of the Eyjafjallajökull volcano, which closed Heathrow, are disruptive to a great many passenger trips that start and end in other places. By contrast, Atlanta's Hartsfield-Jackson Airport ranks highest on Page-Rank. As the top hub in the United States, it gets traffic from all over the world—and in particular from other hubs. Since hubs themselves are considered highly endorsed, getting a lot of traffic from other hubs has the effect of greatly improving Atlanta's ranking.[30]

Table 3-1 shows the ranks for the United States and China on betweenness centrality and PageRank for several cross-border activities. On merchandise trade, China has overtaken the United States in terms of betweenness centrality but still lags the United States a bit on PageRank. While the United States trades less than China, the US's trade partners are evidently more central to the world trade network to an extent that more than offsets China's lead in value of merchandise trade. The United States, however, does receive a very large endorsement from China, the second-ranked economy in terms of PageRank.

On FDI, China is a bit weaker overall, but the pattern of variation across the two centrality measures is reversed. China doesn't even make the top forty in terms of betweenness centrality but does make the top ten in PageRank. The high PageRank comes from the heavy investments that the other major attractors of FDI have made in China.

TABLE 3-1

Ranks of the United States and China on betweenness centrality and PageRank, 2015

Cross-border activity	Betweenness centrality		PageRank	
	United States	*China*	*United States*	*China*
Merchandise trade	3	1	1	2
Services trade	2	19	1	9
FDI stocks	2	47	1	9
Portfolio equity assets	1	8	1	10
Phone calls	1	5	1	4
Printed publications	2	5	1	12
Migration	1	13	1	43
Tourists	1	66	1	6

Source: Based on data collected for the 2016 DHL Global Connectedness Index.

On information and people interactions, data coverage is more hit-or-miss, but China tends to fare significantly worse on both types of centrality measures. These categories are also where current conditions raise the most doubts about China's openness to additional internationalization. Again, the United States generally ranks number one or two.

Overall, given China's relatively limited centrality on these measures of civil interactions, as well as its weaknesses relative to the United States militarily (compare the US worldwide network of military bases with China's single overseas base in Djibouti), talk of its trading places with the United States as the global hegemon looks like an exaggeration. Even just in terms of the sheer aggregate size of its economy, the United States is expected to stay close to China for some time after being overtaken. And since the United States has far fewer people than does China, US citizens are expected to continue to have much higher per-capita incomes than the Chinese. So despite some downward pressure on the salience of the United States, a complete switch of positions seems unlikely. The major caveat to that conclusion is that it is possible to imagine a brew of US policies that are dysfunctional enough and Chinese policies that are smart enough to lead to a switchover.

TPP, NAFTA, Brexit . . .

As discussed earlier, President Trump fulfilled only two campaign promises related to trade and immigration during his first two hundred days in office, according to the *Washington Post* "Trump Promise Tracker": he abandoned the TPP and started to renegotiate NAFTA. The abandonment of TPP marked the end of a US pivot toward Asia—a move aimed partly at ensuring that Asia did not coalesce around China. (China was never going to join the trade deal, given the restrictions membership would place on Chinese state-owned enterprises and state planning.) Between US disengagement and local disenchantment, a bulwark against China now seems a more remote possibility.

Of course, the United States continues to have security agreements with Japan and South Korea, but both countries are on Trump's short list of nations that run unacceptably large trade surpluses with the United States and are concerned about how committed he actually is to their security—and what he will try to charge for it. Halfway around the world, the North Atlantic Treaty Organization (NATO) has been shaken by, among other things, Trump's complaints about how its economic burdens are shared, as well as Europe's internal problems. And, of course, the credibility of a military alliance can be damaged much faster than it can be built up again.

The broader point is that if established security relationships were subject to the strict calculus of economic self-interest, the narrowed focus could totally transform them—and, at a fundamental level, weaken them. The United States would become security for hire rather than a security guarantor. And over the long term, old alliances would fade away. As an extreme scenario—requiring persistently and perhaps implausibly poor decision making by the United States—the geopolitical map might come to look more like the economic one. Such an outcome would play to China's strengths and apparent strategy.

To see how this scenario might pan out, look at the two-pole trade map in figure 3-8, with countries shaded according to their larger trading partner (the United States or China). The United States leads in a few places, particularly in the more proximate parts of the Americas, but China leads more broadly. Extrapolations indicate that by 2025, the Chinese sphere of trade leadership will extend even further, with the United States forecast to lead only in the part of the Americas that is north of the equator. Some might find such a projection far-fetched, but its logic was recognized by the Look South export strategy that the US Department of Commerce developed under the Obama administration.[31]

The same map should remind us of the dangers around NAFTA. As described in chapter 2, Trump could potentially squeeze Canada and Mexico very hard, and Mexican policy analysts have even talked of

FIGURE 3-8

Preponderant and dominant trading partners between the United States and China, 2015

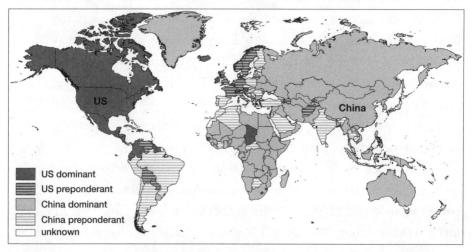

Source: Data from United Nations *Comtrade* and International Monetary Fund *Direction of Trade Statistics (DOTS)*.

Note: "US dominant" refers to the US having more than twice as much trade as China with a third country. "US preponderant" refers to the US having between one and two times as much trade as China. "China dominant" and "China preponderant" have parallel definitions.

playing the "China card." A US retreat from globalization would, obviously, boost China's chances of trading places. And in Europe, although Brexit hasn't been followed by a general populist wave, anti-immigrant, protectionist, and Eurosceptic parties of the far right did win the second-largest vote totals in both the Dutch general elections and the French presidential elections in 2017, followed by strong showings in the German and Austrian elections. If the whole West, not just the United States (and the United Kingdom), were to turn its back on globalization, the south-by-southeast dynamic would presumably become even more pronounced.

The Chinese Road to Globalization

The Chinese government certainly seems to have scented an opportunity: Xi Jinping positioned China as the staunchest defender of globalization at the World Economic Forum in Davos in 2017.

China-watchers also point to increasing talk of "China wisdom" and "community of common destiny (for all humankind)" by the Chinese leadership. This talk apparently reflects lessons China learned about how the United States exercised its soft power and wielded influence through global institutions. The Chinese leadership seems intent on building a different kind of image around themes such as "peaceful rise" and "common destiny."

China has also initiated and invested in institutions for the new global governance that parallel the Bretton Woods institutions. Massive state funding has gone to the Asian Infrastructure Investment Bank (which had more than fifty members by mid-2017, as well as another twenty-four prospective members), the Silk Fund (China's IMF), and the New Development Bank (BRICS Development Bank). Geographically, toward the south and east, China's Regional Comprehensive Economic Partnership (RCEP) trade plan has emerged as a leading regional contender to replace the TPP process. And perhaps most impressive in terms of its scope is the ongoing One Belt, One Road initiative toward the north and west. The initiative held its first summit, with leaders from twenty-nine countries attending, in the spring of 2017.

One Belt, One Road is an umbrella description for an array of projects—total investment is currently touted at $1.4 trillion—that aim to tie China more closely to Eurasia through improved maritime and rail links (figure 3-9). There is a bit less emphasis on Africa, apart from big port investments in Kenya, perhaps because the Chinese are already confident that they have locked in the leading role there with trade and aid. But either way, the idea is to bring the old world together, under China's auspices—and with a China-centric geometry. Considering that Eurasia itself accounts for 70 percent of the world's population and that adding in Africa boosts the amount to above 85 percent, the ambition of One Belt, One Road, is enormous. And the extent to which this initiative has become a national economic project—something that is referred to at every level by the Chinese—is hard to overstate. If this grand design works, it would

FIGURE 3-9

Infrastructure development along One Belt, One Road

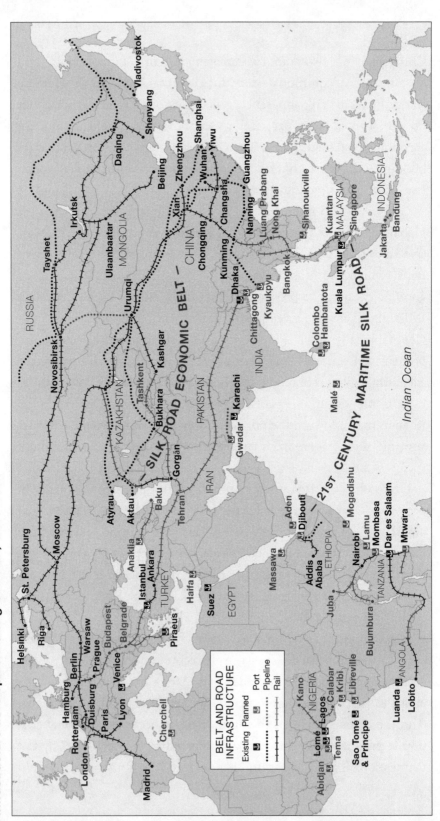

Source: Based on maps produced by Mercator Institute for China Studies (MERICS) and Journal of Commerce (JOC.com), with additional details and updates from news reports.

boost Chinese centrality scores—including on people, perhaps, given a people-to-people bonding component. But whether One Belt, One Road will work is still unclear, given that much of the belt and the road is yet to be built, some partner countries remain quite wary, and trade is suffering unusual headwinds.

This discussion has focused, by design, on what China is doing well and what the United States and the West are doing poorly. China faces huge systemic problems, ranging from internal political tensions to massive demographic challenges. And the US system has shown great flexibility and creative flair over the past few decades. So awarding China the winner's belt because of One Belt, One Road would be reaching beyond what the evidence warrants.

There *is* a safer prediction than China's overtaking—or not overtaking—the United States in the contest for global influence. One can anticipate trouble between the two countries over the next few decades—what political scientist Graham Allison calls a *Thucydides trap*. The original reference is to the Greek historian Thucydides, who wrote that it was the rise of Athens, and the fear that the event instilled in Sparta, that made war inevitable. In his view, situations in which an established power is confronted by a rising one tend to be structurally problematic.[32] Given the Thucydides trap, a US-China relationship that works to an extent but is subject to ongoing disagreements is not an unreasonable baseline for the long run. (It is certainly not a failure scenario: that would be war.) Of course, the prospect of ongoing disagreements does raise diplomatic issues at both the company level and the country level, as discussed further in chapter 7.

Global Generalizations

1. Since the turn of the millennium, growth rates have diverged between advanced and emerging economies, with emerging economies taking off while growth in advanced economies has been sluggish.

2. The center of the world economy is moving from the North Atlantic toward Asia. In 1980, the geographic center of world GDP was above the North Atlantic, but today it is over Iran and is projected to be over Tibet by 2050.

3. While trade may not again grow twice as fast as GDP over an extended period, there is still large, untapped potential for trade depth to increase.

4. Since emerging economies lag far behind advanced ones on the depth of their information, people, and capital flows, further development in emerging economies could power large increases in these aspects of globalization.

5. Although China is a larger exporter than the United States, it remains somewhat behind in terms of its networks. The United States continues to dominate in some measures of network centrality, even in trade. In other cross-border activities, the United States is clearly ahead.

6. China is beginning to assert itself on the world stage. These efforts include initiatives ranging from massive infrastructure projects abroad to the development of alternatives to US-led institutions.

7. From a geopolitical perspective, China's rise presents the concern that a rising power rarely challenges an existing hegemon without war ensuing—a pattern that has been dubbed the *Thucydides trap*.

8. Although China's growth is phenomenal, China is not the only rising power; nor is the United States the only current power. We are moving toward an increasingly multipolar world, in which many countries are forced to share power.

9. There continues to be a great deal of heterogeneity among emerging economies, and although some are rising in economic power and stature, many have yet to take off at all.

10. Although the highest growth rates are in developing coun-
    tries, advanced economies are still projected to account for
    roughly a quarter of growth between 2017 and 2050. Thus,
    we are looking less at a shift from the United States to
    China than we are at a complex world with many powerful
    nations and regional groupings.

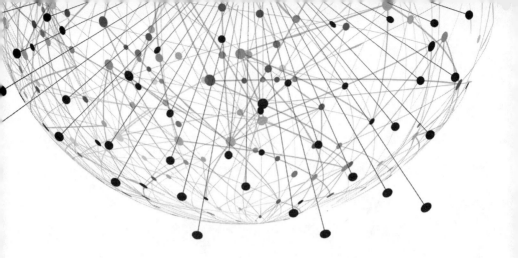

Managing Globalization

SPANning the World

Part two traces the implications of part one's characterization of the global environment and recommends ways for firms to cross borders more profitably. The recommendations target strategy, presence, architecture, and nonmarket issues (SPAN), with one chapter devoted to each of these four areas of the management agenda. These chapters all highlight limits to the localizing or deglobalizing moves that have been proposed in response to globalization-related headwinds. Therefore, the recommendations extend well beyond typical responses such as emphasizing a strategy of adaptation (chapter 4), narrowing presence (chapter 5), empowering local management (chapter 6), and cultivating more of a local face (chapter 7). These chapters jointly articulate a much richer palette of possible responses from which firms can draw to bolster performance.

4

Strategy
How to Compete

The introduction to this book discussed the globalization yo-yo effect: the relation between swings in sentiments about globalization and shifts in supposed imperatives for global companies, as illustrated by Coke before and after the Asian financial crisis. Coke focused its strategy on standardization and scale economies (aggregation) under Roberto Goizueta before the crisis and then shifted to localization and market responsiveness (adaptation) under Douglas Daft, who went as far as to make "Think local, act local" his mantra. The introduction also noted that pure adaptation hadn't worked out any better for Coke in the early 2000s than pure aggregation had earlier.

Similar calls to localize are, however, in the air again. I have already mentioned how GE's then-chairman and CEO Jeff Immelt called for a "bold pivot" toward localization in the face of rising protectionism in May 2016.[1] To cite another example, Larry Fink, CEO of BlackRock, the world's largest asset manager, sent his staff a memo in early 2017 saying, "I have frequently talked about the need to be

The author wishes to thank Steven Altman for his collaboration on the writing of this chapter.

local in every market where we operate. The current environment makes that more urgent than ever. While we need to operate as One BlackRock across the globe, we also need to be German in Germany, Japanese in Japan and Mexican in Mexico."[2] Might localization in response to globalization's travails make sense this time around, even if it didn't the last time?

Three points from the *tour d'horizon* in chapters 1 through 3 suggest that the answer is probably no. First, globalization hasn't (yet) gone into reverse. Second, even if it experiences shocks, the depth of globalization, and particularly the globalization of trade, is unlikely to go to zero—and its breadth is likely to continue to exhibit predictable patterns. Third, in terms of the long run, it makes more sense, for most purposes, to focus on success scenarios rather than on a globalization apocalypse of some sort. None of these points suggest a focus on adaptation in the long run, except as a backup strategy.

Competitive considerations corroborate this sense derived from the consideration of the environment in part one. Pure adaptation or localization is unlikely to be optimal for most global companies because a strategy of copying the locals everywhere leaves no room for advantages over them. To decide what strategies to pursue, multinational firms need to consider three fundamental strategy archetypes they can use to create value across national borders and international distances. I call these the AAA strategies: *adaptation*, which involves adjusting to differences; *aggregation*, which involves finding some ways of overcoming them to exploit cross-border scale and scope economies; and *arbitrage*, which exploits differences—as in when a company sources where inputs are abundant and sells where they are scarce—rather than treating them as constraints to be adjusted to or overcome. Aggregation and arbitrage directly advantage multinationals over local rivals, whereas adaptation mitigates multinationals' disadvantages, expanding the scope over which they can successfully implement aggregation and arbitrage.

Because a detailed examination of these time-tested strategic approaches lies outside the scope of this book, I will only summarize them here.[3] I draw on contemporary examples and then consider how firms should think about rebalancing among the three strategies in the present era of heightened resistance to globalization. Finally, I examine how these strategies should be deployed—differently—by "incumbent" multinationals from advanced economies and by "insurgents" from emerging economies.

Aggregation

Aggregation strategies overcome the effects of distance and differences by leveraging tangible or intangible assets across countries. Aggregators seek out and ride similarities—rather than differences—across countries, because differences tend to constrain or at least complicate the exploitation of international economies of scale and scope.

To start with a very simple example, think about production scale economies enabled by tangible assets. If a product is manufactured most efficiently using a machine with capacity that exceeds national demand, the most efficient setup will involve scaling up production to make efficient use of that machine and exporting a portion of the output. Even if an asset—in this case, the machine—is leveraged across only two countries, aggregation is occuring.

Aggregation strategies become far more powerful when intangible rather than tangible assets are involved. Multinational enterprises firms that actually operate in foreign countries rather than just exporting to them—typically exploit intangible assets such as knowledge, technology, or reputation across borders. Research from the 1970s up to the present has consistently shown that firms' spending on R&D and advertising relative to their revenues—proxies for investments in intangible assets—are strong predictors of the extent to which they operate internationally.[4] In the Coke case, the primary intangible asset leveraged abroad is the company's brand portfolio. Coke spent almost 10 percent of its net revenues on advertising in 2016, and the Coke brand was ranked as the world's third-most valuable (after Apple and Google), at $73.1 billion.[5]

Why the special interest in exploiting intangible assets abroad? These assets underpin strategies that are more difficult for competitors to copy. Some intangibles, such as patented innovations, even enjoy legal protection. And because of intrinsic problems with trading or licensing many intangible assets abroad, they are often exploited across borders most efficiently within multinational firms. Additionally, the rising prominence of multinational firms since the 1970s has coincided with a takeoff in the importance of intangible assets in business. In the US private sector, for instance, investment in intangibles doubled from 6 percent of GDP in 1977 to 12 percent in 2011.[6]

While Immelt's remarks cited earlier on GE's pivot to localization suggest boosting adaptation, my view is that aggregation remains that firm's primary source of international value creation. The power of GE's intangible assets is what gives GE the capability to compete effectively in some 170 countries worldwide and the potential to localize more within them.[7] Immelt also seems to have recognized that localization alone could not work for GE, clarifying in May 2017 that the firm's strategy involves "connected localization."[8] A month later, GE announced that John Flannery would replace him as CEO, but news reports suggest Flannery is "unlikely to reverse course on localization."[9]

To elaborate, GE spent $5.5 billion in 2016 on R&D and regularly ranks among the world's fifty largest corporate R&D spenders.[10] And this R&D investment does seem to be effective in the sense of giving GE a large technological and knowledge-driven edge. PwC Strategy& ranked GE as the world's ninth-most innovative company in 2016; GE is one of only two industrial companies on a top ten list dominated by firms in computers, software, and other internet businesses.[11] It also ranked seventh on the list of companies granted the most US patents in 2015.[12] Without international scale economies, GE could not fund such large R&D investments, which give it a huge leg up against potential local competitors. And here I have to say *potential* local competitors, because the scale effects are so large in some GE businesses (such as aircraft engines) that most countries cannot support any national firms at all.

GE's brand represents another source of aggregation advantage. *Brand Finance* valued the GE brand at $35 billion in 2017, making it the world's twenty-second-most valuable brand and the top brand in the industrial sector.[13] Even where GE lacks a technological edge in a given market, its reputation may provide an advantage over competitors. And a third intangible source of aggregation advantage for GE is its famed capability to develop senior executive talent. Before its current difficulties, the company had long been called a CEO factory, and when other companies hired former GE executives as CEOs, their stock prices often spiked. This reputation for talent development elevated GE's capacity to attract top talent around the world.

GE also exemplifies aggregation advantages based on scope rather than scale. In aviation, for example, the company's sales of jet and turboprop engines, its financing capabilities, and its global service network give it clear advantages over potential competitors. GE can also cross-sell to customers around the world and leverage its global footprint across multiple industries to deter or respond to competitive threats.

To summarize, GE's strengths in aggregation—in technology, brand, talent development, and so on—underpin its capacity to localize. If GE had no advantage over local competitors, it would have no basis to overcome border and distance effects to beat them in their home markets. GE will never become a mirror image of local competitors in all its markets around the world. Rather, its localization strategy is best understood as retaining a core strength in aggregation while toning down the company's prior emphasis on arbitrage and improving its position on adaptation.

Other major multinationals—particularly those from advanced economies—also tend to compete abroad primarily on the basis of aggregation. Their strong intangible assets propel them across borders and distance. Leading pharmaceutical companies, for example, exemplify global strategies predicated almost entirely on R&D assets.

And newer online aggregators have rapidly expanded abroad using scalable platforms. LinkedIn (founded in 2002) says it operates in 200 countries, Airbnb (2008) in 191, and Uber (2009) in 81. This is a striking contrast to the few conventional multinationals that have such broad footprints and that typically took decades or longer to build up such a presence.

The laws of globalization do, however, impose limits on aggregation. The constraining power of borders and distance implies that strategies of pure global aggregation are seldom feasible or desirable. Aggregation is typically most effective within the confines of similar groups of countries. The CAGE framework provides a useful guide in this regard: companies can boost aggregation among countries with cultural similarities (e.g., Ibero-America), administrative linkages (e.g., via free-trade agreements), geographic proximity (e.g., by region), or economic similarity (e.g., advanced versus emerging economies). Even new platform plays like Uber can't scale without any limits. Uber ended up selling its Chinese business to Didi Chuxing for a 20 percent stake in the local competitor plus a $1 billion investment in Uber's operations in the rest of the world.[14]

Region-based aggregation strategies are by far the most common, which prompted me to explore them at length in my 2005 *Harvard Business Review* article, "Regional Strategies for Global Leadership."[15] The big shift toward emerging markets described in chapter 3, however, has boosted interest in aggregation that's based on economic similarities. I will return to this theme and to related applications of the CAGE framework for setting a company's geographic scope in chapter 5 and for making choices about how to organize a company in chapter 6.

Arbitrage

Whereas aggregation strategies exploit similarities across countries to realize scale and scope economies, arbitrage strategies exploit differences to achieve absolute economies. Arbitrageurs treat differences across borders as opportunities rather than constraints. And notwithstanding a curiously phrased observation by the *Economist* in January 2017—"The end of the arbitrage"—its end is not near.[16]

One's sense of the longevity of arbitrage is enhanced by noting that it is the original cross-border strategy. Many of the great traders throughout history got their start by trading luxuries that were subject to extreme differences in absolute cost and availability. Europe's spice trade with India arose because spices could initially sell in Europe for several hundred times what they cost in India. Furs and fish that were abundant only in North America helped create a transatlantic trade and, incidentally, led to the colonization of the continent.

In today's classic example of arbitrage, a firm produces where wages are low and sells where prices are high. Labor-cost arbitrage provided the original impetus for China's manufacturing miracle and India's offshore services boom. A fundamental reason why such arbitrage opportunities are not going away is the persistent gaps in economic development around the world, as exemplified by the per-capita GDP trends in the three largest developed countries and the three largest developing countries (figure 4-1). Despite huge gains in emerging economies—particularly China—output per person in 2016 in the United States, Japan, and Germany was still, on average, seven times higher than output per person in China, India, and Brazil.

The power of labor-market arbitrage is illustrated by the rise of India's offshore IT sector. The sector barely existed as recently as the 1980s, and in 1998, it accounted for just 1.2 percent of the country's GDP. But today it generates nearly 8 percent of India's GDP as well as 49 percent of the country's services exports, while directly employing 3.9 million people and an additional 10 million indirectly.[17] At the company level, the offshoring wave propelled vendors such as Tata Consultancy Services into the ranks of the world's ten largest IT services firms by revenues. Because of their large lead in both profit margins and growth rates, the market capitalization of the top four India-centric IT services firms has consistently outstripped that of their four closest Western competitors since 2009.

FIGURE 4-1

GDP per capita in current US dollars, 1980–2016

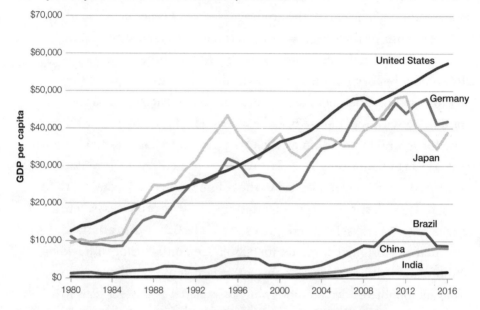

Source: Data from International Monetary Fund, *World Economic Outlook Database*, April 2017.

The offshoring of IT services to India was, of course, underpinned by arbitrage of the cost (and availability) of skilled labor. According to Radford, a unit of Aon Hewitt, fixed compensation for entry-level and midcareer IT professionals in India averaged only 15 to 25 percent of US pay for similar jobs in 2014.[18] In a 2016 survey, around 60 percent of companies indicated that they outsourced both as a cost-cutting tool and as a way to focus on core businesses, while roughly half of them reported that outsourcing helped them solve capacity issues.[19]

Beyond illustrating the power of arbitrage to create large business opportunities, the Indian IT example also helps to draw out three broader lessons about arbitrage. First and particularly salient in the present environment is the political and societal sensitivity of arbitrage. In an October 2016 survey conducted by the Pew Research Center, 80 percent of Americans said that "increased outsourcing of jobs to other countries" hurts American workers, and 77 percent felt the same way about "more foreign-made products being sold in the United States."[20] In response to these sentiments, President Trump has promised changes to the H-1B visa regime used by Indian vendors to send employees to the United States. (Indian IT firms would not be able to easily eliminate their requirements for US work visas by switching entirely to hiring American citizens or permanent residents, since prevailing salaries in the United States often exceed these firms' revenues per employee.) Additionally, the potential of arbitrage to provoke a large societal backlash is not restricted to economic arbitrage. It can be even more severe when companies exploit administrative or legal differences across countries. The sidebar "Ten Tips for Dealing with Arbitrage Sensitivity" offers suggestions to help companies deal with these kinds of issues.

GE's pivot to localization reflects—at least from a rhetorical standpoint—a relative de-emphasis of arbitrage. Before Immelt took over as CEO from Jack Welch, he ran GE's healthcare business from 1997 to 2000. In addition to pushing acquisitions and R&D expenditure to increase the unit's scale economies (in line with GE's primary focus on aggregation), Immelt emphasized arbitrage as a key component of the unit's international strategy. He spoke of a "pitcher-catcher concept," whereby a pitching team at a high-cost existing plant would work together with a catching team at a new, low-cost location until the new plant matched or exceeded the existing plant's performance. But in a 2017 interview, Immelt played down such moves. "I think these things like wage arbitrage, that's 1980s. That's what GE did in the 1980s. Now when we globalize, it's to sell more."[21]

Will GE really reduce (or scale back the growth of) its arbitrage strategy? It's too soon to say, but Immelt's remarks do fit with several of my tips about dealing with resistance to arbitrage: public sensitivity, emphasis on growth, and trying to become more robust to changes in the political environment. And the fact that Immelt's successor, John Flannery, previously served as president and CEO of GE India would seem not to boost the likelihood of GE's entirely de-emphasizing arbitrage.

Ten Tips for Dealing with Arbitrage Sensitivity

Macro approaches

1. Recognize the full costs of arbitrage and societal concerns about it.

2. Be sensitive in your public remarks about arbitrage.

3. Try to be concrete rather than abstract about economy-wide benefits.

4. Support job-retraining programs and, more broadly, a social safety net.

5. Emphasize upgrading as the centerpiece of domestic economic policy.

Micro approaches

6. Rather than (just) talking about cost reductions, emphasize viability and growth as objectives and talent shortages as constraints on achieving them.

7. Be cautious about taking advantage of health, safety, and environmental standards in foreign markets that are looser than in your home base.

8. Recognize the (other) implicit constraints on your freedom of action. Otherwise, they are likely to be made explicit for you.

9. Think through a range of mechanisms—lobbying, working with natural allies (who may, in this context, include product market competitors), investing in job creation, and so forth—as ways of preserving or expanding your freedom of action.

10. Place a premium on strategies that are robust to changes in the political climate.

The second broad lesson about arbitrage strategies relates to their sustainability. Constraints imposed by societal sensitivities represent only one potential limit on the sustainability of arbitrage strategies. In financial markets, one tends to think of arbitrage opportunities as opening and closing almost instantaneously as speculators leap into the markets to take advantage of them. Real-world arbitrage, however, is more complicated and potentially far more sustainable. When the Indian IT boom started to take off, skeptics assumed that fast wage escalation in India (double-digit annual salary increases there were typical) would quickly slow the industry's growth. Instead, companies shifted their strategies to contain their costs. They moved a rising share of work to smaller "tier two or three" Indian cities with lower costs, broadened their hiring beyond traditional labor pools, shifted more work from onsite to offshore, constrained the growth of entry-level salaries, and flattened employee pyramids.

Many also erroneously assumed that once foreign multinationals started arbitraging out of India, the India-based firms would be unable to compete against the multinationals. What they missed was that in India, the local firms—in line with the laws of globalization—have advantages that are hard for foreign companies to match. Even after running large-scale service centers in India for a decade, foreign IT firms still have higher-cost operations there than local firms do. According to one study, US-based multinationals paid their technology professionals in India 50 to 70 percent more than India-based companies paid similar levels of employees.[22]

Third, even though arbitrage strategies are motivated by cross-country differences, they are also normally constrained by them as well. Just as aggregation tends to work best at levels between the country and the rest of the world—often within regions—arbitrage strategies also tend to hit a wall before they become completely global. Figure 4-2 juxtaposes the worldwide composition of the IT and business process outsourcing (BPO) services market versus where the Indian industry earns its revenues. The contrast is stark. Nearly 80 percent of Indian IT and BPO exports go to the United States and United Kingdom alone (the bottom map), almost double those countries' combined 44 percent

FIGURE 4-2

World IT and BPO services market versus Indian revenues, 2016

Map with countries sized according to their IT services and BPO market sizes

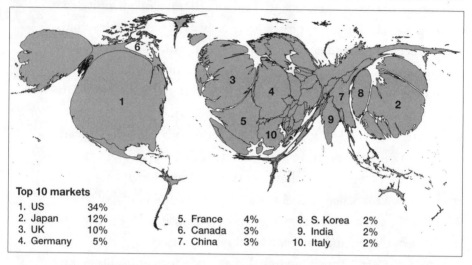

Top 10 markets

1. US	34%					
2. Japan	12%	5. France	4%	8. S. Korea	2%
3. UK	10%	6. Canada	3%	9. India	2%
4. Germany	5%	7. China	3%	10. Italy	2%

Source: Data from Marketline global and regional IT services industry profile reports, March 2017.

Rooted map with countries sized according to India's IT services and BPO exports to them (and India sized based on its domestic IT services and BPO revenues)

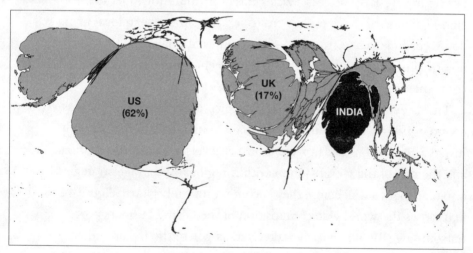

Source: Data from Nasscom, "The IT-BPM Sector in India: Strategic Review 2017."

share of the world market (the top map). Indian firms found it much harder to compete outside the English-speaking world, were only starting to gain traction in Continental Europe after years of investment there, and barely registered in Japan, the world's second-largest market. Adaptation—the third component of the AAA strategies and still to be discussed—is typically required when firms seek to expand the reach of their arbitrage strategies.

Before concluding the discussion of arbitrage, we should look beyond labor-market differences. Arbitrage opportunities exist across all four dimensions of the CAGE distance framework. Culturally, favorable effects related to country or place of origin have long supplied a basis for arbitrage. For example, French culture—or, more specifically, its image overseas—has long underpinned the international success of French haute couture, perfumes, wines, and foods. Administratively, legal, institutional, and political differences between countries open up another set of strategic arbitrage opportunities, but companies must pay special attention to ethical and societal issues when considering such opportunities. Geographically, arbitrage across climate zones motivates agricultural trade as well as tourism. And economically, there are opportunities that range well beyond only labor-market arbitrage. Capital-cost differentials might seem, at first blush, to offer slimmer pickings than do labor-cost differentials. But most companies (at least in the United States) earn returns within two or three percentage points of their cost of capital, so small savings on capital costs can make a large difference.

In summary, the exploitation of differences across countries remains alive and well. There are arbitrage opportunities across all four dimensions of the CAGE distance framework, and the economic value of arbitrage can be very large. However, arbitrage can also provoke a big backlash. I dealt briefly with responses to societal constraints here, and I will return to that topic in chapter 7. In this chapter, however, having noted the constraints that differences and distances impose on both aggregation and arbitrage, I turn next to adaptation as a strategy to expand the scope across which the first two strategies can be effectively pursued.

Adaptation

Considering the limits that cross-country differences and distances impose on aggregation and arbitrage strategies, virtually every company operating internationally needs to engage in at least some adaptation or adjustment to differences. The most obvious form of adaptation is what I call *variation*, as in the adage "When in Rome, do as the Romans do." But variation is costly, and, in the extreme, it results in operations so different across countries that there is no value gained by keeping them together in a single company. Smart adaptation therefore typically involves not only appropriate decisions about the amount of variation but also the use of one or more complementary levers—focus, externalization, design, and innovation—that help improve its effectiveness (table 4-1). The sheer variety of the levers and sublevers for adaptation suggests room to broaden strategic discussions beyond the usual tug-of-war between headquarters and the field over centralization versus decentralization. Note that these levers can also be applied to deal more effectively with changes over time as well as across space, as discussed in chapter 2.

TABLE 4-1

Levers and sublevers for adaptation

Variation	Focus: reduce need for variation	Externalization: reduce burden of variation	Design: reduce cost of variation	Innovation: improve effectiveness of variation
• Products	• Products	• Strategic alliances	• Flexibility	• Transfer
• Policies	• Geographic areas	• Franchising	• Partitioning	• Localization
• Repositioning	• Industry verticals	• User adaptation	• Platforms	• Recombination
• Metrics	• Segments	• Networking	• Modularity	• Transformation

Source: Adapted from Pankaj Ghemawat, *Redefining Global Strategy* (Boston: Harvard Business School Press, 2007), table 4-2.

Variation encompasses changes not only in products, but also in policies, business positioning, and even metrics (e.g., target rates of return). Product variation is the most visible aspect of adaptation. Japan's Panasonic Corporation, for example, released a new clothes-washing machine in India in 2017 with wash cycles specifically designed to remove stains that are especially common in India—stains such as curry and hair oil. Unilever offers more than a hundred variants on its global Lux brand of soaps. And while Apple's iPhone and iPad look the same worldwide, the devices' user interfaces are localized.

Beyond varying products across markets, companies often benefit from tailoring various other aspects of their marketing—and their internal operations—across countries. Sir Martin Sorrell, CEO of WPP, the world's largest marketing services company, estimated in 2013 that "no more than 15 percent of the business we do at WPP is truly global—if by global you mean that we use the same marketing methods throughout the world."[23] In the luxury sector, product variation is often very limited, but there is great variation in how those products are sold. Even the architecture varies across luxury boutiques within a given brand: Tiffany & Co.'s New York flagship presents a refined and understated image, while the company uses a much bolder design for its boutiques in China.

The costs associated with variation, however, can be substantial. Panasonic spent two years analyzing the ingredients of curry dishes in various parts of India and assigned a Japan-India team to study how a washing machine could be tweaked to remove these food stains most effectively.[24] And beyond the up-front investment, the India-specific washer presumably cannot be sold in other markets, restricting economies of scale. This variation thus boosts complexity in Panasonic's production, supply chain, marketing, and other areas of its operations.

Focus, a complementary lever, helps keep the cost and complexity of variation under control. A company can purposefully narrow the scope across which it operates to bite off a manageable mouthful and thereby reduce the amount of variation required. For instance, companies can focus on products or services that require less variation. India's IT services companies, for example, have focused on application development and maintenance (capturing almost one-quarter of the world market for that service). But a focus on consulting would have required far more attention to differences in clients' business contexts, implying larger variation requirements (a mere 3 percent of IT consulting is offshored to India).[25]

Externalization is related to focus, but instead of narrowing scope, it deliberately splits activities across organizational boundaries to reduce the internal burden of adaptation. For example, a company can involve customers and other ostensibly independent third parties in the challenge of adaptation. On a platform such as Airbnb, those who are offering a residence for rent have wide latitude in how they wish to present it. With owners in each residential market destined to have more localized knowledge than those at Airbnb, the customization that can be offered will ultimately prove more attractive to consumers and thus redound to the company's benefit.

Design decisions can deliberately reduce the cost of variation. One method is partitioning. In the simplest form of partitioning, a company clearly separates elements that can be varied across countries from elements that are integral to a complex system and that therefore should not be tampered with on a piecemeal basis. With platforms, companies can go a step further and produce a wide variety of products or services from a common base. Automotive and home appliances companies, among others, have emphasized platform strategies—and boosting the flexibility of their platforms. Thus, Ford simplified from twenty-seven car and truck platforms in 2007 down to nine in 2016.[26]

Innovation is conceptually a very broad lever, but cross-border differences often imply innovation that is somewhat narrower in scope. For example, firms can reduce the *need* for adaptation by seeking to shape or transform the local environments in which they operate, instead of trying to enhance their abilities to fit in. Consider Starbucks. Although the Seattle-based coffee chain is frequently cited as being in the vanguard of American cultural imperialism, CEO Howard Schultz paints a fascinating picture in his autobiography of his original attempt to recreate an Italian espresso bar experience in the United States—right down to recorded opera music and bow-tied waiters.[27] Although the opera music and bow ties soon disappeared, Starbucks *transformed* US coffee drinkers, who now expect easy chairs, hip music, and a smoke-free environment to enhance their coffee-drinking experience. IKEA, the Swedish retailer of low-cost home furnishings, also innovated with its flat-pack design, reducing transportation costs. And Cemex, with its time-based delivery guarantees, demonstrated the power of marketing innovation even in a commodity business.

I could list myriad examples of the creative ways that companies have pursued adaptation to address cross-country differences—my 2007 book, *Redefining Global Strategy*, presents many more examples—but the basic concept should already be clear. The differences and distances between countries loom large enough that aggregation and arbitrage can seldom be executed across a broad footprint without some amount of adaptation. This observation might seem obvious, but it's a lesson that is all too easy to forget when companies come under pressure to speed up their growth and boost their margins. In my 2017 survey of managers, 79 percent agreed with the statement "competing the same way everywhere is the highest form of global strategy."

Many of the greatest blunders in international business come from under-adaptation to important differences. And the missteps can come at a cost that extends beyond profits and losses. When companies fail to appreciate the uniqueness or even the sovereignty of the countries in which they operate, they open themselves up to charges of market imperialism, tarnishing the business environment for foreign firms in general and contributing to political pressures for protectionism. So, adaptation is almost always a necessary ingredient in international strategy.

Adaptation amid the Backlash Against Globalization

Having introduced each of the AAA strategies, I can now return to the question posed at the opening of this chapter: should firms localize (or, in AAA terms, amp up their adaptation) in response to the antiglobalization backlash? In answering that question, companies need to remember the limits of adaptation. Aggregation and arbitrage strategies directly generate value across borders and distances, and adaptation is what extends their reach. Thus a strategy, in contrast, that focuses exclusively on adaptation and leaves no room for aggregation or arbitrage will deliver little value. So the key is to determine how much (if at all) a given company should increase adaptation within its overall approach to the AAA strategies.

It can be helpful to visualize the three strategies on a triangular diagram, and to keep in mind the implications of industry characteristics for the relative attractiveness of the strategies. Data on the intensity of particular types of expenditures can serve as rough proxies for the headroom afforded by each of the AAA strategies. The percentage of sales spent on advertising indicates how important adaptation is likely to be; the percentage spent on R&D signifies the importance of aggregation; and the percentage spent on labor suggests the potential for labor-cost arbitrage. Figure 4-3 provides calibrations of these metrics based on US data. If an industry scores above the median along a particular dimension of intensity—delineated by the small, solid-line triangle in the figure—the corresponding strategy merits at least some attention. If it scores close to or past the larger dashed-line triangle—which delineates the 90th percentile—the strategy may be too important to ignore.

The AAA triangle can also be used to visualize firms' strategies over time. Figure 4-4 employs such an AAA triangle to depict my interpretation of GE's pivot to localization. Both today and in my view of where GE is trying to migrate, the triangle extends farthest along

FIGURE 4-3

AAA strategies and industry expenditure intensity benchmarks

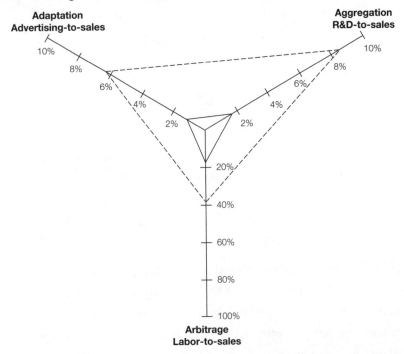

Adaptation
Advertising-to-sales

Aggregation
R&D-to-sales

Arbitrage
Labor-to-sales

Sources: R&D and advertising intensities from Schonfeld & Associates (2017 data), https://saibooks.com/); Labor intensity from US Census Bureau (2012 data), https://www.census.gov/econ/snapshots/index.php.

the aggregation axis, reflecting how aggregation remains GE's primary source of value creation. Adaptation and arbitrage are secondary strategies, with adaptation targeted to become more important while arbitrage recedes or at least becomes something the company pursues more discreetly. Companies can use the AAA triangle to plot their own strategies and to compare them with those of their key competitors, with an eye both to present positioning and to changes over time.

As companies contemplate their strategies using the AAA triangle, they are inevitably faced with trade-offs. Table 4-2 highlights some of the differences that generate tensions among the AAA strategies. They tend, for example, to align with different organizational structures. Aggregation implies greater centralization of authority

FIGURE 4-4

AAA triangle interpretation of GE's pivot to localization

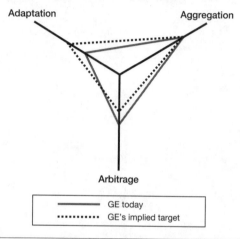

in global business units, regional structures, global account teams, and the like. Arbitrage is often facilitated by vertical or functional structures that help track the flow of products or work through the organization. And adaptation requires vesting more authority with local decision makers.

Given these tensions, firms need to understand the relevant trade-offs and agree internally about how they are to be managed. They should also recognize that because of the different organizational structures involved, switching from one strategy to another can be a long process, with no guarantee of success. In the 1950s, Unilever responded to the European Union's regional integration by promoting pan-European integration—but even five decades later, the company still struggled to integrate the production and marketing facilities of its European firms.[28] Unilever's experience further underscores the importance of employing a rigorous process that will guide the trade-offs between one strategy and another.

Given such findings, strategies should not be adopted or abandoned simply on the basis of short-term changes in the economic climate, the public-policy environment, or industry trends. Companies are frequently criticized for failing to anticipate changes in the

TABLE 4-2

Differences across the AAA strategies

Characteristics	Aggregation	Arbitrage	Adaptation
Competitive advantage: Why globalize at all?	To achieve scale and scope economies through international standardization	To achieve absolute (nonscalar) economies through international specialization	To achieve local relevance through national focus (while exploiting some scale)
Configuration: Where to locate overseas?	To limit the effects of cultural, administrative, geographic, and/or economic differences by concentrating on foreign countries that are similar to home	To exploit (selected) differences by operating in a more diverse set of countries	To limit the effects of cultural, administrative, geographic, and/ or economic differences by concentrating on foreign countries that are similar to home
Coordination: How should international operations be organized?	By business; emphasis on horizontal relationships to achieve economies of scale across borders	By function; emphasis on vertical relationships, including across organizational boundaries	By country; emphasis on adjustments to achieve a local face within borders
Checks: What to watch out for strategically?	Excessive standardization	Narrowing spreads	Excessive variety or complexity
Corporate diplomacy: Which public issues need to be addressed?	Appearances of, and backlash against, homogenization or hegemony (especially by US companies)	The exploitation or displacement of suppliers, channels, or intermediaries; potentially most prone to political disruption	Potentially discreet and robust, given emphasis on cultivation of a local face

Source: Adapted from Pankaj Ghemawat, *Redefining Global Strategy* (Boston: Harvard Business School Press, 2007), table 7-1.

markets where they are operating, but they can also be too quick to switch their long-term strategies in response to changes that may only call for minor adjustments. Small tactical steps can often be pressed into service to powerful effect, especially when rhetoric and action are coupled effectively. They can signal—internally and externally—that while the company is not standing still, it is also not committing to an overhaul of strategies that may still have considerable value.

For some companies, of course, longer-term trends do call for major shifts among the AAA strategies. One driver of such longer-term changes was examined in chapter 3—the big shift toward emerging economies. Building on that material, the final section of this chapter discusses approaches to the AAA strategies for "incumbent" multinationals from advanced economies and for "insurgents" from emerging economies.

AAA Strategies in the Battle Between Incumbents and Insurgents

The faster growth taking place in emerging economies since the early 2000s—growth expected to continue, as discussed in chapter 3—has already reshuffled the ranks of the world's largest corporations. Before 2004, less than 5 percent of the five hundred largest firms by revenues (the *Fortune* Global 500) were based in emerging economies. In 2016, one-quarter were from emerging markets, and researchers have predicted that this proportion will grow to about half by 2025 or 2030.[29] The implication is that insurgent firms from emerging economies will increasingly challenge incumbent multinationals for global industry leadership across an array of industries. Let's look at the strategies that each set of firms can employ in this giant joust for global industry leadership.

The rising share of emerging-market-based firms among the world's largest corporations does *not* mean that the outcome of this competition is a foregone conclusion in favor of the insurgents. Size is not the same as leadership. The emerging-market-based firms on the *Fortune* Global 500 are far *less* globalized than their advanced-economy counterparts. As of 2014, not a single insurgent on the list could be classified as global, based on the criterion of having at least 20 percent of its sales in each of the three broad triad regions of North America, Europe, and Asia-Pacific.[30] Less than half of these firms even report data on their international sales—mostly because they focus almost entirely on their home markets. Additionally, only 16 percent of the world's top five hundred firms by market capitalization were from emerging markets in 2015, as were just 6 percent of the hundred largest nonfinancial firms based on foreign assets.

It would also be a mistake, however, to prejudge the outcome in favor of the incumbent multinationals from advanced economies. These firms *do not* currently hold dominant positions across a broad range of sectors in emerging markets. According to one study, the top two multinationals have smaller market shares than do the top two local companies across several industries in the BRIC countries (Brazil, Russia, India, and China).[31] Trend analysis from 1999 to 2008 indicates that emerging-economy companies not only grew 10 percentage points faster at home than did companies from advanced economies (18 versus 8 percent) but also enjoyed a similar edge (22 versus 12 percent) in advanced economies and an even bigger one in other (foreign) emerging economies (31 versus 13 percent).[32] And a survey by the Boston Consulting Group indicated that while 78 percent of multinationals expect to gain market share in emerging economies, only 13 percent say they have an advantage over local competitors. Also, more respondents cited local competitors as a major threat in emerging economies than multinationals from either advanced or emerging economies.[33]

AAA Strategies for Incumbents

The greatest advantage incumbents typically have over insurgents lies on the aggregation leg of the AAA triangle. In a study of which firms were winning in which industries in China, Thomas Hout and

I found striking evidence of the competitive benefits of aggregation for incumbents. As figure 4-5 shows, the more intensive in R&D and advertising an industry is, the more likely foreign multinationals are to lead it.[34] As the earlier example of GE indicated, intangible assets in technology (supported by R&D) and branding (supported by advertising) are frequently used bases for aggregation strategies. The patterns in China are particularly powerful because it, unlike just about any other emerging market, is large enough for local firms to achieve substantial scale domestically. In addition, China's public policies focus on strengthening local firms. Yet this basic pattern of competitive outcomes has been fairly stable over time.[35]

FIGURE 4-5

Industry leadership: Chinese companies versus foreign multinationals (MNCs), 2012–2013

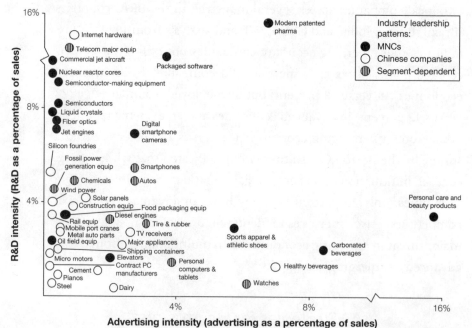

Source: Pankaj Ghemawat and Thomas Hout, "Globalization, Capabilities, and Distance: Theory and a Case Study (of China)," in Oxford Handbook of Dynamic Capabilities, ed. David J. Teece (Oxford: Oxford University Press, 2015).

Note: Segment-dependent industries are those in which leadership varies by segment within an industry, often with foreign multinationals leading in high-end segments and Chinese companies leading in low-end segments.

The ability of incumbents to retain their leadership positions in industries with high R&D and advertising intensity in China suggests that it would be a grave mistake for most of these firms to abandon aggregation strategies. Rather, they will need to protect these advantages as they devote increasing attention to the adaptation and arbitrage legs of the AAA triangle. To consider adaptation first, while insurgents are normally better "adapted" to their own home markets, incumbents usually have more general advantages in managing adaptation across locations. Think, for example, how adroitly global leaders in consumer products such as P&G and Unilever manage how much of the marketing mix to vary, product by product, across countries. Since advertising-intensive industries typically require substantial adaptation, the incumbents' lead at the high end of the advertising-intensity axis in China also suggests that incumbents must work to preserve their leads in this area as well. The specific adaptation challenge for incumbents involves becoming better adapted to key emerging markets or segments rather than increasing adaptation in general.

In contrast, arbitrage is where incumbents typically find themselves at a clear disadvantage relative to insurgents. Insurgents tend to excel at arbitraging from their home bases and sometimes can extend this advantage to arbitrage from other emerging economies. The greatest challenge for incumbents when they are facing threats from insurgents, therefore, often involves strengthening their own capacity for arbitrage. Fortunately for the incumbents, there are many examples of firms that have successfully boosted their arbitrage capacity—and often in ways that strengthened their positions on adaptation at the same time. GE Healthcare, for example, has made India a hub for low-cost medical devices.[36] In response to the threat from Indian IT services firms, IBM and Accenture built up large operations in India. These facilities supported the firms' global market positions, increased the costs of their Indian competitors by bidding up salaries in India, and even opened up domestic sales opportunities for these firms. IBM has become the largest IT services vendor to Indian clients.[37]

One incumbent that has gone even further with adaptation and eventually arbitrage from emerging markets is the Japanese automaker Suzuki. The Suzuki subsidiary in India (Maruti Suzuki India) became the company's biggest unit. After mastering the adaptation required to become India's leading passenger car manufacturer, Suzuki turned to arbitrage, making India its global small-car hub, churning out a quarter of Suzuki's global production. It exports entry-level vehicles to over one hundred countries (including Japan).[38] In 2013, Maruti's chairman, R. C. Bhargava, said that all of Suzuki's future investments in overseas assembly operations would be made by Maruti.[39] This is a rather stunning turn of events for a Japanese company—or, for that matter, for almost *any* incumbent.

To summarize, incumbents typically start with a core aggregation advantage, including considerable market experience, and seek to become able arbitrageurs (or, more likely, to neutralize an arbitrage disadvantage) and to better adapt to big emerging markets. Even as incumbents pay more attention to adaptation and arbitrage, they will typically fare better by continuing to emphasize aggregation because creative application of superior intangible assets in new markets is often the best antidote to a lower-cost local insurgent. Or—to make the same point another way—innovation around existing advantages is a major reason why lower cost does not always prevail. Great multinationals seldom give up on earning premium prices in emerging markets. Instead, they apply their superior scope, know-how, and experience.

AAA Strategies for Insurgents

As we already saw in the Indian IT example, competitors from emerging economies typically start off with advantages in arbitrage (and in adaptation at home and sometimes in other emerging markets). While they will have to do a lot of work on dealing with arbitrage sensitivity, given current trends, their primary challenge in the pursuit of global industry leadership is to build up advantages in aggregation. And secondarily, they have to strengthen their capacity for adaptation to extend the reach of their arbitrage and aggregation strategies. In the next chapter, I'll come back to the question of whether these firms should aim to compete across both advanced and emerging markets or should stick with just one or the other—or even just stay at home. Here, I assume they are trying for a broad international footprint.

The arduous task of upgrading beyond arbitrage must be accomplished while a company is still competing effectively with both the incumbent market leaders—which have more power to set the terms of competition—and other insurgents. In this context, it often makes sense for insurgents to find ways to strengthen their positions without having to go up against the incumbents head-to-head, at least not until an insurgent's capabilities have matured enough to give it a shot at winning the ultimate battle. The possibilities in this regard are multifarious, but they fall broadly into two approaches: either maneuver around the incumbents or make deals with them. In both cases, the objective in AAA terms is to build up intangible assets that can form the basis for aggregation advantages while also gaining valuable international-market experience that can inform better adaptation to differences.

Most insurgents gain their initial footholds in developed markets by maneuvering around the market leaders. They focus on market segments that aren't central to the leaders' strategies and then broaden their capabilities and market positions from there. The routine coding and debugging work that gave Indian IT firms a start in the United States and United Kingdom was at the bottom of the priority list for the global market leaders. The Chinese appliance giant Haier got a foothold in the United States selling compact refrigerators that were popular in college dorm rooms and sold in big-box stores rather than the appliance retailers that were the key channels for incumbents such as Whirlpool. Another company that achieved some success via this route is Mahindra & Mahindra, India's market leader in both SUVs and tractors. While Mahindra hasn't (yet) gained traction in the SUV market in advanced economies, it has maneuvered around incumbents, such as John Deere, to become a major seller of small tractors in the United States. To avoid competing only on price, Mahindra has offered industry-leading warranties and financing and has deftly adapted its marketing to appeal to American "gentleman farmers" working small plots of land.

Flanking strategies take time, and there is no guarantee that a foothold at the low end of a market can be parlayed into a leadership position. Haier, for example, went as far as buying a landmark building in Manhattan and building large refrigerators at a factory in South Carolina, only to continue to struggle in the US market for full-size refrigerators for almost two decades. In 2016, Haier went down the deal-making route, buying GE's appliances business for $5.4 billion. In the acquisition, Haier gained nine US manufacturing facilities, state-of-the-art sales and distribution channels, and the right to use the GE brand on its products for forty years. If the acquisition is integrated and managed effectively, Haier will have substantially accelerated the upgrading of its aggregation and adaptation capabilities by taking on intangible assets that GE cultivated over decades.

Acquiring capabilities abroad, however, requires far more than simply signing a contract and wiring funds. One study of Chinese acquisitions of majority stakes in German machinery companies between 2000 and 2010 found that by the end of 2010, only 30 percent of the acquisitions were still clearly operating successfully. Roughly 35 percent had already been dissolved, and another 35 percent were "barely successful," as indicated by cutbacks to their product range or labor force.[40]

What can insurgents do to boost their chances of successfully acquiring capabilities abroad? For starters, they need to have enough expertise to accurately assess the value of the capability they're seeking to buy. That's a big part of where one of the first big acquisitions from China—TCL Corporation's deal with France's Thomson in 2003 to become the majority partner in the world's largest manufacturer of televisions—went wrong. TCL's chairman Li Dongsheng "admitted that he had underestimated the challenges involved in rescuing

Thomson's business."[41] The biggest problem was that Thomson (like TCL) focused on traditional cathode ray tube TVs, as opposed to the flat panels that consumers were starting to demand.

But let's assume that a firm has found a target with the right capabilities—and managed to negotiate a good price on the deal—as Chinese automaker Geely did for its acquisition of Volvo. Can the firm successfully absorb the target? Research on firms' absorptive capacity emphasizes the importance of people who play interface or boundary-spanning roles.[42] Lenovo's acquisition of IBM's PC division in 2004 provides a powerful example. The company's head, Yang Yuanqing, moved temporarily to the United States and learned English—and even installed an executive of the acquired firm as CEO. Lenovo subsequently created a chief diversity officer role—held by Yolanda Conyers, an American—whose job was to "figure out how to align the company behind common goals while respecting everyone's differences." Conyers lived in China from 2009 to 2012 to make sure she learned enough about Chinese culture to play the required bridging role.[43]

Since big acquisitions involve large risks, firms can also consider other variants of the deal-making route that have worked for insurgents. Brazil's Embraer surpassed its Canadian archrival Bombardier to become the world's largest supplier of regional jets. To get there, Embraer mitigated its capability gaps by focusing on the cockpit and on integration while outsourcing aggressively wherever its own know-how fell short (or when capital intensity was high). And Taiwan's Hon Hai (better known as Foxconn) represents another global leader with basically the mirror image of Embraer's outsourcing strategy. As the firm to which Apple and a host of other consumer electronics companies outsourced labor-intensive manufacturing and assembly, Hon Hai has become China's largest exporter and the world's 27th-largest firm by revenues—well above other tech companies with venerable brands, including Microsoft (69th), IBM (81st), and Sony (105th).[44]

To summarize, arbitrage is a key strategy for insurgents. And as the Indian IT discussion earlier highlighted, arbitrage strategies are more sustainable than many presume. But to really make a run at global market leadership, insurgents have to develop superior intangible assets—to build up aggregation advantages—and to achieve the capacity for adaptation required to successfully deploy those superior capabilities around the world.

Figure 4-6, which sums up the situation for both incumbents and insurgents, implies something of a race toward the middle, even though neither side is likely to give up entirely on its initial advantages. Incumbents try to arbitrage more effectively out of emerging economies and seek to become better adapted to those markets. Meanwhile, insurgents continue to use their arbitrage advantages as they strengthen their aggregation and adaptation capabilities. Given the inherent tensions among the AAA strategies, success for both incumbents and insurgents also requires careful choices about where to compete (the topic of the next chapter) and how to organize and connect internally to manage the tensions (the topic of chapter 6).

FIGURE 4-6

AAA strategies for incumbents versus insurgents

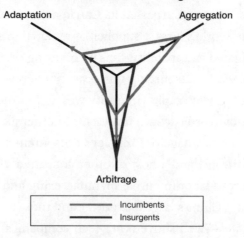

Note: Incumbents are shown here as stronger than insurgents on adaptation because of their generally greater capacity to manage adaptation across a wide variety of contexts. Insurgents, however, would be expected to be better adapted to their home markets.

Managerial Maxims

1. As globalization has come under increasing pressure, business leaders are thinking through how to adjust their international strategies in response to the changing environment.

2. Firms can employ three fundamental types of strategies to create value across national borders and international distance: aggregation, arbitrage, and adaptation (the AAA strategies).

3. Aggregation exploits similarities across countries to create value from scale and scope economies. This is the primary international strategy for most *incumbent* multinationals from advanced economies.

4. Arbitrage exploits differences such as when a company sources where its inputs are abundant and sells where they are scarce. This is the primary international strategy for most *insurgent* multinationals from emerging economies.

5. Adaptation adjusts to differences to expand the scope over which aggregation and arbitrage strategies can be success-fully employed. Incumbents typically have stronger capabil-ities than insurgents for managing adaptation across a large number of countries.

6. Boosting adaptation can help firms deal with globalization-related headwinds. But since aggregation and arbitrage are the primary bases of cross-border value creation—adaptation extends their reach—it would be a mistake for firms to abandon aggregation and arbitrage.

7. The longer-term rise of emerging economies implies differ-ent approaches to the AAA strategies for incumbents ver-sus insurgents.

8. Incumbents will need to preserve their aggregation advantages while shoring up weaknesses on arbitrage and becoming better adapted in key emerging markets.

9. Insurgents will need to continue leveraging arbitrage as they focus primarily on building aggregation advantages of their own and secondarily on strengthening their capacity for adaptation.

10. In light of the inherent tensions among the AAA strategies, firms must pay careful attention to where to compete and how to organize as they pursue the more complex strategies that prevailing trends often require.

5

Presence

Where to Compete

The previous chapter focused on how to compete; this one focuses on where to compete. The two questions are obviously related: with a strategy of pure localization, for instance, the choice of where to compete could be made on a country-by-country basis. But as explained in the previous chapter, since pure localization is *not* the right strategy for dealing with recent developments, the question of where to compete becomes more complicated as well.

The gloom around globalization, with its suggestion that borders might start to matter more again rather than less, has mostly generated calls for multinational companies to narrow their global presence—at the extreme even to pack up and come home, relying on trade to vend their wares. The January 2017 cover story in the *Economist*, "The Retreat of the Global Company," stops just short of arguing as much. Such injunctions cover both horizontal multinationals focused on selling abroad and vertical ones employing international supply chains in sourcing and production.

Calls to retreat from international markets gain plausibility from the observation that significant amounts of restructuring of this sort have been or are being attempted by companies in a diverse range of industries. In banking, both Citibank and HSBC have withdrawn from retail banking in more than a dozen markets since 2012, and major pullbacks have also been announced by Royal Bank of Scotland and Barclays.[1] And while restructuring in financial services might be attributed to more stringent regulations in the wake of the global financial crisis, similar moves in more global or globalizing industries cannot be chalked up to such factors. Consider, for instance, autos. In the spring of 2017, General Motors mostly exited Europe by selling its Opel and Vauxhall brands to Peugeot. And such narrowing of scope isn't confined just to "old" industries. In telecom services, Vodafone had earlier capped a string of withdrawals from joint ventures and partnerships by disposing of its 45 percent stake in Verizon Wireless, the largest US mobile phone company, for $130 billion, leaving Vodafone half its previous size.[2]

But before moving to imitate such moves by narrowing cross-border scope, one should recognize that many such restructurings actually respond to performance problems that predate Brump. Thus, Opel's cumulative losses since 1999, thanks to a fourth-ranked position and a weak brand image in a European market mired in overcapacity, exceeded $20 billion![3] The impression the Opel case presents is that of an overdue move rather than an agile response to recent developments.

Since case examples such as these do not add up to a general prescription for firms to narrow their geographic scope, we must dig deeper to uncover what Brump and other changes in the international political climate mean for firms' choices about where to compete. This chapter does so by first reviewing the facts about firms' cross-border presence, their performance, and relevant managerial intuitions; all these elements help explain why both expansion and contraction are live issues. Then, building on the law of distance and the CAGE framework presented in chapter 1, I propose a series of screens at the country, industry, and firm levels—which lend themselves to the mnemonic "CIF screens"—for guiding firms' choices about where to compete.[4] And finally, with these ideas in mind, this chapter concludes with alternative approaches to restructuring firms' presence abroad.

Global Presence and Performance

Consistent with the law of distance, multinationals, even large ones, tend to have narrower geographic scope than one might presume. A good starting point is provided by data for US companies, which are required to report details of their foreign direct investments to the US Department of Commerce. In 2012, the modal US multinational operated in just one foreign country, and the median multinational in three countries. In contrast, US respondents in my multicountry survey estimated the median number of countries of operation to be ten times as high as the actual number![5] In fact, only 10 percent of US multinationals operated in twenty-plus countries—a percentage that had held steady since before the global financial crisis. Moreover, since only 0.01 percent of US companies engage in FDI, the 10 percent of them operating in twenty-plus countries account for only 0.001 percent of all US companies.

The percentage of US firms that export *is* significantly higher—closer to 1 percent than 0.01 percent. But of the US companies that do export, 58 percent export to only one country.[6] Like the FDI data, the export data indicates that where to expand to remains a significant agenda item for many companies in the United States. And despite somewhat higher levels of multinationalization and engagement in exports in some other parts of the world, notably the European Union, the pattern of limited cross-border activity applies around the world.

Of course, if one focuses on the very largest firms, one does see companies that operate in 100 or even nearly 200 countries. Thus, Sam Palmisano, the former chairman and CEO of IBM, once mock-complained to me, "Our problem is that we just ran out of countries." While IBM operates in 170 countries, it presumably still faces issues about where to allocate more versus less resources. And although IBM does not report its revenues at the country level, other multinationals with broad footprints do. For example, Oracle has customers in 195 countries—but in 2016, about 61 percent of its revenues came from the United States (its domestic market) and its top three foreign markets.

In terms of its revenue distribution, Oracle is representative of the top hundred companies with the most assets located outside their home countries.[7] While these companies tend to operate in dozens of countries, their top four markets—including their home market—account, based on somewhat fragmentary data, for about 60 percent of their revenues (figure 5-1) and, according to even more fragmentary data, a larger slice of their profits. And as discussed in chapter 1, only a single-digit percentage of *Fortune* Global 500 companies—the world's largest firms by revenue—earn at least 20 percent of their revenue in each of the broad triad regions of North America, Europe, and Asia-Pacific.[8] Again, this presence across regions is far smaller

FIGURE 5-1

Average revenue distribution of firms ranked among global top one hundred based on foreign assets, 2015–2016

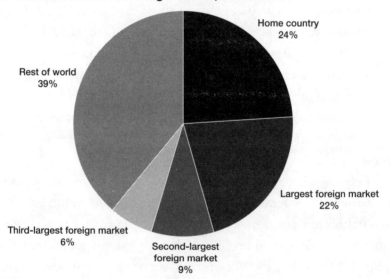

Source: S&P Global *Capital IQ* and company annual reports.

Note: Based on thirty-three companies with available data, from UN Conference on Trade and Development's list of one hundred largest transnational corporations.

than one might presume: the average guess by managers in my multicountry survey was that 44 percent of the *Fortune* Global 500 would meet this test!

Somewhat similar characterizations also apply to internet companies, which often claim near-ubiquity. An analysis of the largest publicly listed internet companies indicates that aside from Alphabet, eBay, and Facebook, they derived the majority of their revenue domestically. And even the exceptions' domestic-versus-international revenue split was close to fifty-fifty. Clearly, they still face issues about where to deepen if not broaden their international presence.

Companies with broad presence, in particular, also confront significant issues about where they should cut back—and have done so for a long time now. Thus an analysis of internal financial data from sixteen multinationals before the global financial crisis indicated that eight of them had large geographic units—units bringing in as much as one-quarter of their revenues—that destroyed value after their capital costs were taken into account. Figure 5-2 shows the distribution of economic profits by country for a fast-moving consumer goods company.

The persistent performance problems of many multinationals across broad swaths of their international operations has been in evidence for decades now, if not longer. In my 2003 article in *Harvard Business Review*, "The Forgotten Strategy," I show that between 1990 and 2001, the foreign operations of *Fortune* Global 500 companies consistently posted lower average returns on sales than did their domestic operations, and an update based on 2016 data affirmed the same pattern.[9]

While such a pattern of multinationals penetrating and persisting in too many markets is not necessarily inconsistent with profit maximization, long-standing biases toward globaloney may play an important role in generating it. Thus, 64 percent of the respondents to a survey I ran in 2007 agreed with the dubious proposition that the truly global company should aim to compete in all major markets. Ten years later, in my 2017 multicountry survey, this percentage had

FIGURE 5-2

Economic profits (EP) by country: a fast-moving consumer goods company, 2005

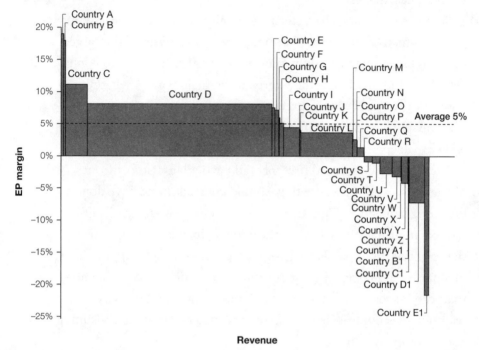

Revenue

Source: Pankaj Ghemawat, *Redefining Global Strategy* (Boston: Harvard Business School Press, 2007), figure 8-2.

actually climbed to 88 percent! And reinforcing this, 85 percent of the respondents agreed with "Global expansion is an imperative rather than an option to be evaluated" and with "Globalization offers virtually limitless growth opportunities."

Multinationalization has always been an option to be considered carefully and, if economic theory as well as past data are any guide, to be pursued by only a few capable firms. What was lacking among most of my survey respondents and in the recent *Economist* article arguing that multinationals should come home was the notion of contingency. The next few sections flesh out how decisions about where to compete should be contingent on a series of country-, industry-, and firm-level considerations, the CIF screens.

Country-Level Screens

In writing about using screens at multiple levels to decide where to compete, I use the word *screens* to conjure up images of the forty-niners panning for gold during the California gold rush. They used a succession of wire-mesh screens of increasing fineness to sift through the sands on riverbeds in search of nuggets, then pebbles, and then flakes of gold. In that spirit, I start with the coarsest screen in the present context, at the country level. Country-level analysis is, of course, fundamental to decisions about which countries to compete in. But firms have long focused just on size—or increments to size—when evaluating countries. As a hopeful Manchester mill owner supposedly calculated 150 years ago, "just adding an inch to every Chinaman's shirttail will keep Manchester's cotton industry going forever." Swap out inch, shirttail, and Manchester for contemporary equivalents, and adjust for more gender inclusiveness, and you get a pretty up-to-date vision statement for many multinationals.

More systematic evidence of firms' tendency to focus on country size is provided by the respondents to my recent multinational survey. Consider the answers to a question I asked managers in the United States: "When US companies establish a single business operation abroad, where do they go most often?" The top-ranked response, from 22 percent of the managers, was China, even though it ranks fifth, representing the first foreign destination for only 3 percent of US companies investing abroad (figure 5-3).

The overblown intuitions about China seem to be based on its place as the second-largest economy in the world, after the United States. Fortunately, the respondents did demonstrate some understanding of the law of distance: the countries they ranked next, the United Kingdom, Canada, and Mexico, all figure in the actual top three, although not in that order.[10] These are obviously proximate countries, albeit in somewhat different ways. And their appearance in the top three is not solely because of their size. The United Kingdom is the fifth-largest economy in the world, Canada the tenth-largest, and Mexico the fifteenth.

FIGURE 5-3

Rooted map with countries sized according to foreign subsidiary locations of US firms with operations in only one foreign country, 2012

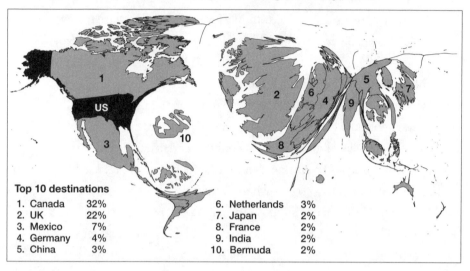

Top 10 destinations

1. Canada	32%		6. Netherlands	3%
2. UK	22%		7. Japan	2%
3. Mexico	7%		8. France	2%
4. Germany	4%		9. India	2%
5. China	3%		10. Bermuda	2%

Source: Data from Jim Fetzer, US Department of Commerce, email to author.

More broadly, many managers intuitively understand the importance of distance. The CAGE framework introduced in chapter 1 aimed to make such thinking about distance explicit, expand the aspects of distance covered, and calibrate their effects. Table 1-1 in chapter 1 identified various types of distance that affect firms when they go abroad, and it emphasized the importance of considering bilateral factors, such as the presence or absence of a common language, alongside unilateral ones, such as economic size.

In chapter 1, I also demonstrated the power of the CAGE framework to explain patterns of international activity by estimating gravity models of trade and FDI. The map in figure 5-3 is based only on US firms that were taking their first steps toward multinationalization, but the CAGE-based models in chapter 1 took into account nearly all trade and FDI worldwide. A small set of variables explained at least two-thirds of the variation in country-to-country flows:

- Distance variables: common official language, colonial linkage, trade agreement or regional bloc, physical distance, common border, and per-capita income ratio

- GDPs of individual countries to capture their sizes

- Country fixed effects to capture other unilateral factors

To conduct an even more concrete test of the CAGE models, consider how well they predict countries' ranks as destinations of US exports and outward FDI stocks. The correlation between predicted and actual ranks is very high: 0.93 for merchandise exports and 0.85 for FDI stocks. This analysis illustrates a pair of patterns that also show up more broadly in the kinds of cross-country analyses discussed in chapter 1. First, CAGE-based models work well to predict both trade and FDI, although they work even better for trade than for FDI. One of the special complications for FDI is the high proportion involving offshore financial centers (Bermuda, for example, is the seventh-largest locus of US FDI stocks). Second, even if one runs a model involving just GDP and physical distance, this more limited model also has high predictive power. These results suggest that even considering just physical distance (rather than all the CAGE dimensions) is far better than basing decisions on size alone.

The CAGE framework, of course, aligns closely with the law of distance: at the firm level, countries that are proximate along multiple dimensions of distance are likely to be easier destinations than distant ones are. Additionally, since the country-level trade and FDI patterns largely reflect the collective behavior of firms, the same analysis implies that most companies focus—with good reason—first on easier markets before moving on to harder ones. When the Chinese appliance giant Haier was in the early stages of its international expansion, it embraced the opposite strategy, which it called "difficult first, then easy," and focused on the United States.[11] But the company nonetheless continues to have stronger market positions in nearby countries such as Vietnam.

The one significant exception to the rule that proximity or similarity eases international expansion involves trade motivated by economic arbitrage. Emerging economies often traverse relatively great distances to sell into developed economies. But even this exception is only partial: while a business might, in certain product categories, try to maximize rather than minimize economic distance, maximizing distance along the other CAGE dimensions at the same time is rarely a good idea. For example, as described in chapter 4, the Indian IT sector does primarily target advanced rather than emerging economies. But within the advanced group, India focuses on the United States and the United Kingdom, which not only have the advantage of being large markets but also have greater cultural and administrative affinities with India than does, say, Japan, Germany, or France.

India also helps illustrate several important contextual points about country-level screens. The country's limited trade and virtually nonexistent FDI with Pakistan highlight how political relationships influence business activity—even though such relationships are difficult to measure and thus excluded from most gravity models. Second, India also exemplifies the importance of considering unilateral factors beyond size and growth. For foreign companies looking to invest in India, the recent liberalization of policies on inward FDI is of particular importance. And third, the assumption that India (and, by extension, the country level) is the only meaningful level of analysis must confront a whole set of issues that get in the way of treating India as a fully integrated market: its cultural diversity (e.g., twenty-two officially recognized languages), internal administrative barriers (particularly between its twenty-nine states and seven union territories), its geographic expanse and poor infrastructure, and economic differences that, when measured using per-capita incomes, are larger than in many developed countries. And the need to consider within-country differences doesn't only apply to emerging giants such as India. Think, for example, of Spain or even Belgium.[12] In internally diverse countries, it is often useful to supplement country-level analysis with sub-country or intra-national analysis.

Two other uses of the CAGE framework in country analysis are also worth mentioning. As discussed earlier, firms can use the

CAGE framework to analyze the effects of shocks such as Brexit or a global trade war. The framework is arguably more important than it used to be because of the elevated policy uncertainty that will be discussed in chapter 7. Additionally, firms often find it useful to map insights from analysis of where to compete into strategies for how to compete in selected markets. Having identified which aspects of distance are likely to prove challenging in a given country, firms can design strategies to address those challenges. Often companies find great value in simply drawing attention to the most salient differences. At a *Fortune* Global CEO forum in Chengdu a few years ago, I presented a CAGE analysis of the differences between the United States and China. One of the other panelists was Carlos Gutierrez, formerly US Commerce Secretary and, before that, CEO of Kellogg. He commented that if he had known about the CAGE framework back when he was at Kellogg, the company might have avoided sinking a great deal of time and money into trying to change Chinese breakfast habits.

While country-level distance analysis is essential and can be performed both qualitatively and quantitatively, companies also generally need industry- and firm-specific considerations—finer screens—to yield actionable results. I turn next to the industry level.

Industry-Level Screens

Unless you are a financial investor, it won't suffice to focus only on distances at the aggregate economy or country level in deciding where to go. You will need a finer-meshed, industry-level screen because the most important dimensions of distance, and how much they matter, vary greatly from industry to industry. For example, movies are more sensitive to linguistic differences but less sensitive to geographic ones than are large home appliances like refrigerators, whose bulk-to-value ratio usually precludes shipping them between continents. See table 5-1 for a summary of the kinds of industries that are particularly sensitive to each dimension of distance.

TABLE 5-1

The CAGE distance framework at the industry level

Cultural distance	Administrative distance	Geographic distance	Economic distance
Cultural differences matter the most when:	Government involvement is high in industries that are:	Geography plays a more important role when:	Economic differences make the biggest impact when:
• Products have high linguistic content (TV programs)	• Producers of staple goods (electricity)	• Products have a low value-to-weight or value-to-bulk ratio (cement)	• Nature of demand varies with income level (cars)
• Products matter to cultural or national identity (foods)	• Producers of other "entitlements" (drugs)	• Products are fragile or perishable (glass, fruit)	• Economics of standardization or scale are limited (cement)
• Product features vary in terms of size (cars) or standards (electrical equipment)	• Large employers (farming)	• Local supervision and operational requirements are high (many services)	• Labor and other factor cost differences are salient (garments)
• Products carry country-specific quality associations (wines)	• Large suppliers to government (mass transportation)		• Distribution or business systems are different (insurance)
	• National champions (aerospace)		• Companies need to be responsive and agile (home appliances)
	• Vital to national security (telecommunications)		
	• Exploiters of natural resources (oil, mining)		
	• Subject to high sunk costs (infrastructure)		

Source: Pankaj Ghemawat, *Redefining Global Strategy* (Boston: Harvard Business School Press, 2007), 50, table 2-3.

The characterizations in the table are drawn from case studies as well as statistical analysis using gravity models that were estimated at the industry rather than country level. In an earlier book, I reported the results of industry-level gravity modeling covering ninety-seven product categories for merchandise trade and thirty-nine sectors, including services, for FDI.[13] I highlight here a small subset of those trade and FDI results. (Readers can conduct and customize similar analyses covering a wide variety of trade, capital, information, and people flows on my website at www.ghemawat.com/cage.) Figure 5-4 covers the impacts of physical distance on merchandise trade by product category, and figure 5-5 summarizes the joint effects of a common language and colony-and-colonizer ties on announced greenfield FDI by sector.[14]

FIGURE 5-4

Physical distance and merchandise trade, by product

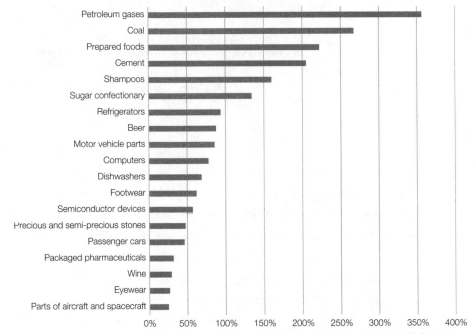

Increase in trade value associated with halving of physical distance

Source: Gravity model estimated using data from United Nations *Comtrade*, CEPII *GeoDist*, International Monetary Fund *World Economic Outlook*, and World Trade Organization *Statistics Database*.

FIGURE 5-5

Cultural/administrative distance and announced greenfield FDI, by sector

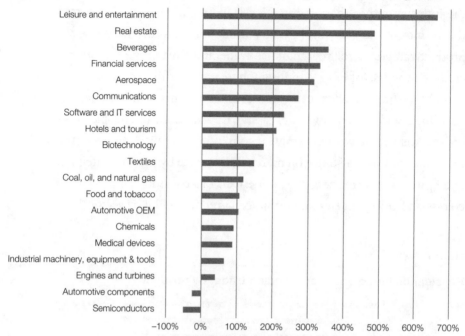

Source: Gravity model estimated using data from Financial Times *fDi Markets*, CEPII *GeoDist*, International Monetary Fund *World Economic Outlook*, and World Trade Organization *Statistics Database*.

As chapter 1 explained, even though per-capita income differences were not significant in aggregate trade models, trade in some industries is motivated by economic differences (arbitrage) while the same differences dampen trade in other industries. Turning to geographic distance, another well-established pattern that shows up in the trade analysis is that high value-to-weight and value-to-bulk ratios tend to reduce sensitivity to physical distance. Among the industries shown in figure 5-4, the one for which merchandise trade is most sensitive to physical distance is petroleum gases, which are difficult and costly to transport over long distances. International trade in this industry increases by over 350 percent when physical distance is halved. And parts of aircraft and spacecraft are the least sensitive to physical distance, presumably because these highly specialized products are themselves components of vehicles for long-distance transportation.[15] For the cultural and administrative dimensions of the CAGE framework, the FDI analysis in figure 5-5 also reveals substantial variation in distance sensitivity across industries. The industry for which common official language and colonial linkage were most important to announced greenfield FDI was leisure and entertainment (with a common language and a colony-colonizer link boosting FDI by more than 600 percent). The strong influence of common language and colonial linkage is unsurprising given that culture is particularly important in such industries. The lowest effect was for semiconductors, an industry dominated by a few countries that mostly have no colonial linkages with each other. And on average, FDI in services (the "tertiary sector") seems to be affected more by cultural and administrative factors than is investment in most of the primary (extractive) or secondary (manufacturing) sectors.[16]

In terms of where to compete, the distance-effect calibrations obviously supply one possible basis for industry-level screening. My team developed the CAGE Comparator tool to help managers conduct this sort of analysis (see the sidebar "The CAGE Comparator Online Distance-Analysis Tool"). But in my experience, firms can reap substantial benefits even from simpler forms of industry-tailored CAGE analysis. Firms often find it useful to nominate and calibrate their own factors under each of the CAGE categories. Thus, Grolsch, the four-hundred-year-old Dutch beer brand, tried to select which markets to emphasize using, in part, CAGE distances. The beer maker analyzed languages (cultural), nonmembership versus membership in the European Union (of which the Netherlands was a founding member [administrative]), transportation costs (geographic), and differences in GDP per capita (economic).

The CAGE Comparator Online Distance-Analysis Tool

The CAGE Comparator at www.ghemawat.com/cage enables businesspeople to generate and customize quantitative analyses of international market opportunities, taking into account where their firms are coming from and in which industries they compete. Start by selecting the type of international flow of interest (for industry-level analysis, choose one of the "Trade by Product" or "Trade by Service" options) and your firm's home country. The CAGE Comparator will then automatically generate a ranking of countries from closest to farthest, according to the historically observed effects of CAGE distance on the flow being analyzed. (The gravity model employed in the analysis is also reported, but no knowledge of gravity modeling—or statistics—is required to use the results.)

The comparator tool will also generate predictions, which may be compared with actual sales or investment patterns to help the user develop hypotheses about untapped international opportunities. Since these predictions are based on historical patterns at the global level, they often vary widely from actual international flows. Some important factors for a particular analysis may be absent from the model. Therefore, the CAGE Comparator also allows users to customize the distance effects incorporated into its analyses, so that executives can build in their own informed judgment and perform sensitivity analysis around the key assumptions.

More often than not, firms consider several factors under each CAGE category. Table 5-2 summarizes the CAGE factors identified by Indian generic-drug manufacturer Dr. Reddy's Labs and UK-based Twinkl Educational Publishing, a digital publisher. Dr. Reddy's specified a range of CAGE factors, some unilateral measures of country attributes and some bilateral (i.e., distance-related) and attached

TABLE 5-2

CAGE distance factors employed by Dr. Reddy's Labs and Twinkl Educational Publishing

	Dr. Reddy's Components	Weights	Twinkl Components
CULTURAL	• Difference in language	5%	• Level of language adaptation
	• Difference in religions/ values	5%	• Religious/social differences
			• Curriculum/pedagogy differences
			• Ethnical differences
ADMINISTRATIVE	• Regulatory barriers	5%	• Level of institutional void
	• Colonial ties	2%	• Colonial ties
	• Political hostility/ protectionism	7%	• Level of political cooperation
	• Local barriers to entry	5%	• Common currency
	• Difference in climate/ environment	5%	• Currency accepted by Twinkl
	• IP barrier	5%	
	• Influence of government on pharma	6%	
GEOGRAPHIC	• Time zone difference	2%	• Shared time zone
	• Physical distance	2%	• Shared land border
	• Population size	12%	• IDI index rank
ECONOMIC	• Per capita income	3%	• GDP per capita
	• Pharma market size	15%	• % of GDP spent on education
	• Payback period	9%	• Relative affordability level
	• Availability of quality HR	5%	• Teacher salary rank
	• Government supported healthcare	7%	• Population size

weights to them. These weights were informed by the manufacturer's sense that, given its generic-drug strategy (a firm-specific factor of the sort that will be discussed in the next section), the administrative and economic categories merited particular attention. (Note that pharma was the industry in which trade was most sensitive to per-capita income in my industry-level gravity models.) Through its analysis, undertaken after the global financial crisis (and a prior mega-acquisition overseas that didn't work out), Dr. Reddy's narrowed its secondary markets, the ones that were in play from the standpoint of additional resource commitments, from thirty-six to five. In alphabetical order, Jamaica, Myanmar, Sri Lanka, the United Arab Emirates, and Vietnam made the cut: there was clearly some degree of prioritization of proximity to India along multiple CAGE dimensions.

The number of CAGE-related factors in the table for Twinkl is roughly the same as those for Dr. Reddy's. But the publisher's factors, not surprisingly, allocate more emphasis to cultural distance. Twinkl anchored itself in England both geographically and in its curriculum (the originally developed materials were aimed at an English audience). Thus, Twinkl's CAGE analysis prompted the company to prioritize the following markets: Scotland, Wales, Northern Ireland, the Republic of Ireland, Australia, New Zealand, and the United Arab Emirates. This example highlights how, even for a digital business, various indicators of proximity influence the choice of where to compete. And also note that Twinkl employed a more qualitative approach: proximity to England for most CAGE factors was ranked low, medium, or high.

These two examples both illustrate the usefulness of customizing CAGE analysis of where to compete to reflect some characteristics of the industry being analyzed as well as some of the approaches that can be employed. But firms cannot stop with an industry-level perspective, because they also vary in their international opportunities and their capacities to bridge the distances and differences required to seize these opportunities. The next section turns, therefore, to firm-level screens.

Firm-Level Screens

The best options for where to compete can vary even among competitors in the same industry and from the same home country. Differences in firms' strategies and capabilities can drive differences in their target markets and so should be taken into account. Additionally, firm-level screens need to reckon with other aspects of firm diversity as well. Thus, while very few firms go abroad at all, some multinationals are already present in nearly every country. For the latter firms, internal distance within the firm may become more important than external distance between the firm and its customers, suppliers, partners, and so on. To deal with this greater complexity, I frame the firm-level screens as three broad questions that firms should ask themselves when making international expansion (or contraction) decisions:

1. How good is your company *really*?

2. How far can your company's competitive advantage travel?

3. How well does your company manage distance?

Note that the relative importance of the three questions varies across firms with different levels of internationalization: starters or would-be starters are likely to find question 1 particularly salient; large incumbents, in contrast, are likely to be more interested in questions 2 and 3.

1. How good is your company really?

Internationalization is the exception rather than the norm. As mentioned earlier, fewer than one out of a hundred US firms is an exporter and only one in ten thousand has direct investments in at least one foreign country. In emerging economies, one might expect even less internationalization, for several reasons: faster growth at home, lags in building up marketing and technological know-how (as detailed in the previous chapter), and a (longer) left tail of inefficient firms that would do well to master the basics of management (e.g., target setting) rather than fantasizing about internationalization.

Theoretical modeling confirms that only the more efficient firms will cross the viability threshold for exporting and that the bar for (horizontal) FDI is likely to be even higher (as evident in the US data). So, it is critical to ask yourself how good your company really is or, more ambitiously, how good it can become. Unless you rank up near the top, staying at home and getting that house in order may be a better option.

2. How far can your company's competitive advantage travel?

The previous subsection implies that if your company doesn't possess or isn't pursuing a significant competitive advantage, it should not pursue a globalization strategy. And even if it does have a competitive advantage, you need to ask yourself how far this competitive edge will travel. I will break down the answer to this complex question into two parts.

Identifying the CAGE dimensions (or subdimensions) to which your competitive advantage is most sensitive. Some types of advantages are relatively insensitive to cross-country differences, whereas others depend delicately on them. For an example of the latter, consider Lincoln Electric, which produces both welding machines and consumable products for them. Lincoln Electric has been one of the most frequently taught Harvard cases of all time because it outperformed its competitors—including much larger firms such as GE—at home in the United States. The key lever was high-powered incentives—bonus plus piecework—supported by other HR policies.[17] In a burst of overseas expansion in the second half of the 1980s, Lincoln Electric focused on establishing its presence in the largest markets around the world and nearly went bankrupt. It might have done better to use the CAGE framework to select markets that resembled the United States in allowing unrestricted use of piecework.

The Lincoln Electric example is far from unusual. From the emerging-economy corner, Mahindra, after frugally engineering and manufacturing an SUV, Scorpio, for the Indian market, tried to take the vehicle to developed markets. But in these markets, emissions and safety standards are more rigorous (administrative differences) and ruggedness is less important than speed (a blend of geographic and economic differences). As an outsider might have guessed, this bold effort backfired, although Mahindra does sell some Scorpios now in other emerging economies with road conditions that more closely resemble India's. As noted earlier, Mahindra achieved more success in the US tractor market—its cost and service-based advantages traveled better in that segment (chapter 4).

Understanding your competitive advantage's sensitivity to distance. Most competitive advantages do decay with distance. Recall the distance-driven limitations to the AAA strategies presented in chapter 4. My research with Steven Altman on the *Fortune* Global 500 provides additional empirical support.[18] As discussed, R&D and advertising intensities are well-known proxies for the ability of firms to transcend borders. Our research shows that *Fortune* Global 500 firms with higher levels on these metrics also tend to support broader footprints. Those categories of "strategic expenditures" are apparently associated with diminishing sensitivity to most of the standard CAGE distance variables.

Simpler calibrations of such distance decay patterns can also be informative. Consider Norwegian Air Shuttle, the fast-growing, low-cost carrier discussed in chapter 2 that is moving beyond intra-European short-haul travel into long-haul travel, primarily between Europe and North America. Norwegian had succeeded in European short-haul by picking routes to avoid too much competition with other low-cost carriers while particularly victimizing Scandinavian Airlines (SAS), which focused on the same region and reported higher costs than just about any other major airline. As European short-haul got increasingly crowded with low-cost carriers, Norwegian contemplated a move into transatlantic long-haul. The trouble was that many of its on-the-ground advantages were specific to Europe. So, the company is targeting a distinct set of long-haul advantages that are partly driven by route and scheduling strategies enabled by a new generation of aircraft. It remains to be seen how sustainable these advantages will be and whether they—as well as feed from short-haul to long-haul routes—will successfully offset reductions to its traditional advantages. But the basic dichotomization between advantages specific to European short-haul and those that might be of broader use helps bring some conceptual clarity.

Finally, even if multinationals can be confident that they will be better positioned than local competitors, they still need to reckon with competition from multinationals from other countries—companies that may face less distance to particular country markets. (This challenge is sometimes tactlessly phrased as "Who is the natural owner of opportunities in country X?") Again, the CAGE framework can help with the perception and analysis of such patterns. For instance, it can help explain the strength of Spanish firms in many industries across Latin America and the fact that, in Mexico, US firms have outperformed even Spanish firms in terms of their rate and scope of success.[19]

3. How well does your company manage distance?

Even firms that do multinationalize—and do so broadly—vary greatly in their ability to handle a given amount of CAGE distance. We can see this variability by adding the diversity of the top management team (TMT) to the firm-level R&D and advertising intensity metrics in the distance analysis of the Fortune *Global* 500 mentioned above. TMT diversity also turns out to be related strongly to broader distance across dimensions of the CAGE framework. Chapter 6 will look in depth at how firms can bridge greater distances and discuss whether TMT diversity enables broader footprints or vice versa. But for now, consider just one company example: BMW.

Figures 5-6 and 5-7 contrast maps of BMW's sales and the national origins of its top management. Despite the obvious discomfort the

FIGURE 5-6

Rooted map with countries sized according to BMW unit sales, 2016

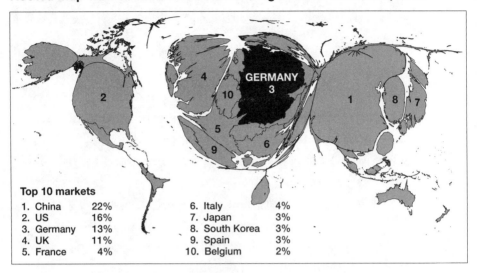

Top 10 markets

1. China	22%		6. Italy	4%
2. US	16%		7. Japan	3%
3. Germany	13%		8. South Korea	3%
4. UK	11%		9. Spain	3%
5. France	4%		10. Belgium	2%

Source: Data from BMW Annual Report and WardsAuto.

FIGURE 5-7

Rooted map with countries sized according to BMW Board of Management, spring 2017

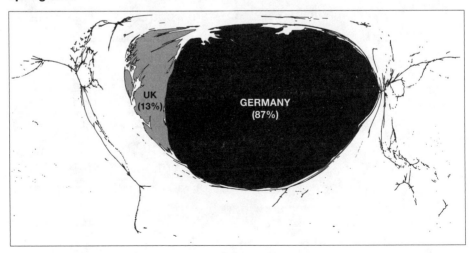

Source: Data from BMW, "BMW Group Profile," BMW website, accessed June 2017.

Using Rooted Maps in Analyzing Companies' International Presence

Rooted maps correct the misperception that the world looks the same regardless of the viewer's vantage point or purpose.[20] They do so by adjusting the sizes of countries or regions in relation to a specific home country or firm, while otherwise maintaining familiar shapes and spatial relationships, which helps managers relate these maps to their existing mental models. This chapter employs rooted maps of US multinational enterprises (figure 5-3) as well as metrics for BMW (figures 5-6 and 5-7) and GM (figure 5-8). On my website at www.ghemawat.com/maps, you can find more than one hundred thousand rooted maps covering country-, industry-, and company-level activity.

Rooted maps with areas colored or shaded according to firms' national or regional market shares often yield interesting insights by blending size-based and share-based perspectives. Furthermore, comparative mapping can also help highlight internal distance within firms. For example, in many multinationals, the stark contrast between maps based on the national origins of the firm's leadership team and its targeted growth markets highlights the need to boost national diversity. It is also often useful to compare rooted maps drawn from the perspectives of a particular firm and its competitors to an industry-level reference map. For example, one may contrast rooted maps of companies' sales to a reference map drawn according to the total sales of a given product by country or region (see figure 5-9 for such a map for the auto industry).

maps caused, I used them in a BMW managerial development program. Even without accounting for future market growth (as opposed to current sales), the two pictures say a lot. And as to whether they mattered, I will simply point to missteps, such as lags in adapting cars' interior space to the Chinese market, where chauffeurs were more prevalent and the ultimate driving experience was less important than space for seating in the rear, or in offering cupholders in the US market despite years of clamor among US owners of BMWs. As somebody from headquarters actually once put it to me, the ultimate driving machine was not meant to be driven in this way.

The portrayal of BMW's relevant knowledge about the world as confined to where its top managers are from is obviously a bit unfair to the company: the automaker also enjoys a wealth of successful operating experience from continents other than Europe. But given the results of my analyses of TMT national diversity, I almost always use some maps to highlight how the globalization of corporate mindsets may often be more limited than the globalization of corporate presence. (For more on using maps, see the sidebar "Using Rooted Maps in Analyzing Companies' International Presence.") The broader challenge of making top management more cosmopolitan will be discussed in the next chapter.

Alternative Approaches to Restructuring International Presence

Having set up a general structure for thinking about where to compete, we can now return to the question with which this chapter began: what if your company does need to restructure its international presence? Firms can pick from five basic approaches to restructuring international portfolios: chopping deadwood, cherry-picking, fortifying regions, manning the bridges, and riding the big shift.[21]

If your organization has large, chronic loss-makers (or a long tail of them), *chopping deadwood* is an obvious place to start. GM-Opel is

mple, not least because it illustrates the difficulties compa-
ace in actually disposing of such operations. To dispose of
had to effectively withdraw from Europe after more than
a century of competing there.[22] *Cherry-picking*, a related approach,
prioritizes a subset of promising markets for managerial focus and
investment, without completely exiting all other markets. Despite
the upsides to these two approaches, chopping deadwood or cherry-
picking based on just financial results should not be allowed to super-
sede consideration of distances in the ways discussed in the earlier
sections.

The restructuring approach that follows most directly from the
law of distance is *manning the bridges*. When a firm employs this approach, it prioritizes, country by country, proximate markets along
the most salient CAGE dimensions for its strategy. Think again, of
the Indian IT firms' focus on the United States and United Kingdom.
At a higher level, *fortifying regions* takes advantage of the greater similarity that exists between countries in the same region than exists
between regions to achieve the same aim at the level of multicountry
groupings. Under the seven-region classification scheme my team developed for the DHL Global Connectedness Index, countries in the
same region were more similar—often by a wide margin—on all but
two of twenty-nine CAGE distance variables.[23] Countries in the same
region, for example, are more than twice as likely to share a common
language, five times as likely to have a free-trade agreement, three
times as proximate geographically, and twice as similar in terms of
scores on the UN's Human Development Index. This pattern of similarity within regions is why the bulk of international flows occurs
within rather than *across* continentally sized regions. And while recent political developments are putting stress on at least two important regional economic groupings (the European Union and NAFTA),
regionalization, after having increased to record levels through most
of the postwar period, is unlikely to disappear suddenly.

Companies can also group countries into emerging versus advanced economies, but this alternative tends not to work as cleanly as

regional groupings. While emerging economies do share unilateral similarities beyond low per-capita incomes (e.g., more hierarchical cultures
and weaker public institutions), when we look at bilateral distances,
emerging economies turn out to share common languages, common re-
ligions, colonial linkages, and, especially, trade agreements more often
with advanced economies than they do with each other. Considering a
full set of CAGE variables, firms from emerging economies actually face
greater resistance because of noneconomic distance when trading and
investing in other emerging economies than they do in advanced economies.[24] Emerging economies thus constitute a relatively heterogeneous
category in many respects—part of the reason why Hal Sirkin and David
Michael of the Boston Consulting Group have proposed relabeling them
"diverging economies."[25] Or to return to the point made in chapter 3
about monopolarity versus multipolarity, an "emerging-markets strategy" generally isn't granular enough today, if it ever was.

Companies *riding the big shift* focus on emerging economies not as
a way of grouping countries but rather with an emphasis on positioning a company's presence for growth. GM has had partial success with
this strategy, as reflected primarily by the fact that it now sells more
vehicles in China than in the United States (figure 5-8). The shading of
countries according to market share in figure 5-8 makes the point even
more dramatically: GM's share of new-vehicle registrations is well
into double digits in the Americas and China but in single digits almost
everywhere else. And GM's lack of success in other parts of Asia is highlighted by contrasting the GM map to a reference map with all countries sized on the basis of their new-vehicle registrations (figure 5-9).
Japan and India, the third- and fifth-largest markets on the reference
map are basically invisible on the GM map. Presumably seeing little potential to fortify Asia as a region, in addition to selling Opel in 2017, GM
also announced its withdrawal from India, Indonesia, and Thailand (as
well as South Africa), although it planned to keep its manufacturing
plant in India open to produce cars for Latin America.[26]

GM has focused on ensuring that the potential of its strong positions in the Americas and in China is maximized, and other moves

FIGURE 5-8

Rooted map with countries sized according to GM unit sales and shaded according to GM's share of new-vehicle registrations, 2016

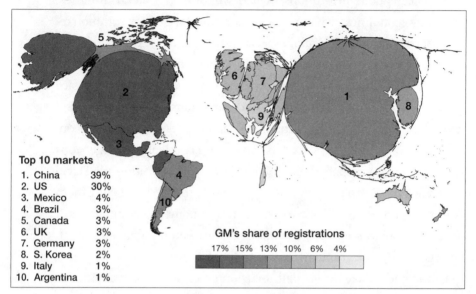

Top 10 markets

1. China   39%
2. US   30%
3. Mexico   4%
4. Brazil   3%
5. Canada   3%
6. UK   3%
7. Germany   3%
8. S. Korea   2%
9. Italy   1%
10. Argentina 1%

GM's share of registrations

17% 15% 13% 10% 6% 4%

Source: Data from GM Annual Report, 2016; Organisation Internationale des Constructeurs d'Automobiles (OICA); and unpublished data provided by WardsAuto.

FIGURE 5-9

Reference map with countries sized according to all new-vehicle registrations, 2016

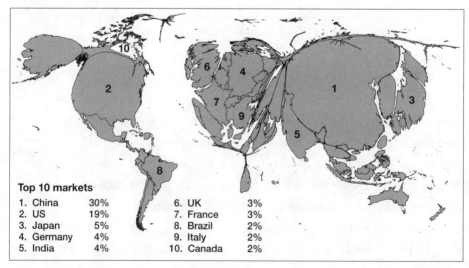

Top 10 markets

1. China	30%	6. UK	3%
2. US	19%	7. France	3%
3. Japan	5%	8. Brazil	2%
4. Germany	4%	9. Italy	2%
5. India	4%	10. Canada	2%

Source: Data from Organisation Internationale des Constructeurs d'Automobiles (OICA).

such as exiting Europe and other Asian countries are presumably looked at in light of that logic. The GM example suggests two additional important points. First, GM was forced to restructure geographically not just because of its track record of continuing to invest heavily—after bankruptcy and a US government bailout—without boosting market value. The automaker also had to restructure because of two new areas requiring large investments: propulsion alternatives to the internal combustion engine and connectivity to enable smart cars (e.g., driverless vehicles). Geographic restructuring is sometimes best understood as a response to deeper changes in the underlying business.

Second, GM builds automobiles in China entirely through joint ventures, many of them with SAIC (formerly Shanghai Automotive Industry Corporation). The joint ventures are not GM's choice but rather the product of regulations on foreign automakers in China. But the arrangement does illustrate that there are a range of ways that companies can participate in international opportunities—full ownership, joint ventures, franchising, other strategic alliances, licensing, and arm's-length transactions. These options also highlight some ways that companies can maintain a broad international presence while still being more selective about where they deploy their own resources.

The broader point is that it is always useful to ask whether one of the alternatives to ownership might be more promising than planting one's own corporate flag on foreign soil. Between the diverse opportunities just outlined and the prospects of varying the scale, scope, or speed of resource commitments (or their reversal), the palette of possibilities offers far more than the binary logic of in or out. And by articulating and analyzing a broad array of alternatives, executives can devise better alternatives than they could thinking of corporate presence in such binary terms.

If these kinds of decisions about where to compete sound complicated, they can be—especially for a large, complex multinational. But the objective is to use the logic of corporate presence to improve performance, not necessarily to optimize it. And especially for the bulk of multinationals that operate in just a handful of foreign markets—two-thirds of US multinationals, for instance, operate in five or fewer countries—as well as the large number of would-be multinationals, there is a very simple heuristic: such a company had better have a good arbitrage-related reason for going, early on, to any country that is distant from home.

Finally, the focus here has fallen on determining a multinational's presence largely based on distance-related considerations. But there is a different (albeit complementary) approach: boosting the company's capacity to operate effectively across greater distances. Ideas for doing so are the focus of the next chapter.

Managerial Maxims

1. Most multinationals do not have a broad geographic footprint; the typical multinational operates only in a small number of foreign countries.

2. Even among the largest multinationals with broad footprints, most earn a high proportion (often the majority) of their revenues in just a handful of countries, and many retain a presence in countries that are chronically unprofitable.

3. Country analysis should complement considerations of unilateral attractiveness factors (e.g., size) with bilateral factors (distances) along cultural, administrative, geographic, and economic (CAGE) dimensions.

4. Except when pursuing arbitrage strategies, the general prescription is to focus first on proximate and similar markets and then expand to more distant and different ones.

5. Country analysis should also take into account internal diversity within countries. Don't treat China, India, or even Spain or Belgium, as homogenous!

6. Because industries vary systematically in their sensitivity to CAGE distances, country analyses need to be tailored by industry.

7. Company-level customization is also essential and should take into account the strength of a firm's competitive advantages, how far those advantages can travel, and the firm's capacity for managing distance.

8. Staying home *is* an option for firms that do not yet have a substantial international presence, and firms that do have an international presence may need to restructure their country portfolios.

9. Chopping deadwood, cherry-picking, manning the bridges, fortifying regions, and riding the big shift represent five approaches to restructuring firms' international presence.

10. To avoid globaloney-induced errors, use rooted maps to strengthen your intuition about international markets (see www.ghemawat.com/maps), and complement qualitative distance analyses with quantitative ones using tools such as the CAGE Comparator (see www.ghemawat.com/cage).

6

Architecture
How to Connect

The previous two chapters focused on how to compete and where to compete in light of what is—and what isn't—changing about globalization. The material covered in both those chapters has challenging implications for how multinational firms operate. Chapter 4 argued that instead of pure localization, which would reduce organizational complexity by putting country managers firmly in charge, multinationals often need to execute strategies incorporating richer combinations of adaptation, aggregation, and arbitrage. And chapter 5 left open the possibilities of expansion *or* contraction of firms' international presence—while warning against the simple alternative of just packing up and coming home.

This chapter will take a broad view of how multinationals get things done. It will consider, in turn, how multinationals are structured, the people who populate them (especially at the top), and the nonstructural "connective tissue" that ties their units together. The first two topics are familiar ones, although this chapter presents

The author thanks Steven Altman for his collaboration on the writing of this chapter.

some fresh insights on them. The third topic is not as familiar and is included here because of the formidable challenges that CAGE distances pose for firms that are or would be global. Especially given the big shift to emerging economies, such firms should think about boosting their organizational capacity to bridge multiple dimensions of distance. Connective tissue is shorthand for a number of ways that firms can bridge these distances more effectively—ways that will be described in this chapter.

Organization Structure—and Stretching

I have already discussed in the introduction how *not* to structure a global company: by oscillating (potentially in perpetuity) between centralization and decentralization, depending on hopes about globalization. While that discussion took place around Coca-Cola, the tendency is general enough to have evoked its own Dilbert cartoon.

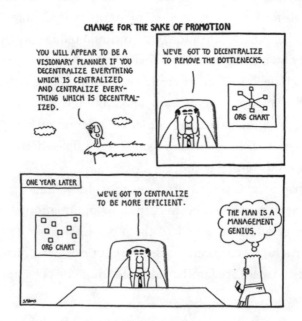

In deciding what to do or not do, firms can start with a fundamental principle of organization design—dating back at least to Alfred Chandler's pioneering research more than half a century ago. Chandler highlighted the importance of aligning an organization's structure with its strategy.[1] Different strategies imply different structures because of the power of organizational structure to shape how and where decisions are made, what kinds of performance get measured and incentivized, how information flows—or doesn't—through a company, and so on. The organization chart is also one of the most powerful devices senior management has to communicate what a company values and how its leaders intend for it to function.

Each of the AAA strategies covered in chapter 4 has clear organizational implications. Adaptation—the strategy some firms contemplate boosting in response to antiglobalization pressures—can best be pursued when firms adopt geographic structures. Adaptation benefits from pushing more decision-making authority out to countries and regions because distance dampens interactions inside firms as well as between firms and external parties such as customers, partners, and governments. Managers who are deeply embedded in a given location are best positioned to adapt a firm's strategy and operations to the local context. At the extreme, think of an organization like Coke during most of its first century, when country managers had nearly complete autonomy.

For firms focused primarily on aggregation strategies, the organizational implications are the opposite of those for adaptation. To maximize economies of scale and scope, a pure aggregation strategy calls for centralizing decision-making authority at headquarters and charging country units primarily with the faithful implementation of the firm's global strategy. If country managers try to make too many changes in response to the distinctive characteristics of their markets, complexity will rise and economies of scale will suffer. Coca-Cola again provides an extreme example. This time, think of Coke in the 1990s under CEO Roberto Goizueta. At that time, even consumer research—the marketing function supposed to get as close to customers as possible—was run out of headquarters.

For multibusiness firms, that is, those competing in multiple industries or product categories, aggregation often implies organizing around global business units. In this type of structure, there are multiple "centers," but power is still centralized and managers abroad are primarily responsible for implementing the business unit's global strategy.

Arbitrage strategies, focused on taking advantage of differences between countries, are facilitated by a third type of organizational structure. Since arbitrage involves splitting up the functional components of a firm's value chain across locations, for example, to produce where costs are low and sell where prices are high, this strategy tends to be facilitated by functional structures. Many Indian IT firms adopt this sort of organization, running their "delivery" functions from inside India while managing most of their marketing and sales activity from inside the United States and other key markets. Walmart represents another example, having long run most of its global procurement function from Shenzhen, China, rather than its US headquarters. Such functional structures allocate decision-making authority to leaders located where key functions are performed, helping track the flow of products and services through the firm and its external networks.

As chapter 4 highlighted, the differences between the organizational structures implied by each of the pure forms of the AAA strategies exemplify the inherent tensions among those strategies. That chapter also cautioned against extreme shifts toward adaptation in response to antiglobalization pressures, because aggregation and arbitrage are the strategies that directly generate value across countries—adaptation extends their reach. It concluded that especially in light of the big shift and the increased distances involved, multinationals aspiring to global industry leadership will often have to pursue combinations of the AAA strategies.[2] Incumbents from advanced economies will need to fortify their aggregation advantages while remedying disadvantages on arbitrage and becoming better adapted in key emerging economies. Insurgents from emerging economies, on the other hand, will need to continue to leverage strengths at arbitrage while building aggregation advantages and becoming better adapted in international markets as well.

Those prescriptions imply that the ideal structures discussed above should primarily guide shifts in emphasis within organizations rather than wholesale organizational restructuring. Additionally, they imply that most multinational firms need more organizational complexity than they would if they pursued just one of the AAA strategies. One approach to help firms manage this additional complexity—closely related to earlier recommendations—is to group similar or proximate countries together. In practice, this tactic has traditionally implied the adoption of regional structures for firms with broad geographic footprints.

Regional structures take advantage of the greater similarity among countries within regions than between regions that was noted earlier. Regional structures can improve information flows between countries and headquarters and help manage the complexity of a global enterprise. And out in the field, they can help with business development, signal commitment, and facilitate cooperation and the pooling of resources.[3]

In addition to geographically focused regional structures, firms have also organized along the other dimensions of the CAGE framework. The previous chapter's discussion of which dimensions of distance are particularly salient for a given firm can guide choices in this regard. While firms can and have grouped countries according to each of the CAGE dimensions, there is rising interest, given the big shift to emerging economies, in organizational structures that more effectively bridge economic distance. IBM, for example, divided its markets into *mature markets* and *growth markets* in 2008, with the latter led by an executive based in Shanghai. GM implemented a similar restructuring in 2009.

Many such organizational changes, however, still reflect experimentation—a fact exemplified by GM's subsequent carving out of China from its international operations division in 2013. The automaker explained the change by saying that this would allow its China operation to focus on China, which is the world's largest automotive market.[4] GM went on to relocate most of the managers of its international division from Shanghai to Singapore in 2014 (and then cut that unit's workforce in half in 2017 because of reductions in the company's international presence). GE also tweaked its reporting structure over time, temporarily giving its India team profit-and-loss responsibility for all business inside the country to accelerate growth there, and then folding India back into the company's normal structure as operations matured. The broader lesson: organizational structures should account for countries' different sizes and levels of strategic importance. It can make sense for some countries to report directly to headquarters while others are folded into regional or other sorts of groupings.

Whether firms employ traditional regional structures or group countries according to other dimensions of the CAGE framework, many large firms—particularly those with diverse product portfolios and broad geographic footprints—find that making country groups the primary axis of their structures is too limiting. Their more complex coordination requirements call for matrix structures that organize along multiple dimensions (e.g., both by product group and by region). A survey that a colleague and I conducted revealed a significant shift among large multinationals toward matrix structures even before the global financial crisis (figure 6-1).[5] Note that matrix went from least to most popular, squeezing all three other structural options. I interpret this as evidence of multinationals stretching their organizational structures to facilitate the pursuit of more than just one of the AAA strategies.

While there are several variants on the matrix, one called the *front-back organization* can be particularly useful for companies attempting to boost adaptation in terms of customer-facing touch points while applying aggregation or arbitrage, or both, behind the scenes.[6] Front-back organizations focus on localizing at the front end (close to the customer) while employing a centralized back-end platform to support integration in R&D, production, and other functions. Com-

FIGURE 6-1

Large multinationals' changing organizational structures

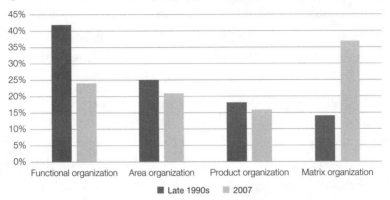

Source: Pankaj Ghemawat and David J. Collis, "Globalization Survey," unpublished, 2007.

panies as varied as P&G in consumer products and Ericsson in tele-communications equipment have adopted front-back organizations.

P&G's recent struggles, however, exemplify the importance of careful attention to where the line between front and back is drawn, as well as the limits of localization. After a six-year reorganization dubbed Organization 2005 divided marketing responsibilities between back-end global business units and front-end market development organizations, innovation and growth sputtered at P&G. In 2014, the company recentralized most of its marketing within the global business units, turning the market development organizations into selling and marketing operations units focused more narrowly on sales, pricing, distribution, merchandising, media buying, and so on.[7]

Within front-back organizations and other matrix structures, the size and relative power of the units represent additional design elements. Charles Handy has proposed "federal" architectures, as distinct from "monarchical" ones, to harness the energy of small units behind a shared corporate purpose.[8] Singapore-based trading and manufacturing group Jebsen and Jesson (Southeast Asia) illustrates the power of federalism as well as the importance of administrative heritage as another input in choices about organizational structure. While the group limits its presence (by choice) to the ASEAN region, its 4,100 employees are spread across seventy-three locations and businesses that span the gamut from nutritional ingredients to construction equipment. Many of the country business units have fewer than twenty people, but those small and highly autonomous units plug into common regional and country-level back-office functions for HR, finance, legal, and the like. Decision making follows a matrix structure in which front and back are—in an unusual twist—given equal authority. Sound like a recipe for gridlock? The company says it beats larger competitors in part by making *faster* decisions, attributing much of that advantage to not having to secure approvals from a headquarters outside the region. Many larger, less geographically focused multinationals do suffer that constraint, leading to both delay and disaffection—and reminding us that structures can be made *too* complicated.

To summarize, as multinationals pursue increasingly complex strategies and, in many cases, target broad footprints, they will need to embrace organizational structures that bridge distances as efficiently as possible. The relative emphasis accorded to each of the AAA strategies provides a starting point for thinking about structural options and potential shifts in how much to emphasize them. To help manage organizational complexity, it can be useful to group countries according to the most salient dimensions of distance and, if necessary, to layer on matrix approaches such as front-back structures. However, reorganizations are costly and time-consuming, and administrative heritage remains a powerful constraint. The next section turns to another approach that may be employed along with or instead of structural change: changing the people who populate—and especially those who lead—the organization.

Leadership Diversity: An Achilles' Heel?

After discussing organizational structure, it is natural to turn to the people within an organization, and particularly its leaders, who disproportionately influence how it functions. Many writers on this topic note as much and then move on to focus on the global leadership competencies that such leaders should have. But the number of competencies that have been proposed significantly exceeds one hundred. And the ones talked about the most—for example, the "big five": extroversion, agreeableness, conscientiousness, emotional stability, and openness to experience—sound as if they might make sense domestically as well. That is, these characteristics lack distinctively global content. I will come back to global leadership development programs later, but will focus in this section on national diversity in firms' leadership teams.

On average, large multinational companies are significantly less globalized in terms of their leadership than they are along any of the standard dimensions (sales, assets, employees, etc.). And there are indications that this lack of leadership diversity may be a constraint on their performance. But first, let's examine the data.

To identify and analyze patterns of leadership diversity in large firms, I collaborated on a project with Herman Vantrappen, who leads the advisory firm Akordeon. We reviewed the biographies of every CEO and top management team (TMT) member across all the 2013 *Fortune* Global 500 firms for which such data was publicly available. The results were striking: only 13 percent of the firms were led by a nonnative CEO, and 15 percent of TMT members (direct reports to CEOs) were nonnative (of which half were from outside the region where the company was headquartered) (see figure 6-2).[9] By comparison, the same set of firms earned 46 percent of their revenue abroad (see figure 1-5 in chapter 1).

The dearth of foreign talent at the top is even more severe when we focus on the subset of the *Fortune* Global 500 based in emerging economies: only 2 percent of those "emerging giants" were led by a nonnative CEO, and the average TMT among those firms had only 3 percent nonnative members. In fact, it was the rising proportion of *Fortune* Global 500 firms from emerging markets that pulled the share of the total that had foreign CEOs *down* from 14 percent in 2008 to 13 percent in 2013.[10]

FIGURE 6-2

Map with countries sized according to *Fortune* Global 500 firms' headquarters locations and shaded according to proportion with nonnative CEOs

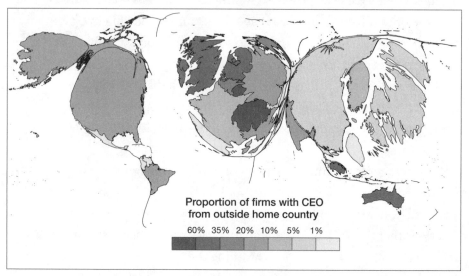

Proportion of firms with CEO
from outside home country

60% 35% 20% 10% 5% 1%

Source: Data from Pankaj Ghemawat and Herman Vantrappen, "How Global Is Your C-Suite?" *MIT Sloan Management Review*, June 16, 2015.

Firms led by a nonnative CEO tend to have far more diverse TMTs, with an average of 45 percent nonnative members, as compared to only 11 percent among firms led by native CEOs. The incidence of nonnative CEOs is also strongly related to large companies' overall levels of internationalization, as measured based on the foreign share of firms' sales, assets, and employees.[11] Firms from countries that are more deeply globalized, according to the DHL Global Connectedness Index, are also more likely to be led by nonnative CEOs. Additionally, similar patterns extend up to the level of boards of directors, where national diversity is also limited and strongly correlated with TMT nonnativity.[12]

One indication that the limited globalization of firms' leadership teams—with respect to both national origins and capabilities—has become an Achilles' heel for many corporations comes from surveys. For example, in a 2014 US survey, 39 percent of respondents admitted

that their firms failed to fully exploit their international business opportunities, because of insufficient internationally competent personnel.[13] The salience of national diversity in TMTs is also supported
by my own analysis with Steven Altman, discussed in chapter 5. We
found that firms with more nonnatives on their TMTs traversed
greater distance along multiple CAGE dimensions.

One can debate the causality here: does TMT diversity drive broader
footprints, or the other way around? I lean toward leaving some room
for the first explanation because of the evidence of benefits associated
with greater national diversity. One study, for example, concludes that
"TMT nationality diversity is among the few diversity attributes that
help increase firm performance," and that "the effects of international
experience and functional diversity diminish over time, whereas the
impact of nationality diversity becomes stronger."[14] Given the difficulties of working across divides, however, the prescription that firms
should boost TMT national diversity *is* contingent on a firm's either
having or targeting a high level of internationalization.[15]

This research also suggests that diversity can boost performance
by increasing group creativity. In the words of University of Mich-
igan researcher Scott Page, "people from different backgrounds
have varying ways of looking at problems, what I call 'tools.' The
sum of these tools is far more powerful in organizations with diversity than in ones where everyone has gone to the same schools, been
trained in the same mold, and thinks in almost identical ways."[16] Another inference is that if a company is to benefit from diversity, it must
reach a meaningful level and be supported by appropriate structures
and processes. Otherwise, a single nonnative on a TMT or board of
directors may have trouble influencing that group's deliberations.

In addition to the direct benefits of national diversity on performance, firms can enjoy indirect but presumably powerful effects
from signaling. If a large share of a global company's assets, sales, and
employees are located outside its home country, yet it consistently
chooses native leaders, that choice signals limited long-term career
prospects both for foreign middle managers already in the company

and for potential hires. The result is that it is hard to attract and retain the right people. Conversely, selecting a nonnative can serve as a very powerful signal as well. Thus, when Indian-born Satya Nadella was named Microsoft's CEO, the announcement was particularly meaningful to the one-third or more of Microsoft's workforce that is estimated to be Indian.[17] It sent a clear signal that national origin was not a barrier to career growth at the company.[18]

The importance of signaling effects is demonstrated by the difficulties Western companies have started to face in recruiting high-potential candidates in emerging markets. Two decades ago, the Westerners had the field almost to themselves. Today they have to compete with fast-growing local companies and constantly confront the question "Why should I work for a company that is run by people who look like you when I could work for one that is run by people who look like me?" For example, the proportion of college students in China saying they want to work for an international company has fallen from almost 40 percent in 2013 to just 18 percent in 2017.[19] Anecdotal evidence indicates that the expectation of greater upward mobility in local companies is an important contributor to their rising attraction.

Returning to the theme of contingency from chapter 5, in addition to linking national diversity goals to decisions about a company's international presence, companies should also think more generally about relating the composition of their leadership teams to choices across the SPAN components (strategy, presence, architecture, and nonmarket issues), around which part two of this book is organized. With regard to strategy, a company focused on aggregation needs a different set of top management capabilities than does a company more focused on adaptation or arbitrage. Within this chapter, choices about organization structure, of course, cascade down to decisions about how to populate a leadership team. And looking ahead to nonmarket strategy (chapter 7), if a company wants to be more of a local citizen, for example, it needs to elevate local managers in key markets.

A common theme across those multiple dimensions of contingency is that most multinationals need more cosmopolitan leadership teams. I have written elsewhere about a variety of levers that firms can employ to cultivate cosmopolitanism—ways that extend well beyond changing the composition of the TMT.[20] They range from adjusting recruitment and development priorities to changing the messages a firm sends via gestures and symbols. Rather than enumerating more of those levers here, I turn next to some of the roles that top management can play beyond acting as connectors themselves to encourage a better sense of connection among key personnel and organizational units.

Connective Tissue: Staying UNITED Across Distance

Besides changing either its organizational structure or the composition of its leadership team, what else can a firm do to bridge distance more effectively? The variety of techniques that can potentially help are limited only by managers' imaginations (and, alas, sometimes their budgets). Here, I will focus on six areas, which I summarize with the acronym UNITED: unifying culture, networked innovation, initiatives and task forces, technology enablers, expatriation and mobility, and (other) development programs.

Unifying culture. Multinationals tend to lag behind local firms in areas such as establishing a shared vision, engaging employees around the world, maintaining professional standards, and encouraging innovation.[21] A strong corporate culture can help multinationals shore up such weaknesses by serving as a bridge across national cultural differences. Investment banks, management consulting firms, and other kinds of far-flung professional services firms tend to emphasize culture as a key unifier. Such firms often have to assemble teams from multiple locations and send them out on short notice to work with high levels of autonomy. Alignment along a set of cultural values helps the teams get up to speed quickly and reassures clients about the consistency of the services they are receiving.

Such emphasis on culture as a unifier isn't limited to professional services. Johnson & Johnson's sixty-plus-year-old credo brings its people together across a diverse array of markets, as well as business units: "We believe our first responsibility is to the doctors, nurses and patients, to mothers and fathers and all others who use our products . . ."[22] Google's culture is also unmistakable: "We hire people who are smart and determined, and we favor ability over experience . . . We strive to maintain the open culture often associated with startups, in which everyone is a hands-on contributor and feels comfortable sharing ideas and opinions."[23] This culture easily transcends national boundaries. When two "Googlers" meet for the first time to collaborate on a project, the company's culture—from its recruitment process through to its office design—helps ease the way. The workers know they have a great deal in common, even if their backgrounds are different.

A corporate common language can also help facilitate communication (and cultural integration). Mexico's Cemex, for example, implemented a single global operating language—in Cemex's case, English rather than the Spanish of its headquarters country—to support its ambitions beyond its home region. Of course, firms that move to a common language must do so with care. They need to avoid losing the valuable perspectives of people who struggle with the selected language. Tsedal Neeley's research on companies that have mandated a corporate official language highlights the enormous efforts—as well as active resource allocation—required to make such initiatives succeed.[24] There's even change required from native speakers, who must counteract the natural tendency to tune out on unfamiliar accents.[25]

Networked innovation. The connections between organizational units in multinational firms should be directed not only to facilitating the execution of a firm's current strategy and reinforcing its culture but also toward creating new capabilities. A focus on organizing for innovation is particularly important in the international context, given the rising importance of intangible assets and their central role in aggregation strategies. Globalization itself also raises the salience of a firm's ability to build new strengths—and shore up weaknesses—since exposure to a wider set of competitors raises the bar on the capabilities required to stay competitive in an industry.[26]

Multinational firms have distinct opportunities as well as challenges with regard to organizing for innovation. Many of the earlier observations about national diversity among a firm's leadership team also apply here. Participation in a variety of markets can boost innovation, but firms need to actively manage and support networked innovation to enjoy the benefits. Donald Lessard, David Teece, and Sohvi Leah advocate involving multiple levels of the organization and opening numerous "ports" through which "partners can co-invent with organizational subunits."[27] To make the most out of such openness, firms will often have to create initiatives or task forces— a topic discussed later—to bring capabilities from other markets to bear on the distinct challenges and opportunities available in particular locations.

Networked innovation can benefit from engagement with a variety of parties both internal and external to a firm. An R&D unit in one country can be put in contact with customers in another country, and new offerings that result can be adapted later on for other markets. Corporate partners of various sorts can also play important roles. According to rough estimates, alliances' share of revenues for the top one thousand US public corporations increased from about 1 percent in 1980 to between 6 and 7 percent by 1990, 15 percent by 1995, and 20 percent by 1998.[28]

Making networked innovation happen and aligning local initiatives with global technology and product road maps demand strong coordination capabilities. The solution is *not* to simply push responsibility for innovation out to the periphery of the organization and let hundreds or thousands of flowers bloom. Strong headquarters support for local initiatives must be coupled with mechanisms for identifying and involving pertinent capabilities from across the network. A firm also needs rigorous processes for allocating resources to the projects with the largest benefits for the firm as a whole.

Initiatives and task forces. In addition to their value for accomplishing priorities that require participation and perspectives from multiple locations, initiatives and task forces can themselves help unite disparate parts of an organization. Such work groups can complement a company's formal structure, setting up temporary or even permanent linkages between units and fostering relationships among people who might otherwise be unlikely to work closely with each other.

When selecting people for standing committees, project task forces, and so on, business leaders should think about both the work that needs to get done and the developmental and relationship-building opportunities that can be provided. At the same time, managers should also think about how to organize cross-border teamwork to minimize unnecessary intrusions on participants' personal time. Global conference calls and meetings will sometimes be required, but times and locations can be rotated to avoid *always* forcing particular people to be up in the middle of the night or to travel halfway around the world.

Some amount of travel, though, especially early in the life of a team, can be highly beneficial. A survey of global teams indicates that "team members can rely too easily on virtual communication and lack an effective balance of virtual and face-to-face contacts."[29] Creating relationships that carry sensitive information flows within an organization often requires people to spend some time together in person. This need is unsurprising, given that trust is highly distance-sensitive, as I will elaborate in chapter 7. There is also evidence that intra-team conflicts are more likely to surface after a team has gone several months without meeting in person.[30]

Technology enablers. While the power of new technologies to overcome distance effects is often exaggerated, many firms have not taken full advantage of existing tools to improve connectivity among far-flung organizational units. As of this writing, corporate social networks are proliferating, as firms seek to learn from and selectively duplicate the tools their people use to keep in touch outside work: Facebook, Twitter, LinkedIn, and so on. Corporate social networks are typically designed to facilitate both vertical and horizontal communication and to provide content that is more dynamic than delivered by traditional knowledge management systems.

The distance sensitivity of interactions on public social networks, however, hints at their limitations in the corporate realm as well. As described earlier, only 14 percent of Facebook friends are located across national borders.[31] Some 25 percent of Twitter followers are located in different countries from the people they follow, but only 14 percent are located in a foreign country that doesn't share the same dominant language.[32]

IT also tends to help more with geographic distance than with other dimensions of the CAGE framework. Misunderstandings due to cultural differences are sometimes made worse by the limitations of online interactions, where facial expressions and other subtle cues are absent or harder to discern. And even the best corporate IT systems and virtual private networks seldom erase the effects of economic and administrative distance that can hinder online collaboration.

These limitations imply that gaining the full benefits of information technologies often requires using them in conjunction with mobility programs—the next topic—as well as some of the other organizational linking mechanisms described here. Thus, Jean-Pierre Clamadieu, CEO of the Belgian chemical firm Solvay, talks of turning on its head the idea of using technology as a substitute for being out in the field: "With the benefit of high-quality video and other technology, these days I think we need to spend less time at HQ and longer periods in different regions of the world."[33]

Expatriation and mobility. Companies also transfer knowledge and build relationships across borders through expatriation. However, there are indications that companies are reducing their reliance on expatriates to save money (expatriates typically cost between two and three times as much as locals) and to improve localization. According to one study, the proportion of expatriates in senior management roles in multinationals in China, India, Brazil, Russia, and the Middle East declined from 56 percent to 12 percent from the late 1990s to the late 2000s.[34] Overall, the data on a small sample of large companies suggests that the proportion of expatriates in large global companies is usually less than 1 percent of total employment—often only around 0.1 to 0.2 percent.[35]

Other studies also suggest that for US and European multinationals, expatriates still take longer, on average, to ascend the corporate ladder than do managers who continue to work within their home countries.[36] These observations indicate a need for greater focus on integrating mobility programs with career paths and talent management strategies. The fact that even at leading international business schools, top multinationals still tend only to recruit graduates to work in their home countries—if they recruit nonnatives at all—suggests that limited integration of mobility into career paths also extends to firms' recruitment policies. To attempt a more strategic approach to the career paths of its senior executives, Solvay treats its top three hundred executives as "corporate assets" rather than as resources belonging to specific organizational subunits.

Firms are also increasingly embracing a wider range of mobility initiatives that extend beyond the traditional model of sending senior-level employees abroad on "expatriate packages." Some large companies distinguish among traditional expatriates, "inpatriates," short-term assignees, international business travelers, and self-initiated assignees and develop different career models for each category of employee. While short-term international assignments can indeed be useful, research indicates that it takes at least three months to become immersed in a new location and appreciate how business works there.[37] This slow acclimation time in turn suggests a need for some caution about what can be accomplished over very short time frames.

Some firms—motivated by the big shift to emerging economies—have also moved entire organizational units, either temporarily or permanently. Starwood Hotels has moved its whole top management team to a key emerging economy for one month every two years: to Shanghai in 2011, to Dubai in 2013, and to Mumbai and New Delhi in 2015.[38] To mention a few permanent relocations: Schneider Electric's CEO moved from Paris to Hong Kong, Halliburton's CEO relocated to Dubai, and KPMG based its new global chairman in Hong Kong. Additionally, companies as varied as ABB, Bayer, Dell, GE, P&G, Philips, and Rolls-Royce all moved the headquarters of particular business units to Asia between 2006 and 2012.[39] Such relocations, however, are still fairly unusual. According to a Boston Consulting Group survey of large multinationals from advanced economies, only 9 percent of the companies' top twenty leaders were based in emerging markets, even though those economies generated 28 percent of the sample firms' revenues.[40]

Development programs. Strengthening the capacity of a firm's top management to lead effectively across countries and cultures can also help unite a firm across distance. Leadership scholars have argued that experience contributes some 50 percent to learning about global leadership.[41] My own investigations of senior executives' perceptions of globalization, however, indicate that experience, while required, is not sufficient for the development of an accurate global mindset. On my 2017 manager survey, CEOs overestimated the extent of countries' and companies' globalization even more than did lower-level managers. And on my 2007 survey, finer-grained data showed that the magnitude of the respondents' errors increased with their years of experience and the seniority of their titles.[42]

Training, as well as education more generally, can be a powerful complement to—and perhaps even a prerequisite for—experiential learning about global leadership. What should be the content of that education? I discuss education in more detail in chapter 7, but in brief, academic thought leaders point to the usefulness of conceptual frameworks that emphasize the multiple dimensions of differences among countries.[43] My own CAGE framework used throughout this book is fairly widely used. Such frameworks can impose order on masses of facts and can fine-tune people's perceptions of foreign countries.

It is worth adding that firms have some advantages over universities for imparting such educational content. They can better integrate training on frameworks with opportunities to connect those frameworks to real-world places and business decisions. A manager receiving tailored, destination-specific training immediately before expatriation, for example, will probably find this training more effective than only a standard framework in isolation. Firms may also benefit from new online learning tools. A major complaint about massive open online courses (MOOCs) is the low commitment of most of the students. It's common for less than 5 percent of the students who sign up for a course to complete it.[44] In the corporate environment—where people have stronger incentives for active participation—low commitment is less often a problem.

Both of these advantages can be tapped in concert. One careful study of blended learning and leadership development concluded that distance learning "can offer significant advantages to those aiming to develop highly situated practices, such as leadership capability."[45] The idea, very simply, is that online learning allows direct application of ideas to workplace contexts, since participants spend much (or all) of their time in the workplace during the term of the course.

To conclude, this chapter has emphasized stretching organizational structures, boosting leadership team diversity, and making investments in a variety of other areas to help a firm stay UNITED across distances and differences. The end goal of adjustments in all three areas is to boost what I have called "corporate cosmopolitanism."[46] Given the inertia that typically exists in large organizations, significantly moving the needle in this direction tends to require very dramatic action from the apex of the firm, as illustrated in the case of

Samsung (see the sidebar "Cultivating Corporate Cosmopolitanism at Samsung").

Cultivating Corporate Cosmopolitanism at Samsung

Samsung's globalization drive was supported by systematic efforts to transform a very Korean organization into a more cosmopolitan one. After six years in charge, Samsung's chairman Kun-Hee Lee started a world tour in 1993 to see his company from an outsider's perspective. Dissatisfied with the company's pace of globalization, he summoned 150 senior executives to a luxury hotel in Frankfurt. He began talking to them at eight in the evening and lectured nonstop for seven hours about the need to "transform Samsung into a true world-class company"—without once going to the bathroom, according to one participant. He concluded with a call to "change everything except your wife and kids," and ordered the participants to stay on in Frankfurt for a week to learn more about conditions outside Korea.[47]

Back at headquarters, Lee's Frankfurt declaration was transcribed, and every employee received a copy of the two-hundred-page document. Samsung even constructed a replica in Korea of the conference room where the Frankfurt meeting took place.[48] And Samsung HR followed up with major policy changes: emphasis moved from seniority to competences, and pay was linked to performance. Recruiting—which had previously been restricted by educational background and gender—was opened up significantly.

Samsung also launched what it called a Regional Specialist Program. Participants went through three months of language and cross-cultural training, and then spent twelve to twenty-one months in a target country, working on a field project without any contact with the local Samsung office.[49] This stint was followed by a two-month debrief in Seoul. The Regional Specialist Program was designed to support growth in new markets, and its focus shifted over time toward emerging economies.[50]

To attract and develop additional non-Korean managers, Samsung established a Global Strategy Group (GSG) in 1997. GSG recruited from leading MBA programs, primarily in the United States and Europe. After two years of training and consulting, participants generally moved on to line-management positions or to the strategic staff of the CEOs of Samsung companies. To attract high-caliber candidates, Samsung offered compensation packages comparable to those provided by international consulting firms.

Given the objective of hiring top global talent for positions at headquarters in Seoul, Samsung also established minimum quotas for foreign employees there. An exception was made, however, for the headquarters leadership team. There were concerns that requiring a minimum number of leaders from outside Korea might lead to the hiring of unqualified candidates or might unduly favor overseas Koreans. Additionally, a policy was instituted in 2009 stipulating that all documents distributed across borders should be prepared in English. Progress to date had been relatively slow—partly because of resistance from Korean employees, who still constituted 99.9 percent of the headcount at headquarters—but Samsung HR stressed that most executives were indeed taking English courses.

To summarize, Samsung utilized many techniques described in this chapter. It created structural mechanisms, such as the Regional Specialist Program and Global Strategy Group, to provide organizational homes for the development of targeted capabilities. It systematically boosted diversity and mobility—setting targets, monitoring its progress, and shifting where it placed people as its business needs changed. All these changes can be traced back, directly or indirectly, to Chairman Lee's Frankfurt declaration, which provides a powerful example of the bold leadership that, when complemented with necessary adjustments to concrete policies, *can* change the culture of a large business group.

Managerial Maxims

1. The AAA strategies have distinct organizational implications: adaptation is amped up when discretion is given to in-country decision makers, aggregation benefits from centralization of authority at corporate or business-unit headquarters, and arbitrage is facilitated when a firm organizes around functions.

2. As firms attempt more complex combinations across the AAA strategies, their requisite organizational complexity will increase. Grouping similar countries together can help make the complexity more manageable.

3. While the most traditional approach is to group geographically proximate countries together (regional structures), the big shift to emerging economies is prompting rising

interest in groupings based on economic development (advanced versus emerging economies).

4. Matrix organizations have also gained popularity. The front-back organization, a variant on the matrix, can help firms become better adapted to customers while supporting aggregation upstream in the value chain.

5. Even among the world's largest firms, national diversity at the top tends to be very limited. Most firms are led by people from the country where the firm is headquartered.

6. The paucity of top management team (TMT) diversity is especially severe among large multinationals from emerging markets, a particular risk for insurgents pushing toward global industry leadership.

7. Boosting TMT diversity can help a firm get closer to its target markets, signal openness to nonnative talent, and generally fits with firms operating across greater distances.

8. For diversity to have positive effects, it must exceed a token level in the team and be supported by structures and processes that ensure alternative viewpoints are considered effectively.

9. Companies can also employ an array of cross-unit linking mechanisms (the UNITED techniques): unifying culture, networked innovation, initiatives and task forces, technology enablers, expatriation and mobility, and development programs.

10. Substantially boosting corporate cosmopolitanism requires strong and sustained commitment from a firm's senior leadership, supported by concrete policy changes, goals, and metrics.

7

Nonmarket Strategy
Anger and Its Management

Market strategy—into which the decisions about how to compete, where to compete, and how to connect across borders can be subsumed—traditionally starts from the assumption that the rules under which firms compete are given. Business leaders who have a reasonable moral compass—or at least want to stay out of jail—are expected to comply with established laws and regulations. And in a democratic society, the market frameworks under which competition takes place are assumed to derive legitimacy from the electorate's control over legislation and regulation.

In the real world, the rules of the game are seldom crystal clear. Business is a powerful actor in the political process, and society expects more from business than just following the law. The realm of nonmarket strategy encompasses firms' engagement with governments, nongovernmental organizations (NGOs), the media, and the public in spheres that extend beyond market transactions and often shape the rules under which market activity takes place.

Yet, nonmarket strategy is often treated as an afterthought to market strategy. Firms decide their market strategies and then try to address any nonmarket issues that arise—even though this reactive approach narrows the scope for nonmarket strategy to make a difference. One possible reason nonmarket strategy doesn't get more attention is because it is often more complicated than market strategy. A broader set of parties is involved in nonmarket issues, and the goals they pursue can be diverse and even contradictory. And especially in the United States, many people subscribe to Milton Friedman's position that "the business of business is business."[1]

But recent developments seem to make nonmarket strategies increasingly crucial for firms and for society at large. Thus, Martin Reeves of the Boston Consulting Group has observed that "in many cases companies are currently seeing bigger impacts from political and economic factors than from competitive considerations, be it from Brexit-driven exchange rate movements, share price shifts following policy pronouncements or the cost of shifting investment plans in the light of anticipated shifts in trade policy."[2] Reeves was talking about the implications of Brexit, but in a more general context, I would add the rise of NGOs, the proliferation of social media, and the unpopularity of globalization to his list. I would also note that when a leading thinker at a consulting firm that has long emphasized the primacy of competitive forces expresses such an opinion, *that* is news.

For businesses to respond and contribute better to society, they must begin to recognize some of the problems that underpin the backlash against both globalization and big business. With this in mind, I begin this chapter with a discussion of the problems out there, both economic and noneconomic. I then discuss fixes, which involve both economic policy and anger management, and the role that businesses might play in their implementation. And if the problems that nonmarket strategy needs to address were all external to firms, the chapter and the book could end there. But in reality, firms and the people within them also need to change. The problems within business—and a set of potential solutions—are thus the final topics of the chapter.

The Problems Out There

Many problems that fuel anger among the public are economic, and they are compounded by a spike in economic policy uncertainty.[3] Scott Baker, Nick Bloom, and Steven Davis's Global Economic Policy Uncertainty Index—based on news coverage across eighteen countries—reached an all-time high in November 2016 (when the US presidential election took place) and remains elevated (figure 7-1). Heightened economic policy uncertainty dampens investment and hiring and increases the salience of nonmarket strategy.

Many economists, including former US Federal Reserve chairman Alan Greenspan, point to slowing productivity growth as the primary culprit behind present economic anxiety.[4] The productivity problem is actually long-standing and widespread. A 2017 OECD report affirms that "a striking feature of the post-crisis period has

FIGURE 7-1

Global Economic Policy Uncertainty Index, January 1997–May 2017

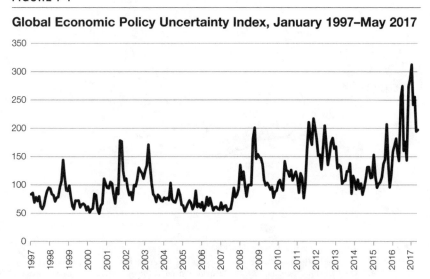

Source: Data downloaded from Scott R. Baker, Nick Bloom, and Steven J. Davis, "Global Economic Policy Uncertainty Index," Economic Policy Uncertainty website, June 20, 2017, http://www.policyuncertainty.com.

been a continuation of a long-term slowdown in productivity growth that has gone hand-in-hand with weak levels of investment. This matters because, as an important driver of growth, productivity has also been an important driver of improvements in living standards primarily through higher wages."[5]

The same OECD report also recognizes rising concern about the distribution of economic gains. And unlike Greenspan, I think that more of the societal anger about economic issues stems from how the pie is shared rather than how fast it is expanding. The United States has recently experienced a rise in income inequality to levels last seen in the 1920s. Other countries, especially developed ones, have registered similar if less dramatic increases (figure 7-2). At the same time, US corporate profits are running close to their highest historical levels (figure 7-3). And that was *before* the large tax cut at the end of 2017.

FIGURE 7-2

Share of total income earned by the top 1 percent, 1913–2015

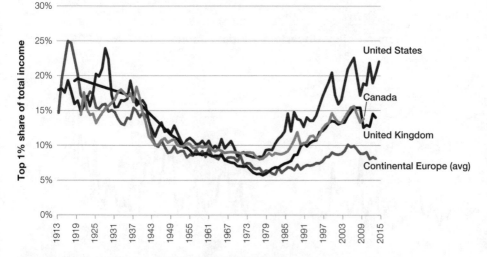

Source: The World Health and Income Database, http://wid.world/data/.

Note: Before 1990, UK data was based on income share of families rather than income share of adults. Continental Europe (avg) is a simple average based on all available data for Denmark, France, Germany, Ireland, Italy, the Netherlands, Norway, Portugal, Spain, Sweden, and Switzerland. The countries included varied from year to year, depending on data availability.

Also worth mentioning in this context is automation, which has replaced globalization as the bogeyman in many recent discussions about job losses. A 2017 update by PwC, building on two widely cited academic studies, predicts that 38 percent of US jobs could be "at high risk of automation by the early 2030s," as well as 35 percent in Germany, 30 percent in the United Kingdom, and 21 percent in Japan.[6] Automation could put further pressure on labor's share of national income, so the anxiety about automation fits with the need to respond more sensitively to distributional concerns.

Job losses due to foreign competition—while smaller than many presume—are large enough that they do demand recognition and sensitivity. A widely cited analysis by David Autor, David Dorn, and Gordon Hanson pegged the US manufacturing job losses from Chinese competition between 1999 and 2011 at 985,000 (17 percent of the 5.8 million job overall drop in US manufacturing employment over that period).[7] The study also usefully draws attention to how the

FIGURE 7-3

Corporate profits' share of GDP in United States, 1948–2016

Source: US Bureau of Economic Analysis, retrieved from Federal Reserve Bank of St. Louis *FRED*. Data Series: Corporate Profits After Tax (without IVA and CCAdj)/Gross Domestic Product.

concentration of those losses in particular locations can devastate affected communities.

Despite these statistics, focusing on economic problems as *the* explanation of prevalent anger might be taking too narrow a perspective. Consider Sunderland, the city in northeastern England that gave the "leave" side its first big win on the night of the Brexit referendum. The British car industry issued a clear warning before the vote: exiting the European Union could put jobs at risk. But 61 percent of the city's voters opted for Brexit, even though Nissan is the largest private-sector employer in Sunderland and more than half its production there is exported to the European Union. Press reports indicated a high level of support for the "leave" campaign, even among employees of the Nissan plant. One employee explained, "I voted Leave because I want Britain to be Britain again."[8]

Or consider American farmers, who, according to a preelection poll, were three times as likely to vote for Trump as they were to pull the lever for Clinton.[9] The US agricultural sector, which exports more than 20 percent of its output—well above the average for the United States as a whole—is particularly vulnerable to Trump's trade policies. And agriculture was among the sectors that stood to benefit the most from the TPP process, from which the United States withdrew on Trump's third day in office. Trump's anti-immigration stance was also at odds with US agriculture's heavy reliance on foreign labor. One Kansas farmer, after the election, said, "I'm puzzled by some of the decisions [Trump] has made. It's hurt me." But he also explained that voting Republican is part of his political DNA: "We bleed red here."[10]

Economic paradoxes such as those revealed in the voting patterns of Sunderland's autoworkers and US farmers suggest that the Brump shocks of 2016 had large noneconomic components. (This conclusion seems to have gained rather than lost weight in the first half of 2017.) We can conceptualize such isolationist (or identity) politics in terms of partiality: the extent to which people favor fellow citizens over foreigners.[11] Some level of partiality is unsurprising, but the degree of it on display in some contexts is staggering. Consider just two strands of evidence.

Look, first, at how much people say they value jobs for their fellow citizens over jobs for foreigners, as reported in a recent survey experiment by Diana C. Mutz and Eunji Kim. The researchers found that among US respondents, a hypothetical trade policy in which the United States gains only one job but a trading partner loses one thousand jobs received much more support than did a policy in which another country gains a thousand jobs and the United States loses one job.[12] The participants' responses imply a partiality multiple of more than one thousand!

Or compare aid to the domestic poor in rich countries with official development assistance provided to the rest of the world's poor. How much we are willing to spend to help other people is, arguably, the most tangible measure of how much we care for them. Branko Milanovic generated such a calculation for seven countries, finding that the "'worth' of a domestic poor expressed in terms of foreign poor" ranged from 32,000 times in the United States to 103,000 times in Sweden.[13] My own simplified version of this calculation, updated and extended to thirty-two rich countries, indicates that redistributive social spending per person in rich countries is on average about 50,000 times larger than official development assistance per person given by rich countries to poor countries.[14]

Some level of partiality can be rationalized in relatively benign terms. The plight of the domestic poor, for instance, is more vivid to voters who elect (and constrain) national governments than is the plight of the foreign poor. But no matter how much partiality is rationalizable, it looms so large that nonmarket strategies must contend with it.

And these nonmarket issues must be addressed against the backdrop of diminishing levels of public trust in business and other major institutions. According to the 2017 Trust Barometer created by the global communications firm Edelman, less than half of the public in two-thirds of countries surveyed trust business, government, the media, and NGOs to "do what is right." It also reports an all-time low for CEO credibility.[15] That fits with the results of a recent US survey by the Pew Research Center, which asked the public how much people in ten occupations contributed to the well-being of society. Business executives ranked next to last, with only 24 percent of respondents thinking they contributed "a lot." Only lawyers fared worse in the public eye.[16]

The collapse of public confidence in governmental institutions and the people who lead them must also be factored into firms' nonmarket strategies. While governmental weakness can sometimes expand firms' freedom of action, it also presents large challenges. If the public does not trust government to regulate business fairly, firms have to devote more attention to NGOs and direct public appeals. Additionally, in countries where there are powerful secessionist movements, firms have to contend with regional governments that may pull in very different directions than national ones. By the end of 2017, 3,000 companies had supposedly moved their head offices out of Catalonia in response to the legal and economic uncertainty created by a push for Catalonia to become independent from Spain.

In the international sphere, multinationals' problems with securing public trust and legitimacy are aggravated by partiality and distance effects. According to Eurobarometer surveys, 48 percent of Western Europeans trust citizens of their own country "a lot," compared with 20 percent who indicated this level of trust in citizens of other Western European countries and only 13 percent who trust people from some Eastern European countries, Japan, the United States, and China.[17] In nonmarket strategy, business leaders should start from the assumption that the farther they get from wherever they are from, the greater the trust deficit they have to overcome.

To summarize, societal problems point to increases in the salience of nonmarket strategy. Alongside economic concerns such as slowing productivity growth and yawning disparities between rich and poor within countries, politics is also complicated by noneconomic issues. And in the international domain, firms have to deal with persistent partiality. What is to be done?

Real Choices—and Recommendations

Nonmarket strategy is often thought of as having two components: corporate political activity (focused on influencing government policy) and corporate social responsibility (focused on responding to societal concerns via choices about how firms themselves operate).[18] In this section, I'll take a broad perspective on the former, considering firms' influence both on government policy and on the wider public discourse about globalization.[19] I'll end the chapter with a discussion of how firms themselves need to change.

Economic Management

To decide what public policies to advocate in response to rising antiglobalization anger, companies should start by asking a more basic question: Would the world be better off with more globalization or less? My 2011 book, *World 3.0*, focused on that question because I expected the present backlash to arrive sooner than it did.[20] On the positive side of the ledger, I found that the benefits of additional flows between countries are actually even larger than pro-globalizers typically estimate. On the negative side, I devoted seven chapters to globalization's alleged side effects: seller concentration, environmental and other externalities, risks of various sorts, chronic international imbalances, economic exploitation, political oppression, and cultural homogenization. Some disadvantages, such as the risks associated with high levels of international indebtedness, are indeed real and significant. Most others, however, turn out to be far smaller concerns given limited levels of international integration.

In debates about inequality, for example, globalization seems to get more blame than it deserves—probably because pinning inequality on an external force is politically convenient. A recent IMF report concurs, finding that technological progress and the decline of unions have both contributed more to the increase in inequality than

globalization has.[21] This finding fits with the law of semiglobalization: since domestic business activity is far larger than international
activity, something as fundamental as distributional outcomes in an
economy would most likely be shaped more by domestic than international causes. We can also point to real-world examples: if the
Netherlands can preserve a relatively reasonable income distribution despite having a trade-to-GDP ratio six times that of the United
States, how can we blame the much higher level of inequality in the
US economy on globalization?

Most of the other alleged harms of globalization I examined in
World 3.0 also had domestic root causes, implying they can be dealt
with most effectively via domestic solutions rather than reductions in
international flows. In other words, international openness should be
coupled with targeted domestic policies addressing undesirable side
effects of globalization. If I were rewriting *World 3.0* today, I would
devote more attention to sensitivities about immigration, but my overall assessment of globalization's pros and cons would be unchanged.
Humanity would be far better off if we continue to expand our circles
of cooperation and competition rather than narrowing them.

How can business leaders strengthen public support for openness
in the current climate? In the economic realm, they can embrace
a very different domestic policy agenda than big business typically
supports—but one that does fit well with the personal views of many
executives. In a 2015 survey of Harvard Business School alumni,
two-thirds of the respondents thought that addressing rising inequality, middle-class stagnation, rising poverty, or limited economic mobility was a higher priority for the United States than was boosting
overall economic growth.[22] Research confirms that sustained public
support for globalization requires safety nets that, in many respects,
seem to have frayed in the United States and the United Kingdom
after the years of Reagan and Thatcher.

The good news is that after cutting through the globaloney, countries have a great deal of flexibility in reducing inequality via a variety of instruments such as tax rates, various support programs, and

increases in the real minimum wage (which, in the United States, has stagnated since the 1980s). In specific regard to globalization, trade adjustment assistance (TAA) is particularly worth mentioning. TAA programs provide aid to people who lose their jobs because of rising imports. As a battle-hardened friend at the US Department of Commerce put it, Republican-oriented think tanks believe that TAA is ineffective, while Democratic think tanks argue it is insufficient. But in public opinion surveys, support for trade agreements clearly increases when there are provisions for TAA. In other words, emphasizing TAA might offer a modicum of reassurance to those who are at risk of displacement, even if the effectiveness of this assistance is contested. And because such policies are not the ones typically favored by big business, the corporate voices advocating them will presumably enjoy more than the usual amount of credibility.

While domestic policy should be the top priority for dealing with globalization's alleged harms, preserving and extending the benefits of globalization demands stronger—although more traditional—business engagement in international economic policy. We need a robust international institutional infrastructure to ensure that we continue to enjoy the (limited) level of globalization that we do despite partiality and distance effects. And although such an infrastructure can take a long time to build, it can be destroyed or damaged very quickly.

From this perspective, the muted business response to the Trump administration's moves against international institutions has been particularly surprising. The administration has withdrawn from the TPP process and the previously signed Paris Accords on combating global warming. It has also announced the renegotiation of NAFTA, declared that the United States would henceforth comply with WTO rulings on a case-by-case basis, and raised doubts about NATO treaty commitments. On top of these moves, there are the (related) strains in relationships with traditional allies as well as adversaries and surveys indicating a collapse in public support for the United States overseas.[23] While one can think up some rationales for the business community's muted response to these developments, in the long run, companies that rely heavily on sourcing from abroad (such as Walmart) and those that export far more than they import (such as GE) would benefit from joining forces to oppose protectionism and preserve international institutions.

Anger Management

An adequate public response to the anger about globalization requires going beyond the economic realm to the sociopolitical realm and, ultimately, into individual psychology. Both of the psychological biases about globalization highlighted in this book, globaloney and partiality, can encourage antiglobalization sentiments. Globaloney causes people to underestimate both the gains from additional globalization and the costs of reducing it, since the (marginal) benefits from strengthening international ties are generally larger when such ties are limited. And the data on partiality multiples regarding job preferences (over one thousand) and aid to the poor (about fifty thousand) directly reveal preferences that are heavily slanted toward co-citizens.

Even worse, when globaloney meets partiality, exaggerated perceptions of how globalized we are can greatly inflame partiality. Considering that strong partiality can get in the way of, for instance, trade agreements that would greatly improve global welfare, we would be better off underestimating globalization levels then overestimating them!

Figure 7-4 summarizes that argument and suggests ways forward. It shows that we are currently stuck in the worst of all worlds, psychologically speaking, with both unwarranted globaloney and partiality. The flip side of that observation is that improvements can be achieved by reducing either globaloney or partiality or, better yet, both. Reduction of globaloney just might by itself reduce the likelihood of antiglobalization horrors. In the paragraphs that follow, I highlight some striking evidence in this regard. Reduction of par-

FIGURE 7-4

Tackling problems with preferences and perceptions about globalization

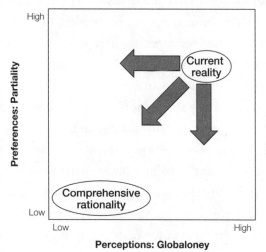

tiality requires revision not of estimated values pertaining to levels of globalization but of what is valued and is therefore harder, and more likely to take place, if at all, over longer time frames. But that is no excuse not to get started, given how damaging high levels of partiality can be.

In my 2016 HBR digital article "People Are Angry About Globalization. Here's What to Do About It," I discuss how to manage this anger. I will summarize here a wide array of approaches subsumed under the acronym FRIEND.

Facts. The role of facts in combating globaloney was discussed at some length in chapter 1. Happily, we can alleviate some public worries about globalization with a facts-based detox. Consider, for example, the results of surveys conducted by the German Marshall Fund of the United States about immigration.[24] They asked respondents if they thought there were "too many" immigrants in their countries—before and after telling them exactly how many immigrants actually lived there. In Britain, for example, where immigration was arguably the key issue in the Brexit referendum, immigrants constitute 13 percent of the population, but three recent surveys indicate that Britons believe that a quarter to a third of the population was born abroad.[25] Informing the respondents about the true percentage of immigrants reduces the share of those thinking there are too many by 40 percent! And in the United States, telling respondents about the actual data leads to an even bigger reduction.

There is also evidence that debunking globaloney may directly influence partiality that constrains foreign aid. For example, a 2015 US poll showed that, on average, respondents guessed that foreign aid made up 31 percent of the federal budget (the correct answer is just 1 percent).[26] And in another poll, half of the respondents were told the actual level of foreign aid and half weren't. Among the respondents who knew the facts, support for boosting foreign aid was 60 percent higher, and support for cutting it was 42 percent lower.[27]

My sense that the globalization debate had become unmoored from facts was a major reason that I decided to become engaged in measuring globalization for the DHL Global Connectedness Index and compiling the other data underpinning the laws of globalization discussed in chapter 1. The firm-level corollary: Business leaders need to rethink the facts they cite about globalization as well as the data they release about their companies' activities at home and abroad—and even the data they measure for internal purposes.

Rhetoric. A better acquaintance with the facts can foster more pro-globalization attitudes but is unlikely, by itself, to be sufficient. As several recent books—for example, Hugo Mercier and Dan Sperber's *The Enigma of Reason*, Steven Sloman and Philip Fernbach's *The Knowledge Illusion*, and Sara Gorman and Jack Gorman's *Denying to the Grave*—point out, impressions, once formed, can be quite impervious to contradictory evidence.[28] Given this problem, another partial antidote is provided by the classical device of rhetoric.

In particular, stories are often more powerful, rhetorically, than references to the elaborate models that economists use to make the case for more globalization. According to the work of neurobiologist Uri Hasson, stories engage the brain in different, more powerful ways than does the simple provision of information.[29] Thus, instead of pointing to one of the many elaborate studies of the welfare implications of large tariffs, businesspeople can make the case through examples.

In one such example, Philadelphia textile designer Kelly Cobb experimented with making a man's suit out of materials produced within one hundred miles of her home. It took twenty people more than five hundred hours to make a very simple suit, which was unlikely to be confused with a typical low-end suit because, among other reasons, it lacked sleeves. And even then, 8 percent of the inputs had to be purchased from farther than a hundred miles away.[30] While Cobb's own conclusion was that viability had been demonstrated, I would point to the more than hundredfold escalation in labor costs, higher materials costs, and horrible quality. And I would remind people that suit manufacture is not subject to strong scale economies. Would there be any way to produce more scale-sensitive products like computers and airplanes locally? Maybe localizers have no need for airplanes, but I'm sure they wouldn't like to give up their computers.

International informational or people interactions. Chapter 1 mentioned that while IT has greatly expanded the potential for connectivity, the depth of internationalization of informational interactions is still quite low. Even the internet, a global network, is still used primarily to transmit information within national borders. And similar or even stronger patterns are visible in social media. Despite the fact that the average Facebook user shares a nationality with only 4.6 percent of the social network's worldwide user base, 86 percent of Facebook friends live in the same country.[31] These figures imply a partiality multiple of nineteen.

Why does all this matter for purposes of anger management? Figure 7-5 indicates a negative correlation between self-perceived cultural superiority and depth on the information pillar of the DHL

FIGURE 7-5

Self-perceived cultural superiority and information pillar depth on the DHL Global Connectedness Index

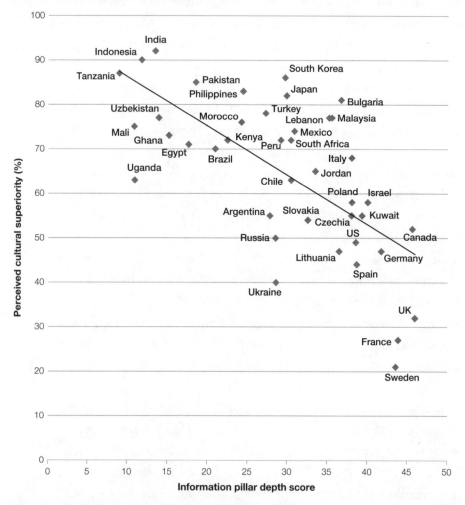

Source: Data from Pew Global Attitudes Survey (most recent data used for each country); and Pankaj Ghemawat and Steven A. Altman, *DHL Global Connectedness Index 2016: The State of Globalization in an Age of Ambiguity* (Bonn: Deutsche Post DHL, 2016).

The information pillar depth score from the DHL Global Connectedness Index captures international telephone call minutes per capita (40 percent weight), international internet bandwidth per internet user (40 percent weight), and trade in printed material per capita (20 percent weight).

Global Connectedness Index (a correlation coefficient of –0.67). Countries that are more deeply connected to international information flows are less likely to view their cultures as superior. And previous surveys have found opposition to trade to be directly related to a sense of national superiority.

A similar but slightly weaker negative correlation also shows up between perceived cultural superiority and people flows. This connection fits with Gordon Allport's famous intergroup-contact hypothesis, which holds that face-to-face contact can—under the right conditions—improve intergroup relations.[32] Allport's necessary conditions include cooperation toward shared goals and equal status between groups, among others. But since contact can also inflame conflict, people flows must be managed carefully if they are to increase openness. Thus, businesses that lobby against broad roll-backs of cross-border people movements should also support policies smoothing integration.

Education. Bernard Bailyn describes education "not only as formal pedagogy but as the entire process by which a culture transmits itself across the generations."[33] This broad concept and its intergenerational emphasis suggests thinking of education as a powerful long-term play. Education levels were apparently the strongest predictor of voting patterns in the Brexit referendum—even though age and income levels tended to get more play in the press. And Donald Trump went so far as to say, "I love the poorly educated."[34] More generally, cross-country evidence shows that higher education levels in a country decrease levels of nationalism and suspicion of outsiders; one study found this connection to hold across the board in ten countries with quite different educational systems.[35] People with lower education levels also tend to worry more about foreign cultural influences, an obvious link back to the discussion of cultural superiority in the previous section.

Beyond the obvious implication that more education is better than less, it also makes sense to delve into educational *content* that can support a more cosmopolitan outlook. Combating globaloney with the real facts about levels of globalization represents an obvious starting point. In addition to dispelling the myth of a "flat world," educational content should also nurture an appreciation for the diversity that persists across countries and how the interactions among countries are shaped by multiple dimensions of distance. For a free course along these lines, see my MOOC, Globalization of Business Enterprise, on the Coursera platform.[36]

To wrap up the FRIEND acronym, the N stands for nonmarket strategy, the focus of this chapter and, as discussed next, an area with large potential for improvement. The D stands for distributional outcomes, which have already been discussed. The FRIEND program is about helping to make the world, and especially particular parts of it, more friendly (again) to globalization. This is an enormous task, given the shifts in the sociopolitical environment required, but we can gain some hope not just from the efficacy of individual levers but also from the diversity and, often, complementarity among them. Also giving us hope, the levers can be pulled by diverse groups of actors: public institutions and policy makers, private businesses, pressure groups, the press, public intellectuals, and individuals acting on their own.

Given how high the stakes are for companies that are, or would be, global, and given their salience in global economic interactions, companies should consider active participation in alleviating the anger about globalization. Some might decide to pursue this objective through collective action under the umbrella of a business or industry group because of their aversion to being singled out as supporters of more globalization in the present environment. But at a minimum, companies with some notion of being good global citizens should avoid fanning the flames of anger.

The Problems Within Business

This chapter has focused, so far, on the anger that prevails out there and, secondarily, on what businesses and others can do to defuse it as participants in the public sphere. (Business reactions from a market rather than nonmarket perspective to what is out there were addressed in earlier chapters.) But there is an internal component to doing better as well: business leaders should think seriously about how their firms—and perhaps even they themselves—might need to change. In particular, three general business infirmities need to be fixed for companies to engage more effectively with society: insensitivity to distributional concerns, inability to acknowledge market failures, and inattention to linkages across local strategies for societal engagement. Consider them in turn.[37]

Insensitivity to distributional concerns. While business leaders frequently acknowledge distributional issues, they are often far less willing to accept that their personal compensation might be part of the problem. The Harvard Business School alumni who agreed—by a two-thirds majority—in a survey that distributional challenges were the leading category of problems facing the United States were, in the words of survey coauthor Michael Porter, often "offended by the discussion saying that somebody is getting paid too much."[38] Although much of the discussion has focused on raising the wages of lower-paid workers, inequality isn't simply about the stagnation of the US minimum wage in real terms since the 1980s. It's also about the top 0.1 percent doing fabulously well for itself over that period. Even though business leaders don't always like to recognize it, under conditions of imperfect competition (i.e., almost always), businesses have a fair amount of discretion in dealing with these issues.

More broadly, a US survey I conducted indicated that businesspeople or, more accurately, people with undergraduate or graduate degrees in business, were significantly more inclined than others to agree that "free markets tend to lead to a fair distribution of income." But even economists, who are generally enamored of the market system, typically praise the efficiency of markets, not their fairness. In fact, they often highlight trade-offs between equality and efficiency.[39] And more recently, a slew of authors have discussed at length the many downsides of distributional inequality: Anthony Atkinson, Thomas Piketty, Joseph Stiglitz, among others.[40]

Linking back more explicitly to globalization, many business leaders themselves need to recalibrate their views about the drivers of rising inequality—nearly one-half viewed globalization as a major contributor in my multicountry survey—in light of the earlier discussion of its real causes. Furthermore, sensitivity to distributional concerns is likely to become even more urgent as technological changes combine with the demographic trends I covered in chapter 3. In the words of World Bank president Jim Yong Kim, "as internet access becomes more widespread, people are increasingly looking outward for their reference income. Keeping up with the Joneses used to be about keeping up with your neighbors. But it's no longer only about the Joneses living around you—because of connectivity, the Joneses could be anywhere in the world."[41] There is probably a bit of globaloney in that last clause, but Kim does have a point, especially regarding Africa, where he notes that GDP growth is failing to keep up with population growth. Given that Africa is projected to account for more than half of world population growth through 2050, all kinds of red lights should start flashing: Would a world order in which Africa ended up even further behind be sustainable?[42]

Inability to acknowledge market failures. Confusing efficiency with fairness is not the only basic economics mistake to which businesspeople are prone. They also tend to forget (or never learned) about the conditions under which markets fail even to deliver efficient outcomes. On the survey I mentioned in the previous subsection, Americans (and, to a lesser extent, Germans) with undergraduate or graduate degrees in business or finance were more prone to discount market failures than were people with similar levels of education in other fields. This blind spot occurs, even though you might expect people trained in business to be more attentive to market failures than other people are, given how frequently business strategies try to exploit these failures.

To provide a bit more detail about the US and German survey, the survey's section on market failures presented the following propositions:

1. Free markets always lead to vigorous competition.

2. Farsighted companies can be trusted to do well by the environment.

3. Smart companies can handle risks and market volatility on their own.

Economists would tend to disagree with all three of these statements because the propositions correspond to three canonical areas where markets are known to fail: (1) when monopolies or oligopolies exert market power at the expense of consumers, (2) when externalities (such as pollution) don't get factored into prices, and (3) when informational imperfections undermine the ability of buyers and sellers to effectively price transactions and the risks associated with them. But across all three questions, business graduates were significantly more likely than other respondents to believe in these fallacies. And this at a time when there's evidence that all three types of market failure have become greater rather than lesser concerns, at least in the United States.[43]

Consider how much better business executives, as well as society, might be served if they took market failures more seriously. The need to be concerned about these failures is obvious if managers care directly about social welfare. But even if they care only about shareholder value, paying attention to market failures can help them understand how collective or coordinated action can boost profitability (e.g., the rationale for the US's Export-Import Bank, which is inconsistent with a simple faith in unregulated markets). By taking market failures seriously, managers can appreciate social concerns and unmet needs and how these issues might be turned into profit drivers—the "business case" for social responsibility. When business leaders grasp the true reasons for their success, they don't overplay the role of their own striving; they recognize the role of market failures in securing economic rents. And even torpid managers need to understand market failures if they want to reduce the odds of getting caught up in sociopolitical backlashes or running afoul of the law (which, in the United States, imposes significant restrictions on how market power can be used). Nonmarket strategy, even more so than market strategy, is likely to work better if it recognizes the nature and extent of market failures.

Inattention to linkages across local strategies for societal engagement. A third area of some confusion concerns the explicitly global parts of nonmarket strategy: how to deal not only with different governments, legal frameworks, and other official requirements but also with citizens of different countries around the world.

The laws of globalization are of some help in suggesting basic design principles. The law of semiglobalization implies that the natural analogue to localization in this context—simply falling in line with what governments want wherever a company operates—is unlikely to work. Even though the world is less globalized than people tend to think, it is too integrated for a pure country-by-country approach. Multinational firms need governmental and societal agendas that are both localized *and* linked across countries. Antiglobalization pressures require firms to deliver more benefits—and communicate about them—in the countries where they operate. The public wants contributions in the form of jobs, technology, and so forth. At the same time, home-country stakeholders typically feel that they have special claims to attention. And the home base also shapes the relevant linkages which, in line with the law of distance, are strongest with proximate and similar countries. Thus, most Mexican firms will probably want to devote considerable thought to Mexico's interactions with the United States and how to influence the outcomes as well as prepare for what might happen.

Additionally, polarization *within* countries where globalization has come under the most pressure exacerbates the inadequacy of purely localized nonmarket strategies. The shrinking common ground in public-policy debates—and increasingly the lack of agreed-upon facts on which to ground them—implies that firms may not even be able to stake out positions with broad local support. Such polarization can impinge on companies in vivid ways: several business leaders faced significant criticism—and their companies some backlash—when they joined President Trump's business advisory councils. And when the polarization is imported into companies, it can even make discussions of what the company is for and why a taboo topic. Avoiding internal conversations about such issues is unlikely to contribute to effective nonmarket strategies.

Finally, I emphasize a historical warning. Harvard Business School historian Geoffrey Jones points out that when the environment got complicated in the 1930s with protectionism, xenophobia, and the like, most companies did not distinguish themselves in their responses. One of his examples is IBM's response to the rise of the Nazi regime in Germany. Rather than pulling back—even as it became clear that the census IBM was supporting was being used to identify Jews for persecution—IBM sought to grow its business with the Nazi government. The decision could be considered a localization response, in a sense. In 1937, then CEO Thomas Watson received a medal from Hitler for "service to the Reich."[44] I hope that such a strategy would not even be considered today. But the example *is* a useful reminder that without some discussion of a company's own values and some effort to live up to them, firms can all too easily succumb to nonmarket strategies that focus purely on catering to local political preferences.

The theme of the inadequacy of pure localization is an appropriate one on which to conclude this chapter and this book. As has been emphasized throughout, localization—of strategy, of presence, of architecture, and of nonmarket strategy—can't be the answer to the present antiglobalization turbulence. Euphoria about globalization has shifted to gloom, but globalization hasn't experienced another great reversal (at least not yet). And even if it did, it would be a mistake to talk about its having ended: the rewind button on a tape recorder shouldn't be confused with the off button. The laws of globalization still hold, and the opportunities available for business and society from pressing ahead rather than retreating are immense. But they require all of us—individually and in our professional capacities—to recognize the borders that still divide us, to become more sensitive to differences and distances, and to embrace the risks that have always been associated with traveling new roads. Bridges are inherently harder to build than walls, but they are what open up the vast expanses of the global map depicted in this book.

Managerial Maxims

1. Nonmarket strategy encompasses firms' engagement with governments, NGOs, the media, and the public in spheres that extend beyond market transactions and often shape the rules under which market activity takes place.

2. The salience of nonmarket strategy is elevated by the backlash against globalization and big business as well as by heightened uncertainty about future economic policies.

3. Internationally, nonmarket strategy is complicated by people's strong preference for their co-citizens over foreigners (partiality).

4. Partiality and globaloney combine to inflame antiglobalization anger, which can be addressed by reducing either partiality or globaloney or, better yet, both.

5. Most alleged disadvantages of globalization—including rising inequality—have domestic root causes, implying that society is best served by coupling international openness with targeted domestic regulation.

6. The benefits of additional globalization outweigh the real harms, so business leaders should advocate for more rather than less international integration.

7. To improve the climate for globalization, firms can adopt the FRIEND program and think about how to contribute to better facts, rhetoric, informational or people interactions, education, nonmarket strategy, and distributional outcomes.

8. Businesses and the people who lead them should also think about areas where they need to change themselves to engage better with society.

9. In particular, business suffers from three general infirmities: insensitivity to distributional concerns, inability to acknowledge market failures, and inattention to linkages across local strategies for societal engagement.

10. As long as the laws of globalization continue to apply, companies will benefit from SPANning the globe with approaches to strategy, presence, architecture, and nonmarket strategy that take advantage of the rich array of possibilities between the extremes of pure localization or pure globalization.

NOTES

Introduction

1. "Jack Ma Talks About Retirement, Anti-Globalization, AI and China," *China Post*, July 26, 2017.

2. Immelt issued his initial call for localization in his 2016 New York University Stern commencement address. His remarks are at https://www.ge.com/reports/the-world-i-see-immelts-advice-to-win-in-the-time-of-globalization/. Immelt subsequently toned this recommendation down a bit, characterizing the strategy as "connected localization."

3. "The Retreat of the Global Company," *Economist*, January 28, 2017.

4. There are some indications, as of late 2017, that the globalization yo-yo may have started to bounce up again. For the first time in twenty years of NBC/Wall Street Journal polls on the topic, more Americans said in August 2017 that globalization was good than bad (49 percent to 40 percent). For additional discussion, see Aaron Black, "The pillars of Trump's nationalism are weakening," *Washington Post*, September 6, 2017. Also, forecasts calling for accelerating global macroeconomic growth provide additional cause for optimism. See, for example, the IMF World Economic Outlook, October 2017 update. And so does the fact that financial markets are cheering "synchronous growth" across both advanced and emerging economies. See Chetan Ahya, "Global Growth Is Finally in Sync—Can It Last?" Morgan Stanley research, March 29, 2017, https://www.morganstanley.com/ideas/global-growth-in-sync.html. Furthermore, preliminary analysis suggests that the tonality of news coverage about globalization rebounded in 2017 (in chapter 1, I will present evidence of a large shift toward more negative news coverage during 2016 in the United States, the United Kingdom, and India).

5. Peter A. Thiel, "The Optimistic Thought Experiment," *Hoover Institution*, January 29, 2008.

6. Harriet Taylor, "Trump's Biggest Tech Supporter: Election Showed 'the Tide Is Going Out' on Globalization," *CNBC*, March 8, 2017.

7. The title of figure I-1, its subheadings, and the yo-yo imagery are new, but the tensions depicted were all highlighted in the original presentation. Figure I-1 can also be used to structure discussions within companies of changing approaches to globalization. Plot where your company and its major competitors were five years ago, where they are today, and where you think they will be five years from now.

8. Muhtar Kent, James Quincey, Kathy Waller, and Tim Leveridge, "2016 Holiday Reception—Prepared Remarks and Q&A," Coca-Cola Company, December 15, 2016.

9. The AAA strategies and CAGE distance framework were discussed at greater length in Pankaj Ghemawat, *Redefining Global Strategy: Crossing Borders in a World Where Differences Still Matter* (Boston: Harvard Business Review Press, 2007, reissued in 2018). The material on these frameworks in *The New Global Road Map* focuses on how to apply them in the present context.

Chapter 1

1. Pankaj Ghemawat, *The Laws of Globalization and Business Applications* (Cambridge: Cambridge University Press, 2016).

2. The term *globaloney* was coined by the late American politician Clare Boothe Luce. See Albin Krebs, "Clare Boothe Luce Dies at 84: Playwright, Politician, Envoy," *New York Times,* October 10, 1987.

3. Robert J. Samuelson, "Globalization at Warp Speed," *Washington Post,* August 30, 2015; "The Post's View: The End of Globalization?," editorial, *Washington Post,* September 20, 2015.

4. Jim Tankersley, "Britain Just Killed Globalization As We Know It," *Washington Post,* June 25, 2016.

5. Paul Mason, "Globalisation Is Dead, and White Supremacy Has Triumphed," *Guardian*, November 9, 2016.

6. Based on analysis conducted using IBM Watson's AlchemyAPI applied to articles mentioning the term "globalization" in the *New York Times,* the *Wall Street Journal,* and the *Washington Post* in the United States; the *Times of London,* the *Guardian,* and the *Financial Times* in the United Kingdom; and the *Times of India,* the *Hindustan Times,* and *Business Standard* in India. Note that local-language newspapers in India with larger circulations than the newspapers used were excluded from the analysis because of the need to restrict the sample across all three countries to English-language publications to ensure accurate cross-country comparisons.

7. Finbarr Livesey, *From Global to Local* (New York: Pantheon, 2017); and Ian Bremmer, *Us vs. Them: The Failure of Globalism* (New York: Portfolio, 2018).

8. Pankaj Ghemawat and Steven A. Altman, *DHL Global Connectedness Index 2016: The State of Globalization in an Age of Ambiguity* (Bonn: Deutsche Post DHL, 2016). Available for free download at www.dhl.com/gci.

9. There are also several other globalization indexes, but the DHL Global Connectedness Index was the only one of the major established indexes to capture the crisis-era decline in its overall measure of globalization trends. The failure of other globalization indexes to capture this decline raises questions about their use as inputs for business and economic policy decision making. The Ernst & Young Globalization Index registered no decline at all, and the KOF Index of Globalization registered only a brief pause.

10. While McKinsey Global Institute's March 2016 report, "Digital Globalization: The New Era of Global Flows," emphasizes how international internet bandwidth has expanded forty-five-fold over the past decade, I estimate that the international *share* of internet traffic has just doubled, as reported in Ghemawat and Altman, *DHL Global Connectedness Index 2016.*

11. World Trade Organization, "Trade Recovery Expected in 2017 and 2018, Amid Policy Uncertainty," World Trade Organization, April 12, 2017.

12. More precisely, the chart depicts the weighted average distance traversed by the flows covered on the breadth dimension of the index, using the weights employed

in the construction of the index itself. The flows and weights on the breadth dimension are as follows: trade pillar (35 percent weight), based only on merchandise trade; capital pillar (35 percent weight), based half on FDI flows and stocks and half on portfolio equity stocks; information pillar (15 percent weight), based two-thirds on telephone calls and one-third on trade in printed publications; and people pillar (15 percent weight), based equally on migrants, tourists, and university students.

13. Gross exports of goods and services as a percentage of world GDP declined from 31 percent in 2014 to 29 percent in 2015 and then 28 percent in 2016, according to trade data from the World Trade Organization (WTO) Statistics Database and GDP data from the International Monetary Fund (IMF), *World Economic Outlook,* April 2017 update. The preliminary characterization of trade depth during the first half of 2017 is from my Quarterly Updated International Connectedness (QUIC) Index, which tracks trade and capital depth in countries for which quarterly data are available. The QUIC Index shows trade depth increasing in 2017 Quarter 1 and declining slightly in Quarter 2, but remaining above the 2016 Quarter 4 level. As of September 2017, the WTO forecasted trade volume to grow faster than GDP over all of 2017. (WTO Press Release, "WTO Upgrades Forecast for 2017 as Trade Rebounds Strongly," September 21, 2017.) Additional trade depth metrics as well as longer-term trend data are covered in the next section.

14. FDI flows surpassed expectations in 2016. UN Conference on Trade and Development, *World Investment Report* (UNCTAD, 2016), forecasted a 10 to 15 percent drop in FDI inflows, but the actual 2016 decline came in at only 2 percent, as reported in the 2017 edition of the same report. FDI inflows as a percentage of global gross fixed capital formation (GFCF) rose from 6.8 percent in 2014 to 9.5 percent in 2015 before falling to 9.4 percent in 2016. FDI outflows as a percentage of GFCF rose from 6.5 percent in 2014 to 8.6 percent in 2015 before falling to 7.9 percent in 2016. My QUIC Index (see the preceding endnote) shows a slight decrease in 2017 Quarter 1 FDI depth as compared with 2016 Quarter 4. However, this still leaves the level higher than in 2016 Quarter 3 and well within the normal range of variation for quarterly FDI flows.

15. For more on how data pertaining to the depth and breadth of globalization support the two laws, see Ghemawat, *Laws of Globalization and Business Applications.*

16. The typical exceptions to this pattern at the country level involve small countries. Note that even with limited depth, there can be a substantial backlash. Immigration-related issues tend to become contentious when the percentage of the population born overseas hits the low teens, although this estimate probably also depends on whether one is talking about a neighborhood or a country, how recently immigrant intensity has built up, and the state of the general economy (anti-immigrant sentiment tends to be countercyclical). The rise of e-commerce and its impact on traditional retailers provides another interesting analogy, from a market rather than a political perspective. E-commerce sales add up to only 8 percent of US retail sales, according to the US Department of Commerce, and after excluding sectors such as autos, a PwC Strategy& estimate puts e-commerce at about 16 percent of its addressable market. Still, this level of e-commerce penetration has been enough to prompt a crisis for traditional retailers. See US Census Bureau, "Quarterly Retail E-Commerce Sales, 2nd Quarter 2017," US Department of Commerce, Washington, DC, August 17, 2017, www.census.gov/retail/mrts/www/data/pdf/ec_current.pdf; and Nick Hodson and Marco Kesteloo, "2015 Retail Trends," *Bricks & Clicks* (blog), Strategy&, accessed September 30, 2017, www.strategyand.pwc.com/trends/2015-retail-trends.

17. An estimated 26 percent of the value of gross exports in 2014 came from foreign sources, according to an exports-weighted average across fifty-nine countries with data

available on this indicator in the Organisation for Economic Co-operation and Development's (OECD's) Trade in Value Added (TiVA) database (TiVA Nowcast Estimates dataset accessed in August 2017).

18. Calculation based on comparison of trade in value added from UN Conference on Trade and Development, *World Investment Report* (UNCTAD, 2013), 137, with sectoral composition of GDP data from World Bank World Development Indicators database.

19. This theoretical benchmark was based on the assumption that buyers in one nation are as prone to obtain goods from foreign producers as they are from domestic ones. Under this assumption, the share of imports in total domestic consumption is equal to one minus a country's share of world output of goods. See Elhanan Helpman, "Imperfect Competition and International Trade: Evidence from Fourteen Industrial Countries," *Journal of the Japanese and International Economies* 1, no. 1 (1987); Jeffrey A. Frankel, "Assessing the Efficiency Gain from Further Liberalization," in *Efficiency, Equity, and Legitimacy: The Multilateral Trading System at the Millennium*, ed. Roger B. Porter, Pierre Sauvé, Arvind Subramanian, and Americo Beviglia Zampetti (Washington, DC: Brookings Institution Press, 2001); and Jonathan Eaton and Samuel Kortum, "Technology, Geography, and Trade," *Econometrica* 70, no. 5 (2002).

20. The Globalization Hotspots index is one of two city-level globalization indexes I produce. Globalization Hotspots focuses on the depth of cities' international interactions. The other index, Globalization Giants, focuses on the magnitude of those international interactions.

21. Calculations based on OECD Trade in Value Added (TiVA) database, December 2016 and IMF, *World Economic Outlook Database*, October 2016. Note that if the law of semiglobalization didn't hold there and Singaporeans bought products and services from abroad as readily as they buy domestic ones, they would get more than 99 percent of the output they consume and invest from abroad (one minus Singapore's share of world GDP).

22. See Edward E. Leamer and James Levinsohn, "International Trade Theory: The Evidence," in *Handbook of International Economics*, ed. Gene M. Grossman and Kenneth Rogoff (Amsterdam: Elsevier, 1995), 1384.

23. HM Treasury, "HM Treasury Analysis: The Long-Term Economic Impact of EU Membership and the Alternatives," UK government website, April 2016.

24. For Germany, the elasticity of merchandise exports with respect to physical distance is about –1. An elasticity of –1 means that doubling distance cuts trade in half—and halving distance doubles trade. To illustrate, consider the intensity of Germany's exports to Belgium, France, and Greece. The distance from Germany to Belgium (based on a population-weighted average of distances between major cities in the two countries) is half as large as the distance from Germany to France. Indeed, the intensity of Germany's exports to France is about half the intensity of Germany's exports to Belgium. The distance from Germany to Greece is a little more than four times the distance from Germany to Belgium (and double the distance from Germany to France), implying the effect should be doubled again ($2 \times 2 = 4$). And so it is—Germany's exports to Belgium are roughly four times as intense as Germany's exports to Greece.

25. The CAGE distance framework was introduced in Pankaj Ghemawat, "Distance Still Matters: The Hard Reality of Global Expansion," *Harvard Business Review*, September 2001, and elaborated on in Pankaj Ghemawat, *Redefining Global Strategy: Crossing Borders in a World Where Differences Still Matter* (Boston: Harvard Business School Press, 2007). The names given to the dimensions of the framework were intended to be

intuitive, although there has occasionally been some confusion about the meaning of the administrative leg of the framework. Rather than administrative, this dimension could have been called institutional or political, but that would have made for a less interesting acronym. Additionally, some drivers of international interactions are not easily classified. Colonial ties, for example, tend to imply both cultural and administrative similarities. That is, they can be thought of as bridges across both types of differences. The CAGE framework is meant to draw the attention of business decision makers to multiple salient dimensions of distance rather than to provide a mutually exclusive classification scheme.

26. Wage differences boost trade between Germany and its eastern neighbors, where German companies have located supply chains, but economic similarity also boosts demand for German exports in Western countries. Products developed for German customers are often affordable and desirable for many buyers in France, the United Kingdom, and elsewhere.

27. Phrased another way, these estimates reflect how much more trade and FDI is expected to take place between a country pair that is half as distant as another otherwise similar country pair. Note that the physical distance effect for trade across all countries is even stronger than Germany's. In comparing these values, however, also keep in mind that the –1 elasticity for Germany was based only on GDP and physical distance, whereas the full gravity model discussed here incorporated explanatory variables based on all four dimensions of the CAGE distance framework. Thus, both the countries covered and the range of explanatory variables differ between the two analyses.

28. The distance effect estimates reported here for trade were generated using data on gross exports. Adjusting for multicountry supply chains does result in some changes to the parameter estimates, but gravity models of trade in value added also strongly support the law of distance. Shifting to trade in value added also results in only small changes to the ranks of countries' largest trading partners. The correlation between trade partner ranks for gross exports and domestic value added embodied in final foreign demand (as an indicator of value added exports) was 0.97 over the period from 2000 to 2011. The gross exports data employed were from the IMF Direction of Trade Statistics (DOTS) and the value added trade data were from the OECD's Trade in Value Added (TiVA) database.

29. The modeling described in this paragraph and the next one is covered in Pankaj Ghemawat and Steven A. Altman, "Distance at the Industry and Company Levels," in Ghemawat, *Laws of Globalization*.

30 These counterintuitive findings have prompted research on what is often termed the "distance puzzle" (see Claudia M. Buch, Jörn Kleinert, and Farid Toubal, "The Distance Puzzle: On the Interpretation of the Distance Coefficient in Gravity Equations," *Economics Letters* 83, no. 3 [2004]) or the "missing globalization puzzle" (see David T. Coe, Arvind Subramanian, and Natalia T. Tamirisa, "The Missing Globalization Puzzle: Evidence of the Declining Importance of Distance," *IMF Staff Papers* 54, no. 1 [2007]: 34–58).

31. The frictionless benchmark of roughly 8,300 kilometers is based on the assumption that each country consumes imports from every other country in proportion to the source countries' shares of world GDP.

32. Keith Head and Thierry Mayer, "What Separates Us? Sources of Resistance to Globalization," *Canadian Journal of Economics / Revue canadienne d'économique* 46, no. 4 (2013).

33. Michele Fratianni, "The Gravity Model in International Trade," in *The Oxford Handbook of International Business*, ed. Alan M. Rugman (Oxford: Oxford University Press, 2009).

34. Thomas L Friedman, *The World Is Flat: A Brief History of the Twenty- First Century* (New York: Farrar Straus and Giroux, 2005).

35. Data employed in this calculation are from Jim Fetzer, US Department of Commerce, email exchange with author, November 2014.

36. Online survey of managers conducted between March 21 and April 6, 2017. These surveys were run in three advanced economies (the United States, the United Kingdom, and Germany) and three emerging ones (China, India, and Brazil). In each country, surveys were completed by at least a thousand respondents holding decision-maker or director/manager roles in companies with at least one hundred employees.

37. The origins of this metric and additional data pertaining to it are covered in chapters 5 and 6.

38. Perceptual bias and motivational distortion extend the analogy between globalization-related sentiments and yo-yo dieting. They are featured in the literature on how people tend to incorrectly estimate their weight. See, for example, Amanda Conley and Jason D. Boardman, "Weight Overestimation as an Indicator of Disordered Eating Behaviors Among Young Women in the United States," *International Journal of Eating Disorders* 40, no. 5 (2007). The final category, technotrances, is an analogy to techno music and its effects on brain activity.

39. Daniel Cohen, *Globalization and Its Enemies* (Cambridge: MIT Press, 2007).

40. Parag Khanna, "Remapping the World," 10 Ideas for the Next 10 Years, *Time*, March 22, 2010.

41. For an extended discussion of digital delusions about globalization, see Pankaj Ghemawat, "Even in a Digital World, Globalization Is Not Inevitable," *Harvard Business Review*, February 1, 2017.

42. Peter A. Thiel, "The Optimistic Thought Experiment," *Hoover Institution*, January 29, 2008.

43. I return to these survey results in somewhat greater detail in chapters 4 and 5.

44. Robert Woodruff, in *The Cola Conquest*, video directed by Irene Angelico (Ronin Films, 1998).

45. Roberto C. Goizueta, remarks made to World Bottler Meeting, Monte Carlo, August 25, 1997, www.goizuetafoundation.org/category/speeches.

46. Roberto C. Goizueta, quoted in Chris Rouch, "Coke Executive John Hunter Calling It Quits," *Atlanta Journal and Constitution*, January 12, 1996.

47. Roberto C. Goizueta, in *The Cola Conquest*.

48. For additional discussion of alleged harms associated with globalization, see chapter 7 of this book and Pankaj Ghemawat, *World 3.0: Global Prosperity and How to Achieve It* (Boston: Harvard Business Review Press, 2011), chaps. 5–11.

49. Julia Kirby and Thomas A. Stewart, "The Institutional Yes," *Harvard Business Review*, October 2007.

Figure 1-4 sources: *E-commerce:* Ivan Chan, "Cross-Border Ecommerce," *Accenture*, 2016. **Services exports value added, Merchandise exports value added:** 2013 UNCTAD World Investment Report; World Bank *World Development Indicators.* **Merchandise and services exports value added:** World Trade Organization *Time Series Statistics*; International Monetary Fund *World Economic Outlook Database*, April 2017; Organisation for Economic Co-operation and Development *Trade in Value Added (TiVA) database* (TiVA Nowcast Estimates dataset accessed in August 2017). **Gross exports of goods and** *services:* World Trade Organization *Statistics Database*; International Monetary Fund *World Economic Outlook Database,* April 2017. *Gross capital inflows:* Susan Lund et al., "The New Dynamics of Financial Globalization," *McKinsey Global Institute,* August 2017. *Foreign direct investment inflows:* 2017 UNCTAD World Investment Report. *Government debt, Patents (foreign applicants):* Euromonitor *Passport Database. Stock market investment, Phone calls (including Skype), Internet traffic, Migrants, Tourists:* 2016 DHL Global Connectedness Index. *Mail:* Universal Postal Union *Postal Statistics. Online News:* Ethan Zuckerman, *Digital Cosmopolitans: Why We Think the Internet Connects Us, Why It Doesn't, and How to Rewire It* (New York: WW Norton & Company, 2013). *Patents (foreign co-inventor):* Organisation for Economic Co-operation and Development, "Science, Technology and Industry Scoreboard," 2013. *Facebook:* Maurice H. Yearwood et al., "On Wealth and the Diversity of Friendships: High Social Class People Around the World Have Fewer International Friends," *Personality and Individual Differences* 87 (2015). *YouTube trending videos:* Edward L. Platt, Rahul Bhargava, and Ethan Zuckerman, "The International Affiliation Network of YouTube Trends," *Association for the Advancement of Artificial Intelligence,* 2015. *Scientific articles:* Pankaj Ghemawat and Niccolò Pisani, "Extent, Pattern, and Quality Effects of Globalization in Scientific Research: The Case of International Management," unpublished working paper, 2014. *Twitter:* Yuri Takhteyev, Anatoliy Gruzd, and Barry Wellman, "Geography of Twitter Networks," *Social Networks* 34 (2012). *TV news:* Media Tenor, "Different Perspective: Locations, Protagonists and Topic Structures in International TV News," *Media Tenor,* April 2006; William Porath and Constanza Mujica, "Las Noticias Extranjeras En La Televisión Pública Y Privada De Chile Comparada Con La De Catorce Países," *Comunicación y Sociedad* 24, no. 2 (2011); Toril Aalberg et al., "International TV News, Foreign Affairs Interest and Public Knowledge," *Journalism Studies* 14, no. 3 (2013). *Popular music:* Fernando Ferreira and Joel Waldfogel, "Pop Internationalism: Has Half a Century of World Music Trade Displaced Local Culture?" *Economic Journal* 123, no. 569 (2013). *Movies:* Motion Picture Association of America; Box Office Mojo. *University students:* UNESCO Institute for Statistics *UIS. Stat Database. Air travel passengers:* International Civil Aviation Organization (ICAO).

Figure 1-5 sources: *Firms (MNEs), employees in large firms:* United Nations Conference on Trade and Development (UNCTAD); Dun & Bradstreet, "Dun & Bradstreet's Data Quality," 2015. *Firms (exporters):* Rough global estimate based on national statistics for various countries. *Multinational enterprise (MNE) foreign affiliates value added, sales of foreign affiliates, exports of goods and services by MNEs:* 2017 UNCTAD World Investment Report. *M&A transactions by number, M&A transactions by value:* Thomson Reuters *SDC Platinum* (note: both based only on deals with values reported). *Debt:* Francisco Cellabos, Tatiana Didier, and Sergio L. Schmukler, "How Much Do Developing Economies Rely on Private Capital Markets?" working paper, July 2010. **Fortune Global 500 revenue:** 2014 *Fortune* Global 500, Bureau Van Dijk *Orbis Database,* company annual reports (note: analysis restricted to firms reporting domestic/international split of revenues). *Stock market listings:* World Federation of Exchanges, 2015. *Bank deposits, bank loans, bank profits:* Stijn Claessens and Neeltje van Horen, "Foreign Banks: Trends, Impact and Financial Stability," working paper, 12/10, International Monetary Fund, January 1, 2012. *Media buying:* Adam Smith, futures director at WPP's media-buying umbrella firm, GroupM, interview with author, 2012. *Marketing services:* Pankaj Ghemawat, Steven A. Altman, and Robert Strauss, "WPP and the Globalization of Marketing Services," case study SM-1600-E, IESE Business School, Barcelona, June 2013. *Brands:* Nigel Hollis, *The Global Brand,* (London: Palgrave MacMillan, 2010). *MNE employment:* World Bank *World Development Indicators,*International Labor Organization, and United Nations Conference on Trade and Development. **Fortune *Global 500 CEOs,* Fortune *Global 500 top management:*** Pankaj Ghemawat and Herman Vantrappen, "How Global Is Your C-Suite?" *MIT Sloan Management Review* (summer 2015). **Business *R&D:*** Organisation for Economic Co-operation and Development, "OECD Science, Technology and Industry Scoreboard 2013: Innovation for Growth" (Paris: OECD Publishing, 2013). ***R&D alliances:*** Melissa Schilling, "Understanding the Alliance Data," *Strategic Management Journal* (September 22, 2008).

Chapter 2

1. Ipsos MORI, "Perils of Perception," survey, 2014 and 2015; and German Marshall Fund of the United States, "Transatlantic Trends: Key Findings 2013," survey, 2013.

2. German Marshall Fund of the United States, "Transatlantic Trends," 2014.

3. Peter Navarro, "Scoring the Trump Economic Plan: Trade, Regulatory, & Energy Policy Impacts," September 29, 2016, https://assets.donaldjtrump.com/Trump_Economic_Plan.pdf.

4. "Trump Promise Tracker," *Washington Post,* last updated October 6, 2017, www.washingtonpost.com/graphics/politics/trump-promise-tracker.

5. Analysis using Google Trends, https://trends.google.com/trends.

6. Mark Zandi, Chris Lafakis, Dan White, and Adam Ozimek, "The Macroeconomic Consequences of Mr. Trump's Economic Policies," *Moody's Analytics,* June 2016.

7. Julian Kozlowski, Laura Veldkamp, and Venky Venkateswaran, "The Tail That Wags the Economy: Beliefs and Persistent Stagnation," working paper 21719, National Bureau of Economic Research, Cambridge, MA, 2017.

8. For a detailed examination of recent developments regarding trade, capital, information, and people flows globally as well as country by country, see Pankaj Ghemawat and Steven A. Altman, *DHL Global Connectedness Index 2016* (Bonn: Deutsche Post DHL, 2016).

9. In discussing this shift, Graham Allison, "Thucydides's Trap Has Been Sprung in the Pacific," *Financial Times,* August 21, 2012, has emphasized the likelihood of clashes due, in part, to the Thucydides trap: the stress inevitably engendered when a rival overhauls a ruling power. However, the US withdrawal from TPP and broader isolationism reduce this risk, as discussed in Pankaj Ghemawat, "If Trump Abandons the TPP, China Will Be the Biggest Winner," *Harvard Business Review,* December 12, 2016.

10. United Nations, "International Trade Statistics 1900–1960," Statistical Office of the United Nations, May 1962. This dataset, employed extensively in this subsection and the next, differs somewhat from the dataset used for this period in figure 1-6, which included data from Mariko J. Klasing and Petros Milionis, "Quantifying the Evolution of World Trade, 1870–1949," *Journal of International Economics* 92, no. 1 (2014). The Klasing and Milionis dataset was specifically developed for measuring trade depth and itself is based on Katherine Barbieri, Omar Keshk, and Brian Pollins, "Correlates of war project trade data set codebook," Codebook Version 2 (2008), which harmonized across different reporting standards used by various countries. While this academic work represents an improvement over the UN data used here, the analysis in this chapter required a dataset that had bilateral trade data, which was unfortunately not available in the improved form.

11. UN, "International Trade Statistics 1900–1960."

12. For further discussion, see Pankaj Ghemawat and Geoffrey G. Jones, "Globalization in Historical Perspective," in Pankaj Ghemawat, *The Laws of Globalization and Business Applications* (Cambridge: Cambridge University Press, 2016).

13. These depth ratio calculations use gross national product (GNP) rather than GDP as the denominator. GNP data from Nathan S. Balke and Robert J. Gordon, "The Estimation of Prewar GNP: Methodology and New Evidence," working paper 2674, National Bureau of Economic Research, Cambridge, MA, 1988; US Department of Commerce, Bureau of Economic Analysis. Export data from UN, "International Trade Statistics 1900–1960."

14. John Ward, "The Services Sector: How Best to Measure It?," U.S. Department of Commerce International Trade Administration, October 2010.

15. Calculation based on data from UN Statistics Division and Angus Maddison, "Historical Statistics of the World Economy: 1–2008 AD," 2010.

16. Barry Eichengreen and Douglas A. Irwin, "Trade Blocs, Currency Blocs and the Reorientation of World Trade in the 1930s," *Journal of International Economics* 38 (1995): 1–24.

17. Alfred P. Tischendorf, *Great Britain and Mexico in the Era of Porfirio Diaz* (Durham, NC: Duke University Press, 1961); and Nora Hamilton, *The Limits of State Autonomy* (Princeton, NJ: Princeton University Press, 1982), as cited in Philip L. Russell, *The History of Mexico: From Pre-Conquest to Present* (Abingdon: Routledge, 2010), 290.

18. Frank Jack Daniel and Adriana Barerra, "Mexico-U.S. Trade Would Survive Any NAFTA Rupture: Mexico Foreign Minister," *Reuters*, September 15, 2017.

19. Tyler Cowen, "One Fact Constraining Globalization: It's a Big Planet," *Bloomberg*, April 7, 2017.

20. McKinsey Global Institute, "Financial Globalization: Retreat or Reset," March 2013.

21. The capital pillar of the DHL Global Connectedness Index excludes debt flows and stocks (including bank lending) because the index is often used to rank countries and assess policies oriented toward taking advantage of benefits of globalization. The inclusion of debt capital would interfere with such uses, because of the widely recognized dangers of high levels of international indebtedness.

22. The decline depicted in figure 2-5 is smaller when calculated in euros instead of US dollars, but still exceeds 30 percent. This analysis, which focuses on the European Union in its current composition, avoids the complication of a changing eurozone composition over time.

23. Feliks Garcia, "Nigel Farage: UK's 'Real Friends' Speak English," *Independent*, February 24, 2017.

24. Josh Lowe, "Commonwealth Day: Why Does It Matter to the U.K.'s Brexit Camp?," *Newsweek*, March 14, 2016.

25. Keith Head and Thierry Mayer, "Gravity Equations: Workhorse, Toolkit, and Cookbook," in *Handbook of International Economics*, vol. 4, ed. Gita Gopinath, Elhanan Helpman, and Kenneth S. Rogoff (Amsterdam: Elsevier, 2014).

26. Since the model is multiplicative, the joint effect is the product of the individual effects: $2.2 \times 2.5 = 5.5$.

27. World Bank, World Development Indicators, https://data.worldbank.org/data-catalog/world-development-indicators.

28. Peter Spence, "Government Faces Worldwide Hunt for Trade Negotiators, Experts Warn," *Telegraph* (London), July 3, 2016.

29. Dan Bilefsky, "Hopes for U.K. Trade Deal with India Hit a Snag: Immigration," *New York Times*, November 7, 2016.

30. Lizzie Stromme, "Sweden BASHES Brexit: EU Exit Will Increase Cost of Trade REGARDLESS of Deal, UK Warned," *Express* (London), March 21, 2017.

31. For further discussion of how industries vary in their sensitivity to each of the dimensions of the CAGE distance framework, refer to pages 49–54 of Pankaj Ghemawat,

Redefining Global Strategy (Boston: Harvard Business School Press, 2007). This topic is also discussed more briefly in chapter 5.

32. Lucy Burton, "Goldman to Add 'Hundreds' of Jobs in Europe Ahead of Brexit as It Starts to Move Staff Out of London," *Telegraph* (London), March 21, 2017.

33. Alan Tovey, "BMW Weighs Moving Production of New Electric Mini Away from the UK," *Telegraph* (London), February 27, 2017.

34. Timothy Aeppel and Mai Nguyen, "Sneakers Show Limits of Trade Policy in Reviving Jobs for Trump," *Reuters*, November 21, 2016.

35. Vodafone Annual Report, 2017.

36. This section benefited substantially from a conversation with Tom Stewart about these themes.

37. Much has been written on the VUCA concept. For a very concise perspective, see Nathan Bennett and G. James Lemoine, "What VUCA Really Means for You," *Harvard Business Review*, January–February 2014. A much more extensive treatment is provided in Oliver Mack, Anshuman Khare, Andreas Krämer, and Thomas Burgartz, eds., *Managing in a VUCA World* (Cham: Springer, 2016).

38. Jasper Jackson, "Sky Will Cost Rupert Murdoch $2.5bn Less After Brexit Vote," *Guardian* (London), December 12, 2016.

39. Arindam Bhattacharya, Dinesh Khanna, Kermit King, and Rajah Augustinraj, "The New Globalization: Shaping Your Own Growth in the New Global Era," Boston Consulting Group, August 17, 2017.

40. See, for example, Hugh Courtney, Jane Kirkland, and Patrick Viguerie, "Strategy Under Uncertainty," *Harvard Business Review*, November–December 1997.

41. Philip E. Tetlock and Dan Gardner, *Superforecasting: The Art and Science of Prediction* (New York: Broadway Books, 2015).

42. Paul Saffo, "Six Rules for Effective Forecasting," *Harvard Business Review*, July–August 2007.

43. "Norwegian took 'all the aircraft'," *News in English*, March 12, 2014. http://www.newsinenglish.no/2014/03/12/norwegian-taken-all-the-aircraft/.

44. Justin Bachman, "Norwegian Air's Global Expansion Draws Fire from a Jilted Rival," *Bloomberg*, September 21, 2017. https://www.bloomberg.com/news/articles/2017-09-21/norwegian-air-s-global-expansion-draws-fire-from-a-jilted-rival.

Chapter 3

1. For more discussion, see Doug Key, "If We Can't Predict Weather Accurately More Than a Few Days Ahead, How Can We Predict Climate Decades Ahead?," Student Guide to Climate Change, accessed May 18, 2017, www2.palomar.edu/users/dkey/Predicting%20weather%20versus%20climate.htm. Another useful source is "If We Can't Predict Weather Two Weeks Ahead, How Can We Predict Climate Fifty Years from Now?," *Climate Central*, November 7, 2009, www.climatecentral.org/library/faqs/if_we_cant_predict_weather_two_weeks_ahead_how_can_we_predict_climate.

2. While 42 percent of a sample of publicly traded companies in the UK conduct strategic planning over a time horizon that extends up to five years, only 13 percent consider time frames beyond five years, according to Keith W. Glaister and J. Richard Falshaw, "Strategic Planning: Still Going Strong?," *Long Range Planning* 32, no. 1 (1999). Even in oil exploration, the longest time horizons employed extended to twenty years, according to data reported in Robert M. Grant, "Strategic Planning in a Turbulent Environment: Evidence from the Oil Majors," *Strategic Management Journal* 24, no. 6 (2003).

3. Peter A. Thiel, "The Optimistic Thought Experiment," Hoover Institution, January 29, 2008.

4. This economic logic for focusing on success scenarios is reinforced by psychological considerations. Thus, psychologist Per Espen Stoknes has argued that apocalypse fatigue gets in the way of our ability to deal with global warming and suggests that strategies that are positively focused are more likely to lead to meaningful action. Something similar may apply to globalization-related challenges in general. See Per Espen Stoknes, *What We Think About When We Try Not To Think About Global Warming: Toward a New Psychology of Climate Action* (White River Junction: Chelsea Green Publishing, 2015).

5. This is an application of what is called dependency-directed backtracking in artificial intelligence. See Richard M. Stallman and Gerald Jay Sussman, "Forward Reasoning and Dependency-Directed Backtracking in a System for Computer-Aided Circuit Analysis," Massachusetts Institute of Technology Artificial Intelligence Laboratory, September 1976.

6. "When Are Emerging Markets No Longer 'Emerging'?" Knowledge@Wharton, May 5, 2008, http://knowledge.wharton.upenn.edu/article/when-are-emerging-markets-no-longer-emerging/.

7. Anita Raghavan, "Head of McKinsey Is Elected to a Third Term," *New York Times*, February 2, 2015.

8. For background on how several organizations have classified countries according to their levels of development, see Pankaj Ghemawat and Steven A. Altman, "Emerging Economies: Differences and Distances," *AIB Insights* 16, no. 4 (2016).

9. This analysis considers "emerging and developing economies" as they are currently categorized by the IMF. The list is updated regularly, and it has changed since the 1992 dip and will presumably change in the future. This analysis, however, is more useful with a static list of countries.

10. Danny Quah, "The Global Economy's Shifting Centre of Gravity," *Global Policy* 2, no. 1 (2011).

11. Data from Euromonitor Passport; Gartner Research, "The World Machine Tool Output & Consumption Survey" (various editions); Global Cement; World Steel Association, "World Steel in Figures 2016"; Cefic Chemdata International, Chemicals Industry Profile Dataset; Innovest, "Overview of the Chemicals Industry," March 2007.

12. Brenda Goh, "Boeing China Plant to Deliver 100 737s a Year, First in 2018: Xinhua," *Reuters*, March 13, 2017.

13. Jackie Cai and Adam Jourdan, "With Maiden Jet Flight, China Enters Dog-Fight with Boeing, Airbus," *Reuters*, May 6, 2017.

14. John Naisbitt, *Megatrends* (New York: Warner Books, 1982); John Naisbitt and Patricia Aburdene, *Megatrends 2000: Ten New Directions for the 1990s* (New York: William Morrow & Company, 1990).

15. See, for example, Richard A. Slaughter, "Looking for the Real 'Megatrends,'" *Futures* 3, no. 8 (October 1993).

16. Dependency ratios are typically calculated by dividing the population aged fourteen or younger and sixty-five or older by the population between ages fifteen and sixty-four (working-age population).

17. See Pankaj Ghemawat and Steven A. Altman, "Defining and Measuring Globalization," in Pankaj Ghemawat, *The Laws of Globalization* (Cambridge: Cambridge University Press, 2016).

18. According to the United Nations Development Programme (UNDP), "2009 Human Development Report," United Nations Development Programme, 2009, "a

report by the ILO counted 33 million foreign nationals in 1910, equivalent to 2.5% of the population covered by the study (which was 76% of the world population at the time)." The same report also indicates the share of migrants in the world population (excluding the former Soviet Union and Czechoslovakia for comparability because their breakup caused people to become reclassified as migrants without actual movement) grew from 2.7 to 2.8% between 1960 and 2010. The International Organization for Migration (IOM) reports that migrants formed 2.5 percent of the world population in 1960 and 3.1 percent in 2010 (International Organization for Migration, "World Migration Report 2010: Costs and Benefits of International Migration," IOM World Migration Report Series 3, 2005 and International Organization for Migration, "World Migration Report 2010: The Future of Migration: Building Capacities for Change," 2010.

19. Jack Hough, "Cheaper Robots, Pricier Stocks," *Barron's*, January 19, 2013; and Ben Bland, "China's Robot Revolution," *Financial Times*, June 6, 2016.

20. Roberto Azevêdo, "Trade and Globalisation in the 21st Century: The Path to Greater Inclusion," keynote address, World Trade Symposium, London, June 7, 2016.

21. Sübidey Togan, "Services Trade and Doha," *Vox* (CEPR Policy Portal), April 1, 2011.

22. Richard Baldwin, *The Great Convergence: Information Technology and the New Globalization* (Cambridge, MA: Harvard University Press, 2016).

23. Comparisons of the relative trade intensity of advanced versus emerging economies are not distorted significantly by variation in the proportion of foreign value added embodied in their exports. While China's exports do contain more foreign value added than do US exports (an estimated 29 percent for China in 2014 versus 15 percent for the United States, according to Organisation for Economic Co-operation and Development's Trade in Value Added [TiVA] database), the export-weighted average on this indicator across all countries with data available is very similar across both sets of economies (25 percent for emerging economies versus 26 percent for advanced economies).

24. For evidence on the relationship between tradability and cross-border M&A, see Bruce A. Blonigen and Donghyun Lee, "Heterogeneous Frictional Costs Across Industries in Cross-Border Mergers and Acquisitions," NBER Working Paper 22546, August 2016.

25. The top five, in ranked order, are population (total), population (ages 15–64), labor force, emigrants (stock), and mobile telephone subscriptions. See Ghemawat, *Laws of Globalization*, figure 11.4.

26. Geert Bekaert and Campbell R. Harvey, "Emerging Equity Markets in a Globalizing World," working paper, April 7, 2017.

27. There is, of course, also a school of thought that does not see long-run GDP growth as predictive of long-run stock market returns. Vanguard, for example, once made such a case to its investors in Joseph H. Davis, Roger Aliaga-Díaz, C. William Cole, and Julieann Shanahan, "Investing in Emerging Markets: Evaluating the Allure of Rapid Economic Growth," whitepaper, Vanguard, April 2010, https://www.vanguard.com/pdf/icriem.pdf.

28. Pankaj Ghemawat, *World 3.0: Global Prosperity and How to Achieve It* (Boston: Harvard Business Review Press, 2011).

29. Arindam Bhattacharya, Dinesh Khanna, Christoph Schweizer, and Aparna Bijapurkar, "Going Beyond the Rhetoric," BCG Henderson Institute, April 25, 2017, https://www.bcg.com/publications/2017/new-globalization-going-beyond-rhetoric.aspx.

30. Analysis of airports based on data from OpenFlights.org route database. See https://openflights.org/data.html.

31. Look South is focused on Latin American countries that have trade agreements with the United States; thus it also includes Peru and Chile, which are south of the equator and currently trade more with China than with the United States.

32. Graham Allison, *Destined for War: Can America and China Escape Thucydides's Trap?* (Boston and New York: Houghton Mifflin Harcourt, 2017).

Chapter 4

1. Alan Murray, "GE's Immelt Signals End to 7 Decades of Globalization," *Fortune*, May 20, 2016.

2. Matt Turner, "Here's the memo Larry Fink, the head of the world's largest investor, just sent to staff on these 'uneasy' times," *Business Insider*, February 2, 2017, http://www.businessinsider.com/blackrock-larry-fink-memo-on-trump-2017-2?r=UK&IR=T. While Fink's memo emphasized localization as a response to the present environment, that call was prefaced by the statement, "First, we must rededicate ourselves to operating as a truly global company. Since our founding 29 years ago, BlackRock has sought to engage with and embrace talent and clients from cultures in all corners of the world. We will not retreat from that commitment." Fink also followed up his call to localize with a reference to scale economies and how they relate to competitive positioning, "Even as we leverage the benefits of global scale, we need to be more relevant to our clients in each market than any local player." Putting all of these statements together, my interpretation (in terms of the AAA strategies discussed later in this chapter) is that Fink targets for BlackRock to boost adaptation while still continuing to emphasize aggregation.

3. For a more detailed discussion of adaptation, aggregation, and arbitrage, see Pankaj Ghemawat, *Redefining Global Strategy: Crossing Borders in a World Where Differences Still Matter* (Boston: Harvard Business Review Press, 2007, reissued in 2018), chaps. 4–7.

4. See Richard E. Caves, *Multinational Enterprise and Economic Analysis* (Cambridge: Cambridge University Press, 2007), 1–13, 29–45, and 105–108, for a more precise statement of the necessary conditions for horizontal MNEs and an overview of the empirical evidence on their incidence.

5. Advertising intensity is based on data reported in Coca-Cola Company's 2016 Annual Report. Brand value from Interbrand, "Best Global Brands 2016 Ranking," http://interbrand.com/best-brands/best-global-brands/2016/ranking.

6. Carol Corrado, "Non-R&D intangibles as drivers of growth," Presentation at the Second IRIMA Workshop, Brussels, December 10, 2013, http://iri.jrc.ec.europa.eu/documents/10180/f90fdba1-bab3-417b-87f0-f401f58d6f6a.

7. GE, "Factsheet," accessed June 13, 2017, www.ge.com/about-us/fact-sheet.

8. Jeff Immelt, "Jeff Immelt: Competing for the World," *GE Reports*, May 4, 2017.

9. Ted Mann and Brian Spegele, "GE, the Ultimate Global Player, Is Turning Local," *Wall Street Journal*, June 29, 2017.

10. GE 2016 Annual Report.

11. PwC Strategy&, "2016 Global Innovation 1000 Study," PwC, accessed June 13, 2017, http://www.strategyand.pwc.com/innovation1000.

12. "Top 300 Organizations Granted U.S. Patents in 2015," *IPO*, June 24, 2016.

13. "Global 500 2017: The Annual Report on the World's Most Valuable Brands," *Brand Finance*, February 2017.

14. Pankaj Ghemawat, "What Uber's China Deal Says About the Limits of Platforms," *Harvard Business Review*, August 10, 2016. Note that the $1 billion that Didi Chuxing invested in Uber Global was equivalent to Uber's annual burn rate in China

before the deal. The 20 percent stake mentioned in the text refers to the total stake in Didi Chuxing received by Uber itself (17.7 percent) and local investors in Uber China (2.3 percent).

15. Pankaj Ghemawat, "Regional Strategies for Global Leadership," *Harvard Business Review*, December 2005.

16. "The Retreat of the Global Company," *Economist*, January 28, 2017.

17. "The IT-BPM Sector in India: Strategic Review 2017," *NASSCOM*, 2017.

18. Marie Brinkman, "Deciphering the Latest Compensation Trends in India," *Aon: Radford Global Surveys*, November 2014.

19. Deloitte, "Deloitte's 2016 Global Outsourcing Survey," Deloitte, May 2016.

20. Pew Research Center, *The State of American Jobs* (Pew Research Center, October 6, 2016).

21. Abigail Stevenson, "GE CEO: I Like What Trump Is Doing So Far," *CNBC*, February 8, 2017.

22. Brinkman, "Latest Compensation Trends in India."

23. Pankaj Ghemawat, Steven A. Altman, and Robert Strauss, "WPP and the Globalization of Marketing Services," Case SM-1600-E (Barcelona: IESE Business School, 2013).

24. "Panasonic Churns Out New Washer Designed to Remove Curry Stains," *Japan Times*, January 26, 2017.

25. Sumeet Jain and Saurabh Thadani, "India: IT Services; Looking for a Silver Lining in the Cloud," *Goldman Sachs Equity Research*, March 2, 2017.

26. Tom Krisher, "GM to Halve Number of Vehicle Frames to Cut Costs," *San Diego Union-Tribune*, August 9, 2011; Raj Nair (Ford Group vice president for global product development), "Product Excellence and Innovation," presentation to Deutsche Bank Conference, 2015, https://corporate.ford.com/content/dam/corporate/en/investors/investor-events/Conferences/2015/2015-deutsche-bank-conference.pdf.

27. See Howard Schultz and Dori Jones Yang, *Pour Your Heart into It: How Starbucks Built a Company One Cup at a Time* (New York: Hyperion, 1997).

28. Geoffrey Jones and Peter Miskell, "European Integration and Corporate Restructuring: The Strategy of Unilever, c.1957–c.1990," *The Economic History Review* 58, no. 1 (February 2005).

29. For the 2025 projection, see Richard Dobbs et al., "Urban World: The Shifting Global Business Landscape," *McKinsey Global Institute*, October 2013. For the 2030 projection, see Mauro F. Guillén and Esteban García-Canal, "The Rise of the Emerging-Market Multinationals," in *Global Turning Points: Understanding the Challenges for Business in the 21st Century*, ed. Mauro F Guillén and Emilio Ontiveros Baeza (Cambridge: Cambridge University Press, 2012).

30. Alan Rugman and Alain Verbeke specify criteria along these lines for firms to be classified as global, drawing on Kenichi Ohmae's work on "triad power." Ohmae highlights the merits of firms having "equal penetration and exploitation capabilities" in each of the triad regions of the United States, European Union, and Japan and "no blind spots" in any of those regions. In recognition of wider regional integration initiatives, Rugman and Verbeke's broad triad focuses on the broader regions of North America, Europe, and Asia-Pacific. For background, see Alan M. Rugman and Alain Verbeke, "A Perspective on Regional and Global Strategies of Multinational Enterprises," *Journal of International Business Studies* 35, no. 1 (2004); and Kenichi Ohmae, *Triad Power: The Coming Shape of Global Competition* (London: Free Press, 1985), 165.

31. José F. P. Santos and Peter J. Williamson, "The New Mission for Multinationals," *MIT Sloan Management Review* 56, no. 4 (2015).

32. Yuval Atsmon, Peter Child, Richard Dobbs, and Laxman Narasimhan, "Winning the $30 Trillion Decathlon: Going for Gold in Emerging Markets," *McKinsey Quarterly*, August 2012.

33. Amitabh Mall et al., "Playing to Win in Emerging Markets," *BCG Perspectives*, 2013.

34. The only major exception to the rule about R&D intensity is internet hardware, currently dominated by Huawei Technologies and ZTE—an exception arguably shrouded in some mystery insofar as links with and support by the Chinese military are concerned.

35. There were only minimal changes from the first time this analysis was conducted in 2006. The 2006 analysis appeared in Pankaj Ghemawat and Thomas Hout, "Tomorrow's Global Giants? Not the Usual Suspects," *Harvard Business Review*, November 2008.

36. Pradeesh Chandra, "GE Healthcare to Focus on Affordable Devices," *The Hindu*, April 2, 2015.

37. Moulishree Srivastava, "Domestic IT Services Market Forecast to Grow 8.4% in 2014: IDC Report," *LiveMint*, May 13, 2014.

38. Aditi Shah, "Maruti Suzuki to Export Made-in-India Car to Japan," *Reuters*, October 26, 2015.

39. Sharmistha Mukherjee, "India to Lead Parent Suzuki's Foreign Investments," *Smart Investor*, March 22, 2013.

40. Waldemar Pfoertsch and Yipeng Liu, "Chinese Jobs in Germany: Do Chinese Mergers and Acquisitions Create Jobs in Germany?," accessed September 30, 2017, https://businesspf.hs-pforzheim.de/fileadmin/user_upload/uploads_redakteur_wirtschaft/Fakultaet_zentral/Dokumente/2013/Turmthesen/TT_Bd2_10_Pfoertsch_Liu.pdf. The same study found that the Chinese had become more successful acquirers during the 2000s.

41. Justine Lau, "TCL to Close Most European Operations," *Financial Times*, October 31, 2006.

42. In more general terms, research on firms' absorptive capacity emphasizes their prior levels of related knowledge. See Wesley M. Cohen and Daniel A. Levinthal, "Absorptive Capacity: A New Perspective on Learning and Innovation," *Administrative Science Quarterly* 35, no. 1 (1990).

43. Caroline Fairchild, "Lenovo's Secret M&A Recipe," *Fortune*, October 31, 2014.

44. Ranks from the 2017 *Fortune* Global 500, based on 2016 revenues.

Chapter 5

1. Citi has been pulling back its retail banking presence since 2012. The company announced plans to drop consumer banking in eleven markets in 2014, and in 2016, it announced plans to exit Argentina, Brazil, and Colombia. Other banks have followed suit. HSBC, which had long styled itself "the world's local bank," withdrew from consumer banking in over twenty countries, including Colombia, South Korea, and Russia. Barclays, which aimed to reduce its noncore business, fully exited its retail banking operations in continental Europe by the end of 2016. The Royal Bank of Scotland also pulled out of around a dozen markets, including the sale of its stake in Citizens Financial Group in the United States in 2015.

2. Amy Thomson, "Verizon Sale Cuts Vodafone's Value by Half to $100 Billion," *Livemint*, February 22, 2014.

3. Aaron Kirchfeld et al., "Peugeot Owner PSA Explores Acquisition of GM's Opel Division," *Bloomberg*, February 14, 2017.

4. As described later in the chapter, the screens are meant to conjure up the image of panning for gold.

5. The median estimate was twenty countries, and the mean estimate thirty-two countries.

6. California Inland Empire District Export Council, "U.S. Exporting Facts," *CIE-DEC*, accessed June 14, 2017, www.ciedec.org/resources/exporting-facts.

7. Oracle ranked 85th on foreign assets in 2015.

8. Sources for this criterion of globalization were cited in chapter 4, endnote 30.

9. In 2016, the number of companies with sufficient data to generate this calculation, however, was more limited. From forty-five companies with sufficient data, the average domestic operating margin was 14.9 percent, and the average foreign operating margin was 9.7 percent. For nine companies, net profit margins were substituted for operating profit margins because of lack of data on the latter metric.

10. The actual order, as shown in the figure, is Canada, United Kingdom, Mexico.

11. Richard McGregor, "China's Companies Count Down to Lift Off," *Financial Times*, August 29, 2005.

12. Internal divisions within both Spain and Belgium have been powerful enough to generate significant secession movements. For some discussion, refer to Pankaj Ghemawat, "To Secede or Not to Secede: The Case of Europe," *The Globalist*, July 2, 2012.

13. Pankaj Ghemawat, *The Laws of Globalization and Business Applications* (Cambridge: Cambridge University Press, 2016). See also the book's online appendix, at www.ghemawat.com/laws.

14. The greenfield component of FDI refers to "investment projects that entail the establishment of new entities and the setting up offices, buildings, plants, and factories from scratch." Source: United Nations Conference on Trade and Development Division on Investment and Enterprise, *UNCTAD Training Manual on Statistics for FDI and the Operations of TNCs* (New York and Geneva: United Nations, 2009).

15. Careful readers may notice that the distance effects shown on figure 5-5 on average are smaller than those implied by the aggregate results reported in chapter 1. This difference is due to the use of a statistical method here called PPML (Poisson pseudo maximum likelihood), which better handles the higher proportion of nontrading country pairs that appear in industry-level analysis. At the aggregate country level in chapter 1, the gravity models were estimated using OLS (ordinary least squares). PPML gravity models tend to estimate smaller distance effects than OLS gravity models do.

16. On average across the industries analyzed, FDI in the tertiary sector increases by 275 percent, while FDI in primary and secondary sectors increases by only 109 percent.

17. Jordan Siegel and Barbara Zepp Larson provide the following brief summary: "The company's industry-leading productivity has been attributed largely to its management system, which consists of four main components: (a) piecework wages, (b) a discretionary annual bonus based on individual and company performance, (c) an individual merit rating used to determine the annual bonus, and (d) a voluntary employee advisory board that works to generate productivity-enhancing innovations." Source: Jordan I. Siegel and Barbara Zepp Larson, "Labor Market Institutions and Global Strategic Adaptation: Evidence from Lincoln Electric," *Management Science* 55 no. 9 (September 2009).

18. I would also like to thank Niccolò Pisani for his collaboration on this and other research concerning the *Fortune* Global 500.

19. Subramanian Rangan and Metin Sengul, "Institutional Similarities and MNE Relative Performance Abroad: A Study of Foreign Multinationals in Six Host Markets," INSEAD working paper, October 2004.

20. Pankaj Ghemawat, "Remapping Your Strategic Mind-Set," *McKinsey Quarterly*, August 2011.

21. Pankaj Ghemawat, "5 Ways Smart Companies Take on the World," *Fortune*, March 25, 2013.

22. That withdrawal also took place almost nine decades after GM's commitment to Europe was significantly escalated by its acquisition of Opel.

23. The seven regions are East Asia and Pacific; Europe; Middle East and North Africa; North America; South and Central America and the Caribbean; South and Central Asia; and sub-Saharan Africa. Countries in each region are listed in the DHL Global Connectedness Index report. For the classification-scheme results described, see Pankaj Ghemawat, *The Laws of Globalization and Business Applications* (Cambridge: Cambridge University Press, 2016), table 10.6.

24. Pankaj Ghemawat and Steven A. Altman, "Emerging Economies: Differences and Distances," *AIB Insights* 16, no. 4 (2016).

25. See Harold L. Sirkin and David C. Michael, "Why It's Time to Reassess Your Emerging-Market Strategy," *BCG Perspectives*, October 29, 2013.

26. Peter Campbell, Simon Mundy, and Joseph Cotterill, "GM to Halt India Sales and Sell South Africa Plant," *Financial Times*, May 18, 2017.

Chapter 6

1. Alfred D. Chandler Jr., *Strategy and Structure: Chapters in the History of the American Industrial Enterprise* (Cambridge, MA: MIT Press, 1962).

2. The sense that multinationals are pursuing more complex international strategies with the organizational implications discussed here draws additional support from research on FDI patterns, which has found that modern multinationals increasingly pursue strategies that do not fit cleanly into the traditional vertical or horizontal categories. See J. Peter Neary, "Trade costs and foreign direct investment," *International Review of Economics and Finance* 18 (2009).

3. Phillipe Lasserre, "Regional Headquarters: The Spearhead for Asia Pacific Markets," *Long Range Planning* 29, no. 1 (1996). For more, see Pankaj Ghemawat, *Redefining Global Strategy* (Boston: Harvard Business School Press, 2007), chap. 5; and Pankaj Ghemawat, "Regional Strategies for Global Leadership," *Harvard Business Review*, December 2005.

4. "GM to Move International HQ to Singapore," *BBC*, November 13, 2013.

5. From an unpublished globalization survey, conducted in 2007 with David J. Collis.

6. Jay R. Galbraith, "The Value Adding Corporation: Matching Structure with Strategy," in *Organizing for the Future: The New Logic for Managing Complex Organizations*, ed. Jay R. Galbraith and Edward E Lawler (San Francisco: Jossey-Bass, 1993).

7. For a rich description of P&G's organizational structures through Organization 2005, see Mikolaj Jan Piskorski and Alessandro L. Spadini, "Proctor & Gamble: Organization 2005 (A)," Case 9-707-519 (Boston: Harvard Business School, 2007). The 2014 restructuring is described in Jack Neff, "P&G's Lafley Tells What Went Wrong with Beauty Division and How He Wants to Fix It," *Advertising Age*, February 20, 2014.

8. Charles Handy, "Balancing Corporate Power: A New Federalist Paper," *Harvard Business Review*, November–December, 1992.

9. Pankaj Ghemawat and Herman Vantrappen, "How Global Is Your C-Suite?," *MIT Sloan Management Review* (Summer 2015).

10. Ibid.

11. This is based on UN Conference on Trade and Development, Transnationality Index, which is calculated as the average of the following three ratios: foreign assets to total assets, foreign sales to total sales, and foreign employment to total employment. For a complete analysis, see Pankaj Ghemawat and Herman Vantrappen, "World's Biggest Companies: Still Xenophobic, After All These Years," *Fortune*, June 24, 2013.

12. Pankaj Ghemawat and Herman Vantrappen, "Become an Ex-Pat and Still Get Ahead: Research on Choosing the Right Company," *Harvard Business Review*, January 9, 2014.

13. Shirley Daniel, Fujiao Xie, and Ben L. Kedia, "2014 U.S. Business Needs for Employees with International Expertise," conference paper, Internationalization of U.S. Education in the 21st Century: The Future of International and Foreign Language Studies, Coalition for International Education, Williamsburg, VA, April 11–13, 2014.

14. Bo Bernhard Nielsen and Sabina Nielsen, "Top Management Team Nationality Diversity and Firm Performance: A Multilevel Study," *Strategic Management Journal* 34, no. 3 (2013).

15. Szymon Kaczmarek and Winfried Ruigrok, "In at the Deep End of Firm Internationalization," *Management International Review* 53, no. 4 (2013). Regarding evidence on some of the challenges of working in diverse groups, see, for instance, Katherine Y. Williams and Charles A. O'Reilly III, "Demography and Diversity in Organizations: A Review of 40 Years of Research," in *Research in Organizational Behavior* 20, ed. B. M. Staw and R. I. Sutton (Greenwich, CT: JAI Press, 1998).

16. Claudia Dreifus, "In Professors Model, Diversity = Productivity," *New York Times*, January 8, 2008.

17. See, for instance, Palash Ghosh, "Microsoft's (MSFT) New CEO Satya Nadella Underscores Rise of Indians in U.S. High Tech," *International Business Times*, February 1, 2014.

18. The Microsoft case does provide a useful reminder that progress on national diversity doesn't automatically translate to gender and other diversity priorities. The fire that Satya Nadella came under in October 2014 for insensitive comments he made about women asking for raises is emblematic of general struggles with gender issues in high tech.

19. Based on surveys conducted by Universum. The 2017 value was reported in Sherisse Pham, "Chinese Students Are Losing Interest in Working at International Firms," *CNN Money*, June 15, 2017. The 2014 value was reported in Colum Murphy and Lilian Lin, "For China's Jobseekers, Multinational Companies Lose Their Magic," *Wall Street Journal*, April 3, 2014.

20. Ghemawat and Vantrappen, "How Global Is Your C-Suite?"

21. Martin Dewhurst, Jonathan Harris, and Suzanne Heywood, "Understanding Your 'Globalization Penalty,'" *McKinsey Quarterly*, July 2011.

22. See the full credo, and the company's writings about it, at Johnson & Johnson, "Our Credo," accessed September 30, 2017, www.jnj.com/about-jnj/jnj-credo.

23. "Our Culture" Google website, accessed June 2016, www.google.com/about/company/facts/culture.

24. Tsedal B. Neeley, "Language and Globalization: 'Englishnization' at Rakuten (A)," Case 412-002 (Boston: Harvard Business School, 2011).

25. Research in neuroscience has found enhanced neural responses in particular parts of the brain when listening to speech in one's own accent and reduced responses when listening to other accents. See, for example, Patricia E.G. Bestelmeyer, Pascal

Belin, and D. Robert Ladd, "A Neural Marker for Social Bias Toward In-group Accents," *Cerebral Cortex* 25 (October 2015).

26. For a theoretical model of how globalization raises the "window of viability" within an industry, see John Sutton, *Competing in Capabilities: The Globalization Process* (Oxford: Oxford University Press, 2012). I also discuss this topic at length in the context of competition between multinationals from advanced versus emerging economies in Pankaj Ghemawat, *The Laws of Globalization and Business Applications* (Cambridge: Cambridge University Press, 2016).

27. Donald Lessard, David J. Teece, and Sohvi Leih, "The Dynamic Capabilities of Meta-Multinationals," *Global Strategy Journal* 6, no. 3 (2016).

28. Data through 1995 based on Cyrus Freidheim, *The Trillion-Dollar Enterprise: How the Alliance Revolution Will Transform Global Business* (New York: Perseus Books, 1998). Data since 1995 based on Warren Company, "Strategic Alliance Best Practice User Guide," 2002.

29. Ernest Gundling, Christie Caldwell, and Karen Cvitkovich, *Leading Across New Borders: How to Succeed as the Center Shifts* (Hoboken, NJ: Wiley, 2015).

30. Eric J. McNulty, "Your People's Brains Need Face Time," *Strategy + Business*, December 12, 2016.

31. Johan Ugander, Brian Karrer, Lars Backstrom, and Cameron Marlow, "The Anatomy of the Facebook Social Graph," November 2011, white paper available at https://arxiv.org/pdf/1111.4503.pdf.

32. Yuri Takhteyev, Anatoliy Gruzd, and Barry Wellman, "Geography of Twitter Networks," *Social Networks* 34, no. 1 (2012).

33. Herve de Barbeyrac and Ruben Verhoeven, "Tilting the Global Balance: An Interview with the CEO of Solvay," *McKinsey Quarterly*, October 2013.

34. William J. Holstein, "The Decline of the Expat Executive," *Strategy + Business*, July 29, 2008.

35. Ghemawat and Vantrappen, "How Global Is Your C-Suite?"

36. Monika Hamori and Burak Koyuncu, "Career Advancement in Large Organizations in Europe and the United States: Do International Assignments Add Value?" *International Journal of Human Resource Management* 22, no. 4 (2011).

37. Gail Naughton, as quoted in Tricia Bisoux, "Global Immersion," *BizEd* 6, no. 4 (2007): 46–47.

38. Craig Karmin, "Hotel HQ: Top Starwood Execs Decamping to India for a Month," *Wall Street Journal*, September 30, 2014.

39. Li Fangfang, "ABB Moves Robotics HQ to Shanghai," *China Daily*, May 4, 2005; Mamta Badkar, "GE Moves Healthcare Division's X-Ray Unit Headquarters to China," *Business Insider*, July 25, 2011; Gordon Orr, "Multinationals Are Slowly Shifting Their Centers of Gravity Towards Asia (Part 1)," *McKinsey Blog*, September 4, 2013; Toby Gibbs, Suzanne Heywood, and Leigh Weiss, "Organizing for an Emerging World," *McKinsey Quarterly*, June 2012.

40. Amitabh Mall et al., "Playing to Win in Emerging Markets," *BCG Perspectives*, September 13, 2013.

41. Bruce Dodge, "Empowerment and the Evolution of Learning," *Education + Training* 35, no. 5 (1993), as cited in Mark E. Mendenhall et al., *Global Leadership: Research, Practice, and Development* (New York: Routledge, 2013).

42. Online survey conducted for Pankaj Ghemawat by *Harvard Business Review* in 2007.

43. See Pankaj Ghemawat, "Responses to Forces of Change: A Focus on Curricular Content," in *Globalization of Management Education: Changing International Structures,*

Adaptive Strategies, and the Impact on Institutions, Report of the AACSB International Globalization of Management Education Task Force (Bingley, UK: Emerald Group, 2011), 105–156.

44. Christian Terwiesch and Karl T. Ulrich, "Will Video Kill the Classroom Star? The Threat and Opportunity of Massively Open Online Courses for Full-Time MBA Programs," Wharton School, University of Pennsylvania, July 16, 2014.

45. Donna Ladkin, Peter Case, Patricia Gayá Wicks, and Keith Kinsella, "Developing Leaders in Cyber-space: The Paradoxical Possibilities of On-Line Learning," *Leadership* 5, no. 2 (2009): 193–212.

46. Pankaj Ghemawat, "The Cosmopolitan Corporation," *Harvard Business Review*, May 2011.

47. "Waiting in the Wings," *Economist*, October 1, 2014.

48. Sam Grobart "How Samsung Became the World's No. 1 Smartphone Maker," *Bloomberg*, March 28, 2013.

49. Nicholas Varchaver and Verne Harnish, "Why Samsung Pays Its Stars to Goof Off," *Smart CEO*, November 18, 2013.

50. Tarun Khanna, Jaeyong Song, and Kyungmook Lee, "The Globe: The Paradox of Samsung's Rise," *Harvard Business Review*, July–August 2011.

Chapter 7

1. Nick O'Donohoe, "What Is the True Business of Business?," *World Economic Forum*, February 25, 2016.

2. Martin Reeves, email exchange with author, March 9, 2017.

3. Scott R. Baker, Nicholas Bloom, and Steven J. Davis, "Measuring Economic Policy Uncertainty," working paper 21633 (Cambridge, MA, National Bureau of Economic Resarcher, October 2015).

4. Erik Sherman, "Is Slow Productivity Growth the Problem, as Greenspan Says, or Is It Selfishness?," *Forbes*, February 20, 2017.

5. *OECD Compendium of Productivity Indicators 2017* (Paris: OECD Publishing, 2017), 9.

6. The two studies on which PwC built its update are Carl B. Frey and Michael A. Osborne, "The Future of Employment: How Susceptible Are Jobs to Computerization?," working paper (Oxford: University of Oxford, September 17, 2013); and Melanie Arntz, Terry Gregory, and Ulrich Zierahn, "The Risk of Automation for Jobs in OECD Countries: A Comparative Analysis," OECD Social, Employment and Migration working paper 189 (Paris: OECD Publishing, 2016). See also "UK Economic Outlook," *PwC*, March 2017, chap. 4.

7. David H. Autor, David Dorn, and Gordon H. Hanson, "The China Shock: Learning from Labor-Market Adjustment to Large Changes in Trade," *Annual Review of Economics* 8 (2016).

8. Chris Tighe, "After a Resounding Brexit Vote, Sunderland Fears for Nissan Plant," *Financial Times*, June 28, 2016.

9. "New Nationwide Poll Shows Trump Leading in Farm Country," *PR Newswire*, October 27, 2016.

10. Shawn Donnan, "American Farm Belt Anxious About Trump Trade Threats," *Financial Times*, April 17, 2017. See also Thomas Frank's best seller, *What's the Matter with Kansas? How Conservations Won the Heart of America* (New York: Holt Paperbacks, 2005), which focuses on the same US state in its examination of why many people seem to vote against their economic self-interest.

11. The manifestation of partiality that has been researched the most in business and economics is home bias in investors' portfolios. For whatever reason, investors seem to leave money on the table by under-diversifying internationally. This pattern has been related to both depth and breadth (and by extension both laws of globalization) in Christopher W. Anderson, Mark Fedenia, Mark Hirschey, and Hilla Skibac, "Cultural Influences on Home Bias and International Diversification by Institutional Investors," *Journal of Banking and Finance* 35, no. 4 (April 2011).

12. Diana C. Mutz and Eunji Kim, "The Impact of Ingroup Favoritism in Trade Preferences," *International Organization*, forthcoming.

13. See Branko Milanovic, "Ethical and Economic Feasibility of Global Transfers," working paper 3775 (Washington, DC: World Bank Policy Research, 2007). Milanovic relied on estimates of the proportion of social transfers in rich countries that are "needs-based" to attempt to generate a fair comparison of those domestic transfers to foreign aid provided by rich countries to poor countries.

14. This calculation is based on 2013 (or the most recent preceding year) figures for total public and mandatory private social spending and net official development assistance, both from OECD.Stat, and population figures from the World Development Indicators (World Bank). The calculation was as follows:

$$\frac{\sum_{i=1}^{n} \dfrac{domestic\ social\ expenditure_i / population_i}{official\ development\ assistance_i / non\ OECD\ population} \cdot population_i}{\sum_{i=1}^{n} population_i}$$

The result of this calculation was 50,854. Similar results were obtained by replacing the domestic population with the number of people living below the national poverty rate and the non-OECD population with the number of people living below $3.10 per day (52,798).

15. Edelman, "2017 Edelman Trust Barometer: Global Annual Study," Edelman website, 2017, www.edelman.com/trust2017.

16. "Public Esteem for Military Still High," Pew Research Center, July 11, 2013.

17. Survey respondents were actually asked to rate the citizens of other countries as well as their own on a spectrum ranging from "no trust at all" to "a lot of trust." An academic article based on this survey summarizes data about the percentage of citizens of each West European country surveyed who report trusting others "a lot." See Luigi Guiso, Paola Sapienza, and Luigi Zingales, "Cultural Biases in Economic Exchange?", *Quarterly Journal of Economics* 124, no. 3 (2009).

18. Kamel Mellahi, Jędrzej George Frynas, Pei Sun, and Donald Siegel, "A Review of the Nonmarket Strategy Literature: Toward a Multi-Theoretical Integration," *Journal of Management* 42, no. 1 (2016).

19. This section does not discuss corporate political activity that is focused only on securing advantages for the firm itself—both because firms already tend to be quite sophisticated about this and because they may want to tone down such activity at least somewhat in the present environment. Traditionally, firms have tried to get as much as they could out of governments, but that may not be so wise in the midst of a backlash against both big business and globalization. Consider, for example, the reaction when Foxconn secured the largest incentive package ever for a foreign company in the US (about $3 billion) in 2017 in exchange for a commitment to build a plant in Wisconsin. For details, see Jason Stein and Patrick Marley, "Wisconsin Assembly Sends $3 Billion Foxconn Incentive Package to Scott Walker," *Journal Sentinel*, September 14, 2017.

20. Pankaj Ghemawat, *World 3.0: Global Prosperity and How to Achieve It* (Boston: Harvard Business Review Press, 2011).

21. International Monetary Fund, "IMF Staff Paper: Linkages Between Labor Market Institutions and Inequality," July 17, 2015.

22. Jan W. Rivkin, Karen G. Mills, and Michael E. Porter, "The Challenge of Shared Prosperity: Findings of Harvard Business School's 2015 Survey on U.S. Competitiveness," Harvard Business School, Boston, September 2015.

23. According to a 37-country survey, the proportion of respondents who were confident in the US president to "do the right thing regarding world affairs" fell from 64 percent at the end of the Obama presidency to 22 percent at the beginning of the Trump presidency, and the proportion viewing the United States favorably fell from 64 percent to 49 percent over the same period. See Richard Wike, Bruce Stokes, Jacob Poushter, and Janell Fetterolf, "U.S. Image Suffers as Publics Around World Question Trump's Leadership," Pew Research Center, June 26, 2017, http://www.pewglobal .org/2017/06/26/u-s-image-suffers-as-publics-around-world-question-trumps-leadership/.

24. German Marshall Fund of the United States, "Transatlantic Trends: Mobility, Migration and Integration," 2014.

25. See the 2014 and 2015 editions of the Ipsos MORI "Perils of Perception" survey and the 2013 edition of the German Marshall Fund of the United States "Transatlantic Trends" survey.

26. Bianca DiJulio, Mira Norton, and Mollyann Brodie, "Americans' Views on the U.S. Role in Global Health," Kaiser Family Foundation, January 2016; Rivkin, Mills, and Porter, "Challenge of Shared Prosperity."

27. Among respondents not told the actual proportion of the budget devoted to foreign aid, 45 percent wanted levels to decrease, 32 percent wanted levels to remain the same, and 20 percent wanted to increase it. Of those who were told the actual level of aid spending, only 26 percent wanted to cut aid (a 19 percentage point drop), 39 percent wanted levels to remain the same, and 32 percent wanted to increase aid levels (a 12 percentage point rise). See Council on Foreign Relations, "Opinion on Development and Humanitarian Aid," in *Public Opinion on Global Issues* (New York: Council on Foreign Relations, 2012).

28. Hugo Mercier and Dan Sperber, *The Enigma of Reason* (Cambridge, MA: Harvard University Press, 2017): Steven Sloman and Philip Fernbach, *The Knowledge of Illusion: Why We Never Think Alone* (New York: Riverhead Books, 2017); and Sara E. Gorman and Jack M. Gorman, *Denying to the Grave* (Oxford: Oxford University Press, 2016).

29. For an introduction to the effect of storytelling on the brain, see Uri Hasson, "This Is Your Brain on Communication," TED talk, February 2016, http://www.ted .com/talks/uri_hasson_this_is_your_brain_on_communication.

30. For more about this project as well as pictures of the suit, see Loretta Radeschi, "The 100-Mile Suit," *Handmade Business*, October 8, 2008, http://handmade-business .com/philadelphiasuit; and *100-Mile Suit* (blog), last post April 16, 2008, http://100-milesuit .blogspot.com.

31. Maurice H. Yearwood, "On Wealth and the Diversity of Friendships: High Social Class People Around the World Have Fewer International Friends," *Personality and Individual Differences* 87 (2015).

32. Gordon Allport, *The Nature of Prejudice* (Boston: Addison, 1954).

33. Bernand Bailyn, *Education in the Forming of American Society: Needs and Opportunities for Study* (Chapel Hill: University of North Carolina Press, 1960).

34. Donald Trump, Nevada Caucus victory speech, Las Vegas, February 24, 2016.

35. Mikael Hjerm, "Education, Xenophobia and Nationalism: A Comparative Analysis," *Journal of Ethnic and Migration Studies* 27, no. 1 (2001): 37–60.

36. For more information, see https://www.coursera.org/learn/global-business.

37. I should note that here, much more than in most other parts of this book, the data available to me is primarily for the United States, so the analysis that follows is primarily US-based. Nonetheless, at least some of the problems with US business that I highlight here probably do apply to other countries as well.

38. Eduardo Porter, "Corporate Efforts to Address Social Problems Have Limits," *New York Times*, September 8, 2015.

39. Arthur M. Okun, *Equality and Efficiency: The Big Tradeoff* (Washington, DC: Brookings Institution, 1975).

40. See, for example, Anthony B. Atkinson, *Inequality: What Can Be Done?* (Cambridge, MA: Harvard University Press, 2015); Thomas Piketty, *The Economics of Inequality* (Cambridge, MA: Belknap Press, 2015); Joseph E. Stiglitz, *The Great Divide* (New York: W.W. Norton & Company, 2016).

41. Jim Yong Kim, "Rethinking Development Finance," speech The World Bank, April 11, 2017.

42. Population growth projection from United Nations, World Population Prospects, 2017 edition (medium variant).

43. For evidence in support of this point as well as a broader discussion of market failures and how they relate to business, see Pankaj Ghemawat, "Market *and* Management Failures," *Capitalism and Society* 12, no. 1 (2017).

44. Geoffrey Jones, "The Future (and Past) of Globalization and the Multinational Corporation," presentation at the annual meeting of the Academy of International Business, New Orleans, June 28, 2016; Jack Beatty, "Hitler's Willing Business Partners," *Atlantic*, April 2001.

INDEX

ACKNOWLEDGMENTS

This book builds on three previous ones: *Redefining Global Strategy* (2007), *World 3.0: Global Prosperity and How to Achieve It* (2011), and *The Laws of Globalization and Business Applications* (2016). It is impossible, as a result, for me to thank all the people who have, in one way or another, shaped my thinking on globalization and business. So I will focus here on thanking those who contributed directly to this particular project. My greatest debt is to Steven Altman, the Executive Director of the Center for the Globalization of Education and Management (CGEM) at New York University's Stern School of Business, who oversaw the project, drafted the initial versions of chapters 4 and 6, and helped substantially with all the remaining chapters as well. I am also greatly indebted to Phillip Bastian and Erica Ng, also at CGEM, for the skill and speed with which they conducted much of the research that lies behind this book. Jordi Canals, Thomas Hout, Guy Pfefferman, Martin Reeves, Heini Shi, and Daniel Simpson, as well as anonymous referees, provided helpful comments on how to improve the manuscript. Finally, I want to thank Melinda Merino, my longtime editor at Harvard Business Review Press, for her enthusiasm for this project and help accelerating it to completion; my longtime assistant at IESE Business School, Marta Domenech, for providing extensive support; and CGEM at NYU Stern and the Division of Research at IESE for very generous funding of my research.

ABOUT THE AUTHOR

PANKAJ GHEMAWAT—globalization and business strategist, professor, and speaker—works with organizations and policy makers to help them anticipate and prepare for major market shifts. He also specializes in emerging markets, sustainable competitive advantage, and strategic investment.

Ghemawat is the Global Professor of Management and Strategy and Director of the Center for the Globalization of Education and Management at the Stern School of Business at New York University. He is also the Anselmo Rubiralta Professor of Global Strategy at IESE Business School. Between 1983 and 2008, he was on the faculty at the Harvard Business School, where, in 1991, he became the youngest person in the school's history to be appointed a full professor.

Ghemawat is also the youngest "guru" included in the *Economist*'s guide to the greatest management thinkers of all time (2008). He ranks among the top twenty management thinkers worldwide (Thinkers50) and among the top twenty case writers (the Case Centre). Other honors include the McKinsey Award for the best article published in *Harvard Business Review*, the Booz Eminent Scholar Award of the International Management Division of the Academy of Management, and the Irwin Educator of the Year Award of the Business Policy and Strategy Division of the Academy of Management.

Ghemawat's prior books on globalization and international business include *The Laws of Globalization*; *World 3.0*; and *Redefining Global Strategy*. The *Economist* recommends that *World 3.0* should "be read by anyone who wants to understand the most important economic development of our time." It won Thinkers50's biennial award for the best book on business.

Ghemawat is the principal author of the DHL Global Connect-edness Index and is Chairman of the Foundation for Practice and Research in Strategic Management (PRISM). He served on the task-force appointed by the Association to Advance Collegiate Schools of Business, the leading accreditation body for business schools, on the globalization of management education, and authored the report's recommendations about what to teach students about globalization, and how.

For more information, including dynamic maps and proprietary tools, visit Ghemawat.com.